MERGING COLLEGES
FOR MUTUAL GROWTH

MERGING COLLEGES FOR MUTUAL GROWTH

A New Strategy for Academic Managers

James Martin, James E. Samels & Associates

The Johns Hopkins University Press   *Baltimore & London*

© 1994 The Johns Hopkins University Press
All rights reserved
Printed in the United States of America on acid-free paper

The Johns Hopkins University Press
2715 North Charles Street
Baltimore, Maryland 21218-4319
The Johns Hopkins Press Ltd., London

Library of Congress Cataloging-in-Publication Data will be found at the end
of this book.

A catalog record for this book is available from the British Library.

Contents

Foreword, by Franklin Patterson   vii

Preface   xi

I   LEADERSHIP
Strategic Initiatives and Governance Structures   1

1 *Achieving Academic Excellence through Strategic Mergers:
   A New Approach*   James Martin and James E. Samels   3

2 *Higher Education Mergers, Consolidations, Consortia, and
   Affiliations: A Typology of Models and Basic Legal
   Structures*   James E. Samels   22

3 *The Role of Trustees and Governing Boards in College and
   University Mergers*   John F. Welsh   42

4 *Presidential Leadership and the Mutual-Growth Concept*   Bryan
   E. Carlson   59

5 *An Academic Action Plan for Faculty Involvement, Curriculum
   Revision, and Professional Development*   James Martin   75

II   OPERATIONS
Financial Planning and External Considerations   101

6 *Strategic Planning for Growth Mergers*   André Mayer   103

7 *The Implications of a Public Institutional Merger*   Donald L.
   Zekan   117

8 *The Business Aspects of College and University Mergers: A Plan
   for Merger Financing and Resource Sharing*   James E. Samels and
   Donald L. Zekan   132

9 *Merger Licensure and Accreditation*   James E. Samels   142

88076

III CONSTITUENTS
Campus Relations and Quality Service   153

10 *Merging Diverse Student Cultures*   Sheila Murphy   155

11 *Consolidating Library Collections and Learning-Resource Technologies*   Patricia Sacks   168

12 *Mergers, Institutional Advancement, and Alumni Relationships*   Victor F. Scalise, Jr.   188

13 *An International Perspective: Recent Growth Mergers in British Higher Education*   Paul Temple and Celia Whitchurch   209

14 *Conclusion: The Mutual-Growth Process—Myths and Realities*   James Martin and James E. Samels   227

Appendix: Principal College and University Mergers   239
Notes   245
Bibliography   257
Contributors   263
Index   267

Foreword

The present volume has a practical aim: to provide a realistic context and clear guidelines for those whose responsibility it is to consider, plan, and carry through to successful completion the merger of one institution of higher education with another. This means that the book is primarily directed at trustees, chief executive officers, faculty, senior staff, alumni, students, and other constituencies of colleges and universities concerned with the possibility or actuality of merger. Such key people, often with long experience in college affairs, may be quite inexperienced in dealing with the processes involved in a successful interinstitutional merger. Lack of such experience, at best, can stimulate anxiety about the nature and possible consequences of the merger process. At worst, it can result in unnecessary mistakes in policy and action related to a merger effort. The purpose of this book is to give those concerned with mergers needed information about the ways and means by which successful mergers can be completed.

The Context of Mergers

A great part of the genius and drive of higher education in American life lies in its strong tradition of *institutional autonomy*. Your institution, now considering merger with another, has undoubtedly been touched by this tradition. The first element of context for every merger is this fact: the institutions involved value the autonomy they have had.

In a nation committed to individual freedom and independence, it was natural for the colleges its people created to reflect similar values. This was the case from the beginning in U.S. private higher education. Church-related colleges, in their variety, displayed the full range of religious freedom in the United States, their sectarian distinctiveness translating into institutional autonomy. Over the years, as church relatedness disappeared or was deemphasized, institutional autonomy gained strength under the boards of trustees and faculties of the country's private colleges.

In public higher education, the traditional principle of institutional autonomy—always overseen by some public authority—similarly took root. The individual identity of public institutions like the City College of New York, Michigan at Ann Arbor, Colorado at Boulder, California at Berkeley, and hundreds of others became part of our academic culture and folklore.

During the twentieth century, new developments have profoundly altered the conditions of higher education in the United States, including those on which the tradition of going it alone was based. U.S. population growth combined with changes in the size and diversity of the population desiring higher education to make colleges and universities a major economic and cultural factor in our national life. In the last quarter of the nineteenth century, the nation had 311 colleges and universities. By 1990 that number, not counting two-year institutions, had risen to over 2,500. In 1870, U.S. institutions of higher education enrolled over 50,000 young men and women. By 1990, the City University of New York alone, a public institution with eight campuses under a central executive, enrolled over 80,000 students. This kind of revolutionary growth plus other dynamic changes, such as those in the status of women and ethnic and racial minorities, and those in technology and employment, altered the place and function of institutional autonomy in U.S. higher education.

Colleges everywhere, naturally, sought to maintain as much of their autonomy as possible. The result at its best has been the establishment of academic freedom, of independence of inquiry and teaching, as the hallmark of all institutions of higher education worth the name in the United States. At the same time, the tradition of ivy-covered Old Siwash—small, bucolic, provincial, and totally on its own—has diminished.

The old order has given way to new solutions in the effort of American society to find workable academic responses to the classic economic dilemma posed by the growth and diversification of demand for higher education: *how best to reconcile apparently unlimited needs with clearly limited resources.* Virtually every college has been whipsawed between the demands of growth and the difficulties of meeting rising costs. To deal effectively with enrollment growth and change, to do so in the midst of an accelerating revolution in the quantity and quality of knowledge, *and* to find the necessary capital and operating resources with which to do the job have been the preoccupations of U.S. higher education in the last part of the twentieth century.

Mergers as a Response to Growth and Change

One response of the country's higher education to growth and change was to build bigger and more complex institutions, with large faculties and huge enrollments. Academic depth and diversity, economies of scale and management, and other ends were sought through this means. Unintended consequences such as impersonality and anomie, bureaucratization, and hangarlike buildings made it clear that campus size had its limits as a solution.

A concurrent response, largely in the public sector, turned its back on the concept of the autonomous institution to create *systems* of campuses. Perhaps the leading example is the University of California, once based solely at Berkeley. By 1988 the school had nine campuses stretching from Davis to San Diego with a total enrollment of 160,596 and still represented only the top tier of a three-tiered public system in California which also included 19 California State University campuses and 104 community colleges.

A third response was found in *consortia*. In the last half of the twentieth century, hundreds of colleges and universities have banded together to create voluntary multicampus cooperatives. Some have been highly specialized, pooling institutional resources in such expensive fields as nuclear research. Many others, some highly successful in achieving both economies and enrichment through interinstitutional cooperation, have grown up on a more general basis. A distinguished example of this kind of consortium is Five Colleges, Inc., in Massachusetts, including the Amherst campus of the University of Massachusetts, Amherst College, Hampshire College, Mount Holyoke College, and Smith College. In this consortium, without relinquishing their individual identities, five institutions have opened up their resources to each other so that students at any one of the colleges may enroll in courses at the others without extra charge. Among the benefits of this arrangement are the increased variety of course work from which students may choose and the avoidance of expensive duplication.

A fourth response, opted for by a growing number of institutions across the nation, has been the *merger*. Some of the most prominent interinstitutional mergers that have occurred in the modern period are Carnegie Mellon University, resulting from the consolidation of Carnegie Tech with the Mellon Institute, and Case Western Reserve University, which combined Western Reserve University and the Case Institute. Less well known are recent examples such as the merger of Tift College with Mercer University and the Delaware Law School, and Boston State College with the University of Massachusetts, Boston. Mergers have occurred and are now occurring among a surprising number of institutions of differing size and prominence, some private and some public.

In this volume, the authors outline the potential in a new approach to college and university mergers: *the mutual-growth strategy*. In this model, mission-complementary institutions combine to enhance the vision and will of each. These mergers are not taking place for the traditional bankruptcy-bailout reasons; rather, the strategies outlined in these chapters reward institutions willing to move forward boldly and to consider merger as one of their most creative planning options in the coming decade.

Lighting the Way

The contributors have sought to throw fresh light on the essentials of mutual-growth merger design, not to compound the complexities of the total field but to make the main features of the merger process clear and tenable for academic managers.

Their conviction that this is both possible and needed comes from wide experience in directing a number of successful mutual-growth mergers, and in this volume they share with readers the information this experience has provided. Few studies specifically dedicated to the subject of managing mergers exist, but the chapters that follow reflect some of the most valuable findings from those that are available.

With the other contributors to this volume, I join in hoping that it may serve you and your colleagues usefully.

FRANKLIN PATTERSON

Preface

This merger handbook was developed for higher education trustees, presidents, academic administrators, strategic planners, faculty leaders, students, and alumni. For too long, institutional managers have operated without a set of clearly articulated, practical guidelines for planning and implementing college and university mergers built on mutual-growth, mission-complementary principles. Each contributor commissioned to write a chapter of this book has participated in one or more institutional mergers; some have directed several.

The concept of a handbook for academic managers on this subject arose in discussions among the contributors when it became apparent that no such book existed and that one was needed. We asked contributors to write from their experience the same chapters for which they had discovered a need during the implementation of their mergers. We then arranged the chapters into a comprehensive set of strategic guidelines which may be used in linear fashion (as the volume presents a complete merger planning process) or through selected chapters.

The handbook addresses theory while emphasizing practice. We believe there is an increasing need to provide coordinated guidelines to the widest range of merger participants, from those exercising the most complex forms of trustee stewardship to first-year students elected to a planning task force. The handbook addresses fourteen areas and concludes with a detailed reading list of higher education merger materials.

In chapter 1, we identify the reasons why we believe a new model of merging complementary educational offerings for mutual growth is superseding the earlier higher education merger for bankruptcy-bailout purposes and why, for a growing number of colleges and universities, this move is a creative and effective way to achieve academic excellence. Chapter 2 outlines for all levels of the academic management structure a detailed description of the forms current higher education mergers may take—consolidation, consortium, affiliation, full merger, and a number of other joint ventures.

Chapters 3 and 4 address mergers from the perspectives of trustee and presidential leadership. Chapter 3 focuses on the role and impact of trustees and governing boards in the development of mergers as an institutional strategy. This chapter was written by John Welsh, associate director of academic affairs at the Kansas Board of Regents, who has held special responsibility for overseeing mergers within the Kansas higher education system. The Kansas system recently completed the merger of its state university with the state's only college of technology. Chapter 4 outlines the impact of presidential leadership on an academic merger and the critical necessity for a chief executive officer to define and control the new institutional mission generated through the merger process. This chapter also describes the emergence of a new higher education management model that uniquely supports institutional mergers as a strategic planning instrument. Chapter 4 was written by Bryan Carlson, president of Mount Ida College, who has directed Mount Ida through three successful complementary mergers since 1986 in the development of this new institutional management strategy.

Chapter 5, by James Martin, discusses the implications of complementary college and university mergers for members of the faculty. This chapter provides a plan for the comprehensive involvement of faculty members, individually, departmentally, and through their committee structures, from the start of the merger process. By focusing on the central issues of curriculum revision, academic standards, and professional development, faculty members become principal architects of the shape and mission of the postmerger institution.

Chapter 6 considers the merger as a strategic decision point for each merger partner as well as for the new institution to be created. André Mayer, former director of planning for the Massachusetts Higher Education Coordinating Council, outlines the aspects of a strategic planning process that will validate the merger among key stakeholders and support its successful completion.

In chapter 7, the broad implications of a merger between large public universities are addressed by Donald L. Zekan, vice president of business and financial affairs at St. Bonaventure University. Chapter 8, written by Zekan and James E. Samels, presents the business aspects of a merger in a detailed plan for building the necessary financial foundation to support the mutual-growth model.

Chapter 9 presents the legal dimensions of institutional mergers and includes specific discussions of the licensing, regulatory, and accreditation reviews that uniformly accompany educational mergers. A legal action plan is provided incorporating regulatory and accreditation requirements as integral steps in the merger process.

Chapter 10, by Sheila Murphy, examines the impact of the merger on the student cultures involved. Currently the vice president for student affairs and the dean of students at Bradford College, Murphy, during fifteen years as a chief student development officer directed a multicampus institution that was the result of an academic merger. Chapter 11 presents a plan to address the complexities of merging library collections and the evolving area of learning-resource materials and equipment. This chapter was written by Patricia Sacks, director of the libraries at Cedar Crest and Muhlenberg Colleges, who has coordinated an unusual library merger at Cedar Crest and Muhlenberg in which the colleges remained distinct.

Chapter 12 reviews an aspect of college and university mergers we have found to be both significant and overlooked in most planning documents: institutional advancement and alumni relationships. In planning a merger, attitudes and opinions of alumni may be considered, but it is rare in our experience that they are effectively used in the decision-making process. We have observed the increasing significance of the alumni factor in mergers, however. One of the most important constituency groups for the *long-term* success of college mergers is the aggregate alumni and institutional development network of the joined institutions. Victor F. Scalise, the author of this chapter, was for thirteen years the president of a small New England college, the New England Institute of Applied Arts and Sciences, until its merger with Mount Ida College in 1988–89. He is presently the director of institutional advancement and alumni affairs for the combined institution.

Chapter 13 offers a contemporary view of higher education mergers in Great Britain. Paul Temple, former head of the Academic Planning Department of the University of London, and Celia Whitchurch, former assistant head, have provided an overview of the significant university and polytechnic mergers of the past twenty years as well as a discussion of the impact mergers and consolidations will have on British higher education over the next decade.

In the concluding chapter, James Martin and James E. Samels consider the future of the mutual-growth merger movement in higher education in the United States and abroad, giving special focus to the identity and self-image of the postmerger institution, to the opportunity mergers create for innovative forms of academic governance, and to the increasing challenge academic mergers pose to institutional leadership.

The chapters in this volume represent the efforts of many higher education experts; however, we want to identify another group of persons as a resource for much of the discussion now occurring on proactive mergers in American higher education. Since 1984, the faculty and administration of Mount Ida College have successfully implemented three mission-complementary, mutual-growth mergers and several more program transfers and affiliations. Details of their institutional planning are discussed in several chapters that follow, and we would like to thank them here for the many times they challenged us to sharpen our thinking on merger design, planning, and implementation. It is with pleasure that we dedicate this volume to them and to their continuing contributions to Mount Ida College. Finally, we would add words of special thanks to Jacqueline Wehmueller, our editor at Johns Hopkins University Press, for her vision and support, and to Carol Chauncey and Deborah Marsh, our word processing assistants, for the many ways they shaped the final draft of this manuscript.

J. M.
J. E. S.

I LEADERSHIP

Strategic Initiatives

and Governance Structures

Achieving Academic Excellence through Strategic Mergers: A New Approach

James Martin and James E. Samels

It has been fifteen years since the last significant treatment of college and university mergers was published in the United States, and a handbook written by academic managers with merger experience has never been published. Still, as one reviews the evidence that academic mergers, consolidations, and affiliations are steadily on the rise in U.S. higher education, the prevailing stereotype associated with these strategies is that of corporate behavior from over half a century ago.

In fact, mergers at the collegiate level have become one of the most creative, effective vehicles academic planners now have to achieve academic excellence, to articulate a broader institutional vision, and to solidify the strategic position of the combined institution locally and regionally. More significantly, the motives behind merging institutions to achieve academic excellence—rather than to avoid bankruptcy—signal the arrival of a new way to think about U.S. higher education managerially and strategically.

Academic mergers in the United States have been characterized by involuntary closings, financial insolvencies, forced reorganizations, and massive human and programmatic retrenchment. Managing decline rather than seizing an educational advantage has been the focus of traditional college and university mergers. Since 1980, as approximately 70 percent of all the literature on decline in U.S. organizations has appeared, over two million manufacturing jobs have been lost in the United States. More surprisingly, proportionally during this period twice as many colleges and universities have failed as businesses.[1]

Higher education institutions are complex interlocking sets of resource systems, and, as greater numbers of academic managers are trained in graduate programs of professional educational administration, as fewer faculty members accept traditional, rotating administrative posts, and as increasingly corporate forms of accountability are required of deans and department chairs, it would be naive to disregard the powerful effect business and industrial factors now exert within the management of education.[2] In the next decade, academic managers must learn powerful new ways to channel energies toward the improvement of teaching and learning activities at each institution, and, contrary to the assumptions of many, mergers are persuasive, effective methods to accomplish these goals.

In response to campus, state, and federal budget cuts, resource scarcities, and shrinking enrollments, greater numbers of U.S. colleges and universities have become conservative in their strategic planning and resource allocation. Many campuses are unfortunately retreating to earlier images and concepts of institutional success in which long-term planning is giving way to short-term solutions.[3]

Against this conservative background, however, a growing number of both public and private entrepreneurial colleges and universities are choosing forms of institutional merger, consolidation, and affiliation to meet these unprecedented challenges while simultaneously raising levels of academic quality.

The American Merger Stereotype: Bankruptcy-Bailout

The stereotypical formulation for a merger in U.S. higher education has been two colleges or universities in financial difficulty coming together and suffering an erosion of both reputations. Consistent with this earlier approach, Joseph O'Neill posed these questions at a 1987 national conference at Wingspread:

> Should merger be considered a preferred way for a college or university to achieve both quality and growth? Is it merely chance that most recent merger efforts involve institutions that were financially *in extremis?* I think not.
>
> Of the 100 top American universities, you can count on the fingers of one hand those that were created by merger. In contrast, you would need several pairs of hands to total up the number of top 100 business firms— General Motors and AT&T come immediately to mind—born from merger.[4]

This view forms a fading counterpoint to much promerger planning now occurring on U.S. campuses; however, only by addressing and moving beyond it can any new view of higher education mergers effectively be articulated. In the new mutual-growth approach, proactive mergers form an entrepreneurial educational management strategy able to rapidly improve academic quality to a degree not feasible through most other planning models, a potential that carries with it philosophical and functional implications that can alter the ways many administrators presently think about their principal responsibilities.[5]

Gail Chambers, an academic merger researcher, describes a new academic and strategic environment in which "services and resources rather than institutional entities" define the system, and, more radically, "the institution itself [serves] mainly as the *negotiator of contracts which control the flow*."[6] Successful joint ventures such as regional computer networks, faculty teaching exchanges, and interlibrary cataloging systems, have served as smaller but effective prototypes for this mutual-growth approach to merging entire institutions. This scenario is clearly distant from the traditional college merger in which one of the campuses finally closes amid a furor of angry professors and demonstrating students. In this new context, we may define academic merger as a creative opportunity to combine significant and powerful educational resources and academic cultures as well as books, microscopes, and sports equipment. Preserving the sovereignty and autonomy of U.S. campuses has preoccupied so many generations of academic leaders that it will take a great deal more than one merger handbook to implement this broad a shift in managerial outlook. It is increasingly possible, however, to discern the openness of many governing boards, presidents, deans, and faculty members to the significant benefits an academic strategy proposing institutional merger can offer.

A New Philosophy: Merging for Mutual Growth

Traditionally, by the time one or both institutions ripe for merging acknowledged the need for retrenchment and a comprehensive financial resolution, many opportunities for achieving new forms of academic excellence had been lost or permanently reduced. A merger plan based on the mutual growth and enhancement of the missions of both institutions can stimulate the members of the combined faculty to new levels of professional development by peer example and increased institutional support. The development and articulation of a set of flexible, concise guidelines for academic managers now contemplating public or private strategic mergers to achieve academic excellence forms the core of this book's intent.

Skeptics will, and should, ask, does the theory work in practice? How can a merger, by its nature, be collaborative, participatory, and ethical? Collectively, the contributors to this book have consulted on or directly managed over two dozen college and university mergers during the past decade, three of them involving one private independent college in Massachusetts. They have repeatedly experienced the necessity to respect personal and professional considerations within strategic parameters. With special conditions such as curricular and faculty integration, accreditation, collegial governance, student credit rationalizations, records confidentiality, financial aid commitments, and lifetime alumni relationships, it is imperative to approach the earliest merger discussions with clearly stated organizational principles followed by procedures for implementation which convey the merger's purpose and practicality even to those on its periphery. In fact, the complementary mergers discussed in the following chapters provide the new institution with an ethical mandate to review developing activities in all of the above areas.

The Emergence of the Mutual-Growth Strategy in the Public Sector

In a few of the largest and latest initiatives in the public sector, state legislators, chief executive officers, and systemwide coordinating boards have explored the benefits of merging universities, state colleges, and community colleges for mutual growth in Arkansas, California, Florida, Georgia, Kansas, Maryland, Massachusetts, Michigan, Minnesota, New Jersey, Oklahoma, Oregon, and Texas.

In Arkansas, the Department of Higher Education in 1991 implemented a plan including four mergers between institutions in the twenty-four-member state vocational technical school system and the nineteen-member state system of technical and community colleges and the creation of ten newly designated technical colleges. The broad scope of this venture is seen as necessary to make postsecondary education as well as enhanced transfer articulation available to a significantly increased percentage of the state's population in the technologically oriented 1990s. Planners determined that two-thirds of the state population did not have access to a two-year college degree.[7]

In New Jersey, Camden County College in partnership with Glassboro State College (now Rowan College) opened a new facility called the Camden City Center. Completed in June 1991, this new facility has become the site for an innovative joint academic program that enables students from Camden City and surrounding areas to earn an associate's degree after two years of study and then, with full transfer of credit and an additional two years of study, a bachelor's degree in selected academic programs without leaving the city of Camden.[8]

In a similar model, Macomb Community College in Michigan opened in the fall of 1991 the University Center at Macomb Community College offering bachelor's degree programs in partnership with Wayne State University, Walsh College, Oakland and Central Michigan Universities, and the University of Detroit Mercy.

Described as a collaborative, cooperative, noncompetitive contractual agreement among a consortium of both public and private institutions, Macomb's University Center has been praised as a "timely concept that has been well-received." Donald Wing, associate vice president for academic affairs at the University Center, states that "the need for such a program in this part of the Detroit metropolitan area has been demonstrated by its tremendous growth so far—in the first two years, over 2,000 students have enrolled, exceeding our initial four-year projection."[9]

In this 70,000-square-foot building, which includes a two-story atrium lobby, university faculty members offer courses in classrooms provided by the community college. County residents will be able to earn undergraduate degrees from five institutions by virtue of a plan in which students complete their associate's degree studies at Macomb or another area community college and then complete one of sixteen bachelor's degree programs at the same site. Nationally, educational and political leaders have viewed the Macomb County plan as a model for communities who wish to encourage more community college graduates to complete four-year degrees.[10]

Referring to the success of this collaboration, Sanford Cohen, former senior vice president for academic affairs and provost at Wayne State University, said, "There [has been] one basic ingredient here that many institutions don't enjoy, and that's good will . . . we've had a long understanding that [Wayne State] wouldn't offer lower division courses in Macomb County."[11] At the same time, Macomb Community College has structured all of its courses to meet the universities' general education requirements. Basing their campaign on the need for increased education among the work force in Macomb County, a manufacturing area in decline, educators and politicians passed a controversial 1988 tax increase to support the initiative, which went on to win the top award for community relations from the Public Relations Society of America in 1989.

The Oklahoma Board of Regents has approved a study of the possible consolidation of the governing boards of three two-year colleges— Oklahoma City Community College, Redlands Community College, and Oklahoma State University Technical Branch—with the intention that all three would retain their own freestanding identities.[12] The state board has met with the boards of the three colleges to determine program needs and program duplications in order to improve coordination of postsecondary activities and enhance college-level education throughout the state. A mandate to raise overall curriculum standards has been followed by a marked increase in enrollment in the state's two-year colleges during the past five years. The proposed merger follows a similar plan implemented among three other two-year colleges in Tulsa in 1969.[13]

In 1990, a commission of higher education in the Portland metropolitan area began exploring possible avenues for collaboration among schools in the Portland area seeking to improve coordination among existing curricula and faculty resources in order to avoid costly expansion.[14]

In 1991, as a result of this commission, Portland State University, Clark College, and Mt. Hood, Clackamas, and Portland community colleges received a three-year joint grant from the U.S. Department of Education entitled "Fund for Improvement of Post Secondary Education." This grant has enabled the faculty of these five institutions to engage in a collaborative effort, sharing methodologies, objectives, and resources in the disciplines of British literature, chemistry, and American history. Portland Community College is working toward institutionalizing this grant so that this model for collaboration can be extended to other disciplines and continue beyond the scheduled three-year time frame.[15]

In 1990, the Kansas legislature approved a proposal for the merger of Kansas College of Technology in Salina and Kansas State University in Manhattan. The new structure would maintain both campus sites, and the smaller institution would be renamed the Kansas State College of Technology at Salina. Enrollments at the College of Technology had remained static in recent years, and the new model would combine and streamline the administrations and allow the College of Technology to draw on the extensive course offerings at the university. The university gains academically and in reputation from the only technology college in the state system.

The University of Maryland system was created in 1988, and in its first three years of existence significant merger discussions have arisen at several junctures. Almost immediately, the state general assembly voted to merge the five campuses of the University of Maryland with the other six campuses of the state college and university systems. In late 1989, a specific plan was considered to merge the University of Baltimore with the University of Maryland, Baltimore County, growing out of multiple requests over the preceding decade from the Baltimore business community for broadened continuing education opportunities for its employees and from the state's desire to coordinate more strategically the educational services provided by its community colleges and larger research institutions. This merger has not been implemented, but institutional and systemwide mergers have been placed on the table as viable options within the Maryland system as it considers plans for future growth.

The International Merger Context

Complementary growth mergers have also found a growing number of public-sector proponents internationally, particularly in Australia and Great Britain. In Australia, a team of several dozen planners has been working since the 1980s on a massive reorganization of the higher education system which would consolidate the nation's community colleges with its four-year institutions. The *Times Higher Education Supplement* reported in 1990 that the current government had set out "to modernize Australia's economy and institutions to adjust to the demands of a knowledge-led post-industrial world." After decades of patterning higher education policies on the British model, the newer colleges and universities in Australia, similar to the polytechnic sector in England, have taken inspiration from more flexible entrepreneurial American examples of institutional development. The *Times* noted, "Today the pattern of undergraduate and post-graduate education owes far more to the new world than the old. . . . The obsolescence of the binary policy has been tackled and a new National Unified System created. . . . Vigorous action has been taken to shape the pattern and scale of this unified system both by setting minimum sizes for institutions and by actively encouraging mergers."[16]

In the 1980s, major mergers have also occurred at the University of Wales, the University of Ulster in Northern Ireland, and, most prominently, the University of London. With its more than forty constituent colleges and institutes, the University of London represents over one-fifth of the total resources dedicated to and students enrolled in university education in Great Britain. Since the late 1970s, the university has developed and implemented an aggressive plan of more than fifteen institutional mergers, significantly altering both its face and inner structure. Recent examples of its merger master plan include the consolidation of Queen Elizabeth and Chelsea colleges into King's College, the combining of Bedford College and Royal Holloway College to form Royal Holloway and Bedford New College, and the creation of the combined Queen Mary and Westfield Colleges near the massive Docklands redevelopment project in East London (see chap. 13).

Recent Significant Mergers in U.S. Private Higher Education

Within a public system in the United States or abroad, the impetus for merging may sometimes follow from fiscal constraints and postaudit activities focused on not duplicating educational services; however, this has not been the case recently in the U.S. private sector. Across the country, recent private higher education merger activity has been impelled by a recognition of complementary missions and the legitimate need to preserve strength and competitiveness.

In the early 1980s, Widener University in Pennsylvania completed a merger with two Delaware institutions, the Delaware Law School and Brandywine College. This unusual venture integrated a law school, a junior college, and a four-year institution into one national comprehensive university whose enrollment increased from 5,000 to 9,000 students and whose budget rose from $7 million to over $70 million. Since the initial three-way merger, the law school has been renamed the Widener University School of Law, with campuses in Harrisburg and Wilmington, and the university has also merged with a doctoral program in clinical psychology at Hahnemann Hospital in Philadelphia.[17]

In 1985, Tift College in Forsyth, Georgia, approached Mercer University in Macon concerning a potential consolidation. At the time, Tift had no short- or long-term debt and an endowment of approximately $6 million. The faculty and administration, however, feared a possible erosion in enrollment. By the end of 1987, Tift had completed a merger with Mercer, a foundational principle being that the new institution would preserve the identity and commitment of Tift in both women's and teacher education in perpetuity.[18]

In 1989, Iona College in New Rochelle, New York, consolidated with Elizabeth Seton College in North Yonkers to form one institution on two campuses. Iona, a large, urban, four-year college founded by the Congregation of Christian Brothers in 1940, joined with Elizabeth Seton, an open-enrollment, two-year college operated by the Sisters of Charity. In the new academic configuration, the smaller institution has been transformed into the Elizabeth Seton School of Associate Degree Studies within Iona College. By this plan, Seton's strengths in nursing and communications will not only be preserved but strategically highlighted through the focused growth of the combined institution.[19]

Also in 1989, Gannon University, a coeducational, 2,400-student university in Erie, Pennsylvania, merged with Villa Maria College, a 600-student Catholic women's college known for strong programs in nursing and education as well as for addressing the special needs of women beyond traditional college age. Both institutions are now developing a number of complementary options that will enhance each of their original missions and the mission of the newly formed university. One new direction includes transforming the Villa Maria operation into a two-year college within the larger structure, through which students would progress before moving to the Gannon campus, a variation of the Elizabeth Seton School model at Iona. The current mission statement of the overall university includes as its fourth and final point: "[To] maintain Villa Maria College as an integral women's college with its own core curriculum and enhance the education of women and their status in society."[20] Whatever the details of its final shape the mutual-growth, complementary-mission concept has created a significantly broader set of educational opportunities for both Gannon and Villa Maria as they jointly face the uncertainties of regional and Catholic student demographics.[21]

After much consideration of a variety of models, the University of Detroit and Mercy College of Detroit agreed in 1990 to merge into the largest private Catholic comprehensive university in Michigan. In its first year, the new university will have a $72 million budget and student enrollments of 7,850. The two institutions, similar in mission and vulnerable to many of the same recruiting and marketing challenges, will keep the dentistry and law schools on their respective campuses, while using the university's former main campus for traditional aged college students and the former college campus for returning adult student programs and continuing education professional student programs.[22] It was reported that the creation of the newly named University of Detroit Mercy would eliminate duplicate programs and save both institutions money without eliminating any full-time faculty positions.[23]

Mount Ida College, an independent Massachusetts college with 1,600 students, over the past five years has implemented the strategies outlined in this chapter, merging with three Boston colleges and a division of a fourth: Chamberlayne Junior College, an institution with a reputation for the quality of its design programs; the Coyne School of Electricity, one of Massachusetts's two largest colleges of technical electricity; the New England Institute of Funeral Service Education, the only college in its region to award a degree in funeral service education; and the Veterinary Science Division and Opticianry Program from Newbury College. In each instance, faculty and administrators jointly developed a comprehensive plan that enhanced the personnel, curricular, and financial resources to be consolidated. More importantly, each step in the merger process validated the willingness of both colleges in approaching the merger with mutual growth rather than simply survival as their primary goal.

During the past decade, it has been more than simply full institutions that have merged, consolidated, and affiliated. In Maryland and Pennsylvania, creative designs have been implemented wherein pairs of smaller colleges have decided to remain distinct while merging library and learning-resource operations. Loyola and Notre Dame colleges in Baltimore, and Cedar Crest and Muhlenberg colleges in Allentown, Pennsylvania, separately developed the concept of joining forces in information-resource areas to form one large, coordinated library housed in two facilities, rather than two competing libraries on neighboring campuses. The Cedar Crest–Muhlenberg agreement formed a separate corporation, Educational Ventures, Incorporated, with its own board of trustess.[24] On all four campuses, the feeling now is that this concept has worked to the benefit of each pair of institutions from resource allocation and financial growth points of view and that this model could have application among other neighboring institutions with complementary missions.

The Mutual-Growth Model: How Excellence Is Achieved

All of the plans for merger, consolidation, and affiliation discussed here required extensive proactive planning as well as commitment to mission review and openness to new answers for familiar questions. Annual planning, planning in a five- or ten-year model, and even strategic planning are not sufficient to accomplish a college or university merger. Mutual-growth planning requires all of the skills of these approaches as well as a willingness to articulate a new model that does not merely reposition the institution within its natural category but develops an expanded institutional identity within a new category of colleges and universities.

The goals of the merger process will be affected by predictable factors such as institutional history, geographic distance, regional traditions, state regulations, the presence of collective bargaining, and specific financial parameters; however, the majority of private and public mergers discussed in the following chapters share ten components, the core principles behind merging colleges for mutual growth.

Enhancement of Complementary Institutional Missions

Traditional American bankruptcy-bailout merger plans were often driven not by a harmony of institutional missions, but rather by the coincidence of a financially secure, aggressive institution located near a weakened, even failing, college that was vulnerable to takeover. These were mergers in the barest sense of the word. At that time, the vocabulary of terms and strategic approaches managers now use to describe models for institutional consolidations, connections, and mergers did

---

The Core Principles of Merging Colleges for Mutual Growth

- Enhance complementary missions
- Encourage mutual growth
- Strengthen academic offerings

  Revise combined curriculum

  Emphasize complementary degree
  programs

  Eliminate redundancies

  Expand faculty resources

- Strengthen financial base

- Stabilize enrollment and student
  market share
- Improve administrative efficiency
- Accomplish economies of scale
- Use public relations opportunities
- Expand alumni base
- Create new institutional synergies

---

not exist.[25] A proactive, mutual-growth merger begins from a distinctly different perspective. First and most important, the missions of the colleges or universities must be complementary; that is, two or more postsecondary institutions join in a common endeavor for the mutual benefit and advancement of both organizations. This agreement demonstrates a shared vision and a stake in collaborative growth and development. One who assumed this to be the foundation of any successful merger would be surprised at the many educational mergers in this century which were forced on one or both participants because of financial considerations and geographic proximity.

A complementary-mission merger is predicated on the reality, rather than the wish or perception, of integration and articulation of the goals and visions of both institutions. This should not imply, however, that successful complementary-mission mergers must be limited solely to schools that offer similar programs or master plans for the future. Widener University simultaneously and successfully merged with a law school and a junior college, and later with a doctoral program in clinical psychology. Mount Ida College merged in succession with a junior college noted for its art and design curricula, a school of technical electricity, and an institute of funeral service education. In all instances, planners at Widener and Mount Ida had developed creative, accurate visions for the future shapes of their institutions which included new directions for mission expansion to serve more effectively enlarged resident and commuter populations during periods of demographic decline. The medium-sized university and the medium-sized college have both prospered in the first decade of their new identities.

Faculty and administrative leaders of merging colleges and universities must skillfully identify and build a common future on the connections between like institutions with separate, even rival, histories who have simultaneously confronted their long-term prospects and accepted the need to increase stability and flexibility by combining their structures, staffs, and reputations. The academic management of this institutional consonance, and its deliberate translation into lasting forms of cooperation by faculty and administrative leaders, are the primary characteristics of a merger undertaken to achieve academic excellence rather than to forestall bankruptcy.

Mutual Institutional Growth

A proactive, mutual-growth merger does not mean that both campuses will remain intact and expand the size of their budgets and enrollments. Rather, such a merger ensures that the *wills* of both institutions, by mutual agreement, are not simply to be preserved in the new educational structure but enhanced to a degree impossible for two freestanding institutions. By institutional *will*, we mean the conviction to place resources in the service of an often controversial merger strategy. Many times, a more timid merger partner will choose a less aggressive course of action in the face of faculty resistance to curriculum revisions and staff recalcitrance toward personnel changes.

Thus, mutual growth may be viewed as both a support and a challenge to the institutions' aspirations. Ultimately, merger can serve as the most effective vehicle to sustain and advance the visionary growth of both partners, even though each institution relinquishes its autonomy—a major hurdle for many American higher education planners. We have observed in more than one instance that colleges and universities able to separate their strengths and potential for long-term contributions to American higher education from dogged belief in institutional autonomy can best grasp the opportunities in this new managerial approach and position themselves for new forms of growth and prosperity.

Strengthened Overall Academic Offerings

Although complementary institutional missions characterize the mergers discussed in the following chapters, strengthening the overall academic offerings of the new institution and developing a sounder financial base constitute the two most important benchmarks in achieving academic excellence through this merger strategy.

When combining the two institutions' academic structures and programs, new strength is achieved in a variety of specific ways.

Review and Revision of Combined Curriculum

A merger causes a massive amount of curriculum review; in fact, developing a joint college curriculum review committee as the initial step in implementing the merger process is recommended in all cases (see Chapter 5, where this model is discussed in detail). A growth merger offers both institutions a once-in-a-generation opportunity to examine in detail each degree program and its relationship to all other degrees as well as its connectedness to the evolving mission of the university. Reviewing combined institutional curricula, even in their roughest state, also allows the revision of recent programs as well as older programs that may have become dated.

Enhancement of Complementary Degree Programs

Following on the comprehensive curriculum review and revision process, specific complementary programs offered by both institutions can be made even stronger in the collaborative articulation of their joint purposes by a transitional Curriculum Review Task Force. The merger provides, again, an unprecedented opportunity to blend the strongest aspects of degree curricula from both campuses in the formation of groups of master programs.

Elimination of Redundancies

The curriculum review component of the merger process also provides the chance to isolate and eliminate redundancies not simply in the combined curriculum but also within individual programs and courses on both campuses which may have survived several annual reviews. Course and program redundancies have a tendency at many institutions to accumulate and become hidden within departmental and program structures. This incremental process daunts and eventually defeats almost every dean and department chair who attempts to revise and improve the system. Experienced academic managers rapidly perceive the opportunities inherent in the forced redundancies that may accompany a merger and manipulate this situation openly and beneficially to bring new order to the aging areas of their curriculum.

Deepened Faculty Resources

Upon merging, the principal chief academic officer may supervise twice as many teaching faculty or more in the merged structure, an opportunity to build departments, programs, and divisions strategically to a depth not available in the separate colleges. Although fears regarding job security accompany a merger in any context, a complementary-mission design provides for the preservation of the greatest number of positions through a philosophy of merging for mutual *growth* and academic excellence. No merger will ever guarantee job security for the entire staffs of both institutions; however, the mutual-growth approach does consider at a much earlier stage the priority of strengthening both colleges through preserving faculty positions rather than eliminating full-time instructors to address financial exigencies.

Strengthened Financial Base

Successful higher education mergers require candid analyses and creative financial planning well before any strategy is implemented. As we note in chapter 8, a mission-complementary college or university merger arises from a congruence of growth opportunities which, when carefully but aggressively managed, produces a financial structure notably different from that of the traditional bankruptcy-bailout model. A plan based on mutual-growth principles approaches the central elements of debt structuring, financing ratios, refinancing options, consolidation of financial reporting, and accounting and management information systems from a more tactical frame of reference.

Analyses by members of the Merger Task Force of assets, liabilities, fund balances, near-term cash flow, and long-range economic consequences are conducted with the goal of preserving and enhancing the educational missions of two institutions that have willingly chosen to relinquish their longstanding autonomies to form a new, more powerful entity. At the same time, mutual-growth mergers remain honest regarding their necessary financial underpinnings and must make persuasive economic sense to academic managers at both institutions by generating returns able to support the projected increase in educational quality.

Stabilized Enrollment and Student Market Share

A strengthened student market share, including stabilized enrollments over a period of years, as a result of the merger of two institutions with complementary missions is another core principle. After controversial issues such as job security, collective bargaining requirements, tenure, and the possible closure of one campus have been addressed, the most prevalent merger-related question in both offices and classrooms will most likely be how many students the new institution will draw in its first three-to-five years of operation.[26]

It is important even during the height of this transitional period to acknowledge that the question is much broader than simply how large the college will be. The concern voiced by students and staff members regards the *stability*, not the growth, of the surviving educational structure. No rule addresses the issue of enrollment growth for all academic mergers. We have observed generally that complementary-mission, mutual-growth mergers maintain in their first year an enrollment level slightly less than that of the combined student bodies at the start of planning discussions. How much less, if any, is of course critical for budget forecasting. Merger managers realize they must take this factor into consideration during the development of their first five-year plan. More importantly, however, while we have seen several combined structures emerge with slightly less than the total prior enrollments, growth *above* this enrollment level even as soon as one or two years after merger often occurs and may be an achievable objective for the project's designers.

Some consolidating institutions understandably do not seek enrollment growth above their original combined levels, and in these cases adding students will necessitate special resource and personnel considerations. Whatever the case, a mutual-growth merger will provide a significant stabilizing effect on enrollment drift or decline. Institutions willing to undertake this change will achieve enrollment success on a scale beyond the scope of one admissions staff, no matter how talented and dedicated.

As a result of its new profile, expanded academic and financial resources, and the significant media exposure accompanying a merger, the newly merged college or university will naturally and rapidly claim a larger market share of local, regional, and even national recruiting areas. From an admissions point of view, mergers eliminate competitors and combine the strengths of at least two sets of veteran recruiters, factors which alone can go far toward stabilizing student market share.

Administrative Efficiencies

Similar to the careful personnel review of faculty, administrative leaders must make certain to collaborate in designing and publicizing a rigorous, authentic staff review for themselves, a practice that has emerged as a core factor in the long-term success of a complementary-mission merger. The perception must not be allowed to develop that administrative staff, particularly at the highest levels, can or should be more protected than line faculty members during personnel reviews and consolidation. In fact, administrators may have less claim to job security than faculty members. Complementary academic programs almost always will preserve necessary faculty positions as long as enrollments remain stable. Administrators often have no such protections, nor could they have. There cannot be two directors of the library or two deans of students. The key to managing a mutual-growth merger successfully in this area is the academic managers' sensitive guidance during the important negotiations that may result in difficult but desirable administrative reductions.

Often, an accurate indicator of a successful merger will be how candidly administrators can view themselves and each other in devising the leadership structure of the combined institution. At all costs, a parity must be preserved between the personnel guidelines developed for administrators and faculty members in the merger. In later years, this parity will represent one of the most formative aspects of the character of the new college or university.

Economies of Scale

Merger-prompted duplications appear in hundreds of areas from financial aid to library collections, and, rather than viewing them as negatives, successful merger managers will use each as an opportunity to upgrade the academic, student, and financial services provided by the merged college or university. New opportunities for academic excellence will form the basis for most decisions dictating reductions in each area of merger implementation.

Administrators and faculty members routinely hear that duplication should be eliminated, but only under special circumstances do they find themselves freed to make decisions regarding retrenchments and redundancies. Mutual-growth mergers challenge academic managers to apply theories they believe are correct but that they may never have observed in practice, much less implemented on their own campuses.

New Public Relations Opportunities

A college or university merger provides the consolidated office of public relations with a media occasion rare in the life of most campuses. Mergers simultaneously provoke welcome and unwanted media review; however, mergers that carry no stigma of bankruptcy or financial exigency create proportionally more positive interest among student consumers and the general public. Mutual-growth mergers, in particular, offer the leaders of the new institution an unusual opportunity to define its identity, image, and even elements of its reputation to a significant degree. Nevertheless, the media attention may prove to be a challenge beyond the resources of even the newly expanded staff. The merger management team must make certain that the designated director of public relations has full access to the highest levels of executive leadership at all times.

Successful merger managers must create a public relations program of press releases and position papers concerning the new educational structure. Traditionally, postsecondary institutions are featured in news stories during the months of September (for orientation) and May (for commencement); proactive college and university mergers provide unseasonal news, and experienced faculty members and administrators utilize this public attention as one more step toward real and perceived academic excellence.

Expanded Alumni Base

Bankruptcy-bailout mergers, like threats of coeducation, can provoke alumni to public demonstrations, letter-writing campaigns, and calls for legislative intervention. As Victor Scalise, Jr., indicates in chapter 12, alumni involvement in both planning and implementation should be viewed as the norm for success in an organizational change as significant as merger. Alumni are, with students, one of the two most overlooked resources in the merger process. While a bankruptcy-bailout merger and the potential closure of one or more campuses can produce a sense of abandonment among graduates, a complementary, mutual-growth merger gives alumni affairs officers together with the expanded public relations staff many opportunities to formulate a set of special programs and gatherings spanning the first one to three years of the postmerger period.

Similar to the public relations area, the alumni office in a mutual-growth merger experiences a sudden and dramatic change in the nature of its agenda and the number of its staff members, and because both of these offices are sometimes distant from the highest levels of leadership during the merger's implementation, events may sometimes seem uncontrollable, heightening tensions. Nevertheless, from a numerical point of view, alumni offices realize mergers are a boon to their development planning. In one year, the staff often inherits at least twice as many prospective contributors. Mount Ida College rose from an alumni base of fewer than 4,000 graduates to a population of almost 12,000 during the six-year period of its merger activity. Mercer University gained 7,000 alumni in its union with Tift College, raising its total to over 30,000 in two years. Widener University, through its merger with Brandywine College, added over 3,500 additional members to its alumni community over the past decade.[27]

Any merger attracts significant attention from all graduates. Older graduates, increasingly attached to memories of a disappearing institutional reality, may view even a growth merger as an acknowledgment of defeat and dissolution; however, it is the responsibility of the merger managers to achieve a balanced, positive approach to the dramatic increase in the number of community members, always building on the opportunities for excellence occasioned by this dramatic growth in human resources.

New Institutional Synergies

This factor draws from all the others in articulating the controversial yet undeniable organizational synergy released during the merger planning and implementation process. In our experience as planners and managers, we have noted the character of the new institution rapidly breaking through in committee meetings, task force planning sessions, and the ongoing business of both campuses long before the merger is legally consummated.

In the past twenty years or so, synergy has become overused to the point of dilution in education literature[28]; however, many of its authentic aspects persist in mission-complementary merger. Although much debate has concerned the factors that may most effectively produce synergy, in our experience, the character of the merged college or university has been distinguished by aggressive faculty and administrative leadership and by an aura of new purpose, even amid a great number of ambiguities. Realizing that a degree of institutional combustion must occur, proactive administrators use this intensity in guiding all levels of the new organization through a stressful but beneficial period of institutional redefinition.

The Key to Successful Implementation: Diversified Planning

With the principal conditions and goals of the merger defined, and with the expected results articulated, academic managers must finally focus their collective attention on the plan for implementation and then on postmerger review. In fact, postmerger master planning may be introduced as the first significant community-building activity to draw peripheral departments and areas, possibly overlooked or underused by the original merger planning team, closer to the center of the new institutional identity. It has been noted that the success or failure of a merger's conceptualization cannot be adequately measured for three to five years; thus, it becomes even more important to develop early, clear guidelines for the implementation process and to assure they are fairly and rigorously followed on both campuses through the first five years.[29]

Critics point out that higher education mergers typically require new buildings that increase fixed costs, that additional students mean additional support services and expenditures, and that a larger college population will include more low-skilled learners, underprepared for true postsecondary work. Yet the trend is toward more and larger growth mergers in education and the corporate sector.[30] The *Harvard Business Review* reported as far back as 1986 that the use of mergers "to redirect and reshape corporate strategy has never been greater."[31]

The more planners have investigated the concept of synergy as well as the broader philosophy of merging colleges for mutual growth, the more they have discovered both to be characterized by at least two core elements: superior planning systems and the work of two or three central managers of change. Meticulous merger planning—a detailed yet imaginative design grounded in a grasp of the unique elements of both institutional cultures—is an essential component of significant, lasting change. Project leaders must immediately identify those who will serve in the long term as managers of this change, as these individuals will finally form the most critical factor in the enduring success of the new institution.[32] A surprisingly small number of faculty leaders and academic administrators will be charged with accepting the great number of unknowns into their personal and professional lives, and they will be responsible for shaping the plan approved by the collective faculties and administrations into the identity of the new institution. Enlightened, effective academic administrators have been in short supply in every merger we have studied. The time demands mergers place on the new leadership are often underestimated, and the challenges these leaders must address and overcome will probably be unprecedented in their careers. Executive leaders on both campuses will also do well to remain sensitive to the risks as well as opportunities mergers present to their subordinates.

A note of caution regarding institutional merger as a planning instrument: merging, for whatever set of reasons, should not be considered by some aggressive colleges and universities. Even with sufficient managers of change and institutional resources, mission complementarity may not exist, and strategic objectives might never be achieved. We propose instead that merging colleges and universities to preserve and extend the visions and wills of two or more institutions should become one element of a broader, more diversified national model of effective academic management in postsecondary education.

The mutual-growth merger strategy has emerged in the past twenty-five years despite the lack of an effective, unified planning model for higher education institutions. With over 3,400 colleges and universities in the United States, the challenge is great to achieve even a small advance in planning systems; however, there is significant agreement that U.S. and European colleges and universities now face greater uncertainties while possessing greater human and technological resources than at any time in their histories. Merging for mutual growth has become integral to entrepreneurial academic planning. Although it should never serve as more than one component in a diversified approach to achieve academic excellence, we believe its potential is now critical.

CHAPTER TWO

Higher Education Mergers, Consolidations, Consortia, and Affiliations: A Typology of Models and Basic Legal Structures

James E. Samels

Central to an informed understanding of higher education mergers is a familiarity with basic merger models and corporate restructuring terminology. When trustees consider legally available merger options, it is counsel's responsibility to explain the full range of alternatives, including advantages and risks to the institution in the near and long terms. At the core of collegiate mergers sits the legal framework of corporate charters, trustee bylaws, contracts, statutes, common law, and regulatory promulgations. Taken together, these legal authorities shape much of the merger plan and process.

This legal component is predicated on the supposition that several other necessary elements are present in the merger plan: complementary educational missions, shared faculty scholarship aspirations, involved student bodies, flexible governance systems, and endowment and resource articulations.[1]

In considering merger as an academic management strategy, college and university trustees should start by closely examining the range of structural alternatives, including pure merger, consolidation, consortium, asset transfers, and educational affiliations. Trustees must try to preserve an institutional mission adaptable to the educational marketplace while also strengthening their institution's academic offerings.[2]

Academic managers and the members of the Merger Task Force must consider risks and benefits with an eye to preserving each institution's distinctive name and reputation. The levels of risk will typically correlate with the up-front investment either institution is willing to make toward pure merger. If one institution assumes the major share of liabilities, the merger agreement will provide it with the bulk of surplus tuition and boarding fee revenues generated over the long term.

In past decades, many colleges and universities considered merging mainly in response to financial exigency or even insolvency. Often, endowment goals were missed and dedicated funds were utilized under the guise of interest-free loans for which repayment was unlikely. Over time, as fiscal matters deteriorated, senior administrators unavoidably delayed payments to product and service vendors, credit lines constricted, and payrolls and debt service obligations were deferred. Annual financial statements painted a steadily worsening picture as auditors began to look more closely at the financial underpinnings of an older, weakened institution or an up-and-coming college that suddenly found itself overextended.

Fiduciary Responsibilities

Establishing legally appropriate fiduciary guideposts with the assistance of independent, experienced legal counsel helps to define realistic parameters for building institutional confidence and monitoring overall merger timing and implementation. Beyond their powers of governance and executive leadership, trustees must assiduously avoid real and apparent conflicts of interest and develop a sixth sense of ethical prerogatives in their internal discussions and external merger relationships.[3] As trustees, they must be the most vigilant to protect, where educationally and financially practicable, the institution's mainstream educational programs.

Board members must also develop a special sensitivity to maintaining the quality and rigor of the institution's particular academic research, publishing, and community service programs. Without fidelity to these central educational purposes, even the institution's most candid expectations for postmerger growth could place one or both of the merging colleges at risk. Trustees must also exercise prudence and due care to ensure that projected revenues, direct and indirect cost estimates, and other related financial, administrative, and legal implications are realistically assessed.

Each board should secure experienced advice in strategic areas such as finances, accreditation, academic policy, and legal issues to guide their deliberations in compliance with applicable provisions of law and fiduciary responsibility. Finally, each trustee should consider all practical alternatives rather than simply conceding the sale or divestment of their institution's educational assets. In a pure merger, one college or university may exercise a certain measure of dominance over its partner institution in light of its faculty numbers, scale of campus operations, diversity of educational programs, student enrollment size, or endowment depth. In some instances, trustees may opt for merger or consoli-

---

A Typology of Higher Education Mergers

- Pure merger
- Consolidation
- Transfer of assets
- Consortium
- Federation

- Association
- Joint venture
- Affiliation

---

dation over affiliation, asset transfer, or simple discontinuance when the college's mission and purposes might be better served by an option short of full merger.[4]

Attorneys representing these institutional governing boards must immerse themselves in the similarities and differences of each partner's campus legal culture by assessing and assimilating a history of recent master plans, mission statements, curricula, collective bargaining agreements, catalogues, personnel policy manuals, and student and faculty handbooks that will inform the merger planning process. Conducting a legal audit of the prospective merger partner promotes mutual trust and confidence between institutional legal representatives and builds a shared understanding of the legal parameters of the prospective merger transaction.[5]

A Typology of Higher Education Mergers

Once the premerger planning questionnaires have been completed and all charters, statutes, policies, contracts, publications, regulations, and endowment trust declarations have been reviewed, and once the basis for collegial dialogue between the merging educational communities has been established, the institutions must select a legally appropriate merger model, a basic choice with which they will live long after the merger pact has been signed.

In the following section, an outline of the most common college and university merger agreements is provided from both strategic planning and legal points of view.

Pure Merger

A pure merger is generally defined as an agreement by which Institution A is *merged into* Institution B, with Institution B serving as the exclusive legal successor. In effect, Institution A is dissolved, leaving Institution B as the sole surviving institution. Dissolution may be either voluntary or involuntary, depending on the legal and governance circumstances leading up to and surrounding the merger transaction. In this kind of pure merger, Institution B inherits both the assets and liabilities of Institution A unless provided otherwise by agreement. Institution B is usually enhanced by another institution's identity, as it typically absorbs the strongest of Institution A's legacies and traditions.

Generally, once consummated, pure mergers are irrevocable, as the merged institution has discontinued its vital operations and lost its former identity and position. Although one institutional partner may consider establishing a defunct campus following a difficult merger implementation, for all practical purposes a simple return to the status quo is not easy once the legal transaction has triggered the discontinuance of that campus's operation.

A variety of financial and academic conditions can affect the choice of pure merger.[6] Often, pride in an institution's identity or longstanding political controversies can obstruct the path to pure merger. Conversely, the academic reputation, faculty credentials, and student preparedness of both institutions can be significantly elevated through this simple and direct approach. In these instances, the merging institution would naturally prefer to inherit the remaining intellectual and real property assets of the merged institution without assumption of corresponding liabilities, threats of litigation, or other claims. In a best-case situation, the merging institution will devise a self-liquidating resolution of outstanding liabilities, with remaining assets dedicated to continuing the merged institution's programs according to collaboratively developed parameters.

In his influential research on higher education mergers, John Millet chronicled a number of examples of pure mergers, including such better-known ones as Case and Western Reserve universities, the University of Missouri and the University of Kansas City, and Western College and Miami University.[7]

Case Western Reserve was arguably a pure merger, even though its name appears to describe a consolidation. The two institutions shared a legacy of close affiliation and common identity, and the merged university has served for over twenty years as a national role model for both its physical integration and complementary academic programming.

In contrast to this more complementary plan, Western College faculty members and students entered the merger process with Miami University thinking that Miami would continue in perpetuity to subsidize Western's operating deficits, without absorbing the college into the university. In a short time, however, spiraling debt and creditors' claims made it apparent that economic reality had overtaken Western's hopes for institutional survival, and it was merged into Miami. These two scenarios offer contrasting examples of traditional mergers prompted by financial necessity. What follows are two examples of mergers for mutual growth based on strategic and academic, rather than purely financial, concerns.

Mount Ida College in Newton, Massachusetts, successfully merged Chamberlayne Junior College, the Coyne School of Technical Electricity, and the New England Institute of Funeral Service Education into its two-plus-two, junior and senior college academic structure over the 1987–90 period.[8] These three mission-complementary, growth-oriented mergers have significantly strengthened the academic quality of the combined college while diversifying its professional, vocational, and business education offerings, expanding its enrollment base, raising the scholarship aspirations of faculty, and increasing academic rigor for students.

In 1986, the College of St. Catherine in St. Paul, Minnesota, accomplished a merger with St. Mary's College in which, through the expanded resources of the new institution, St. Catherine has completed a successful postgraduate degree approval process and will begin to award its first master's degrees in four health science areas, building on the legacy and strengths of St. Mary's academic tradition. This merger reflects a successful, clearly defined implementation process with neither institution contemplating a singular postmerger role or function.

Also of note is the 1989 merger of the Swain School of Design in New Bedford with Southeastern Massachusetts University.[9] Three years after this merger, the university's new College of Visual and Performing Arts was selected as one of Massachusetts's outstanding community arts projects by the *Boston Phoenix* newspaper and has been widely acclaimed as a critically important educational and cultural resource in the southeastern quadrant of the state.

Consolidation

Higher education consolidations involve two or more institutions that are *collapsed into* one new college or university, usually with a different name, mission, and scale of operation: Institution A and Institution B become Institution C. The new institution typically houses multiple schools or colleges and reflects a diversity of degree program offerings at undergraduate and graduate levels. Several variations of corporate governance structures are available to accommodate separate but coordinated or reconstituted trustee boards.

In this model, an institution seeking to preserve its academic heritage might see potential in either a new or shared institutional name identification. Whatever the choice of nomenclature, consolidations are often motivated by many of the same academic quality, administrative efficiency, and demographic realities that impel pure mergers and often duplicate pure mergers once the respective campus cultures are fully integrated.

In *Colleges and Corporate Change: Merger, Bankruptcy, and Closure,* Barnett and O'Neill cite the consolidation of the New School for Social Research in New York and the Parsons School of Design as a leading example in which two freestanding institutions retained their separate legal identities and corporate charters but became a single new operating unit.[10] Both preserved most of their respective academic missions and degree programs but with separate budgetary and revenue retention processes. Parsons agreed to an eventual phaseout of split governance by which New School trustees would be appointed to fill vacancies when these occurred on the Parsons board.

Similarly, in 1977, the consolidation of Becker College in Worcester, Massachusetts, with Leicester Junior College in neighboring Leicester left intact both campuses and boards of trustees, with major policy-making, governance, and academic stewardship powers transferred to the Becker board. The members of the Leicester board remained to oversee specifically designated endowments left in trust for the betterment of the Leicester campus.[11]

Transfer of Assets

In transfer transactions, Institution A *transfers* and assigns its right, title, and interest in some or all of its assets to Institution B, which provides, as consideration, the continued maintenance and operation of some or all of Institution A's programs. In certain cases, these reciprocal covenants for consideration may be used in combination with monetary payment in exchange for use or ownership of academic programs, curriculum, faculty, library resources, archives, development network, and alumni lists. Depending upon the transfer objectives of the participating institutions, Institution A may continue to operate, albeit reduced in its educational focus and offerings, or may discontinue entirely after completing the resolution of its corporate affairs and voluntary dissolution process.

Transfer transactions can be motivated by a broad range of academic, financial, and administrative considerations. Frequently, the host institution has developed a significant market penetration and student following. At the same time, the transferring institution may have found that the programs to be transferred are no longer cost-effective or germane to its academic mission. Whatever the motivations, asset transfers have become an increasingly popular merger mechanism for promoting proactive, creative, and growth-oriented collaboration between colleges and universities.

The merger between the Delaware Law School and Widener University in Chester, Pennsylvania, precipitated several years of legal challenges that influenced the structure and contractual framework of Widener's subsequent merger with Wilmington's Brandywine College.[12] In the view of some observers, Brandywine faced becoming a heavily indebted two-year institution acquired potentially to provide an additional campus for the university's new law school. Simultaneously, Widener wanted to protect its assets from Brandywine's creditors and residual liabilities. While many of the operations were consolidated and faculty and academic concerns merged, because of the preexisting debt obligation of Brandywine and the legal challenges of Delaware Law School, it was deemed legally imprudent to complete a statutory merger and subject all of the assets of Widener University, the parent institution, to the claims of existing or potential creditors of the new subsidiaries. Legally, both Brandywine and Delaware Law School continued to maintain separate corporate existences as wholly owned subsidiaries of Widener. The law school then encouraged Widener to establish a separate corporate presence in Delaware, and it became dually incorporated, remaining under Pennsylvania jurisdiction and creating a shell corporation in Delaware that was consolidated with the Pennsylvania structure to form a single entity.

Peabody College in Nashville, Tennessee, a freestanding institution merged by transferring its assets to Vanderbilt University. As a school of education, however, Peabody College still exists, one of ten schools at Vanderbilt. Although the college can no longer claim any freestanding legal existence, it remains a freestanding institution on the site of its original campus with its physical identity preserved intact.[13]

Other examples of successful asset transfers have been completed by Boston University in its acquisitions of the Wang Institute, a midcareer computer science graduate program, and of the *Partisan Review* literary journal, which was transferred from Rutgers—The State University. In the other direction, Boston transferred its own graduate nursing program, ranked at the time among the best in the nation, to Northeastern University in 1989. From Boston University's viewpoint, it was no longer economically feasible to deliver graduate nursing education following the closure of its undergraduate program, which occurred at the same time that the University of Massachusetts at Boston had been permitted to expand its undergraduate program at a significantly subsidized tuition rate. For its part, Northeastern was intent on building a serious graduate level program in the specific fields of nursing education that Boston University had maintained, and its cost-effective budgeting system was able to provide sufficient revenues to permit a major cash investment at the critical moment. In so doing, Northeastern has attracted a core of aspiring graduate nursing students and enhanced its reputation for graduate studies in the allied health field.

Consortia, Federations, and Associations

Frequently referred to by their acronyms, these forms of collegial collaboration usually involve a series of mutual covenants and obligations that have common resource-sharing objectives. These aims can include avoiding duplicate course offerings, increased library access, shared use of facilities, computerized data bases, applied technologies, and cooperative procurements. Often, such consortia, federations, and associations are chartered on a regional, statewide, or county basis to capture the advantages of geographic proximity, similar campus cultures, and common regulatory frameworks. The Council for Inter-Institutional Leadership, a national clearinghouse for higher education consortia in Kansas City, lists 150–200 multipurpose college- and university-based consortia now operating in the United States.

These collaborative arrangements also can go beyond the sharing of educational resources for the development of common academic and public policies or interaction with the licensing and accreditation process. If properly conceived and focused, these forms of institutional bonding can lead to more effective use of finite campus resources and the advocacy of common educational and political positions. Members of consortia typically assume financial responsibility only for activities specified in the joint venture. Ordinarily, consortium membership does not imply financial support for the broader institutional goals of other member colleges.

Among the more well known, longstanding examples of this structure is California's Claremont Group, which stands as a leading model of merged efficiency. The group's schools (Claremont Graduate School, Pomona, Pitzer, Scripps, Harvey Mudd, and Claremont McKenna) have developed a flexible, collegial plan to share library, business, and maintenance operations. A second example is The Great Lakes College Association, one of the country's oldest consortia, was founded in 1961 as an academic consortium of twelve liberal arts colleges (Albion, Antioch, Denison, DePauw, Earlham, Hope, Kalamazoo, Kenyon, Oberlin, Ohio Wesleyan, Wabash, and the College of Wooster) and provides among other services and resources the sponsorship of extensive off-campus study opportunities for students and professional development opportunities for faculty members.[14] Third, the Consortium of Vermont Colleges (Bennington, Castleton State, Champlain, College of St. Joseph, Green Mountain, Johnson State, Lyndon State, Marlboro, Middlebury, the New England Culinary Institute, Norwich, St. Michael's, Southern Vermont, Sterling, Trinity, the University of Vermont, and Vermont Technical College) has established joint admission programs to recruit out-of-state students.

A fourth instance is the Lehigh Valley Association of Independent Colleges, founded in 1969, which includes Lehigh University, Allentown College of St. Francis de Sales, Cedar Crest, Lafayette, Moravian, and Muhlenberg colleges. The association provides program and resource support in the following areas, among others: student cross-registration, reciprocal library borrowing privileges, study abroad programs, student recruiting programs, cooperative academic planning, and cultural events.[15] Lastly, Five Colleges, Inc., in Massachusetts provides interinstitutional course registrations, intercampus bus service, and extensive joint academic and cultural programs for Amherst, Hampshire, Mount Holyoke, and Smith colleges and the University of Massachusetts.

Joint Ventures and Educational Affiliations

Sometimes overlooked is the simple joint venture affiliation, one of the most productive formats for the mutual-growth merger concept. This shared investment and campus-sensitive approach offers the distinct advantages of preserving the respective identities and governance structures of the participating institutions while promoting creative, specific collaborations in areas of academic programming, administrative efficiency, and complementary growth.

A basic affiliation agreement typically involves a set of mutual promises and anticipated academic benefits which, when gathered together, can provide mutual faculty exchange opportunities, joint enrollments, transfer articulations, shared library resources, joint externships, and other related advantages. In consideration of these several benefits, the institutions may receive a share of the surplus proceeds generated from the joint educational endeavors and potential enrollment growth. A key point regarding affiliation agreements is that, unlike the other merger structures, they have the least intrusive impact on the participating institutions by providing a period of collegial confidence and trust building in preparation for potentially more permanent educational partnerships.

The Legal Steps of a Mutual-Growth Merger

- Engage experienced merger counsel
- Complete strategic plan
- Assess educational complementarity
- Coordinate trustee governance models
- Determine post-merger institutional name
- Develop non-competition covenants
- Clarify residual liabilities
- Articulate human resource systems
- Assess collective bargaining implications
- Conduct legal audit
- Structure negotiations

- Complete merger contract development
- Consummate merger contract
- Arrange for capital outlay financing and new facilities development
- Anticipate educational consumer claims
- Prepare combined financial aid model
- Conserve student records
- Secure appropriate licensure and accreditation

Variations on this affiliation format run to the hundreds, even thousands, in the public and private higher education systems of many states and are not coordinated through a national resource bank. The Council for Inter-Institutional Leadership projects their number in the tens of thousands.

The Legal Structure of Successful Mutual-Growth Mergers

Independent and Experienced Merger Counsel

It has not been uncommon in the past for some institutions considering merger to drift into the negotiation process with a geographically convenient, apparently complementary partner without the benefit of experienced, disinterested legal counsel. In many cases, before either institution realized it, their boards of trustees were caught in a morass of legal liabilities, restrictive obligations, governmental regulations, and endowment erosion that effectively drained any support for merger as a strategy to achieve educational excellence.

In still other situations, a well-meaning trustee, faculty member, or senior staff member who happens to hold a law degree and has some general practice experience may offer pro bono advice and consultation to guide the merger process. It may not be surprising that such well-intended efforts to strike a harmonious chord of informality and near-term cost savings can result in undue delay and significant long-term financial loss.

Whatever the reasons for donated legal services or delayed engagement of experienced counsel, the results can be uncertain legal consequences for one or both institutions—untoward contract liability, unnecessary and distracting litigation, adverse court judgments, and protracted settlement negotiations over ambiguous or unlawful merger pact provisions that were well intentioned but the product of legal naïveté or inadvertence. Experience has shown that positive merger results are typically preceded by early legal intervention, preplanning, and strategic guidance in order to avoid issues such as contract breach, litigation, collateral attack by endowment donors, and judicial restraint by various groups of institutional stakeholders.

Retained counsel should be familiar with higher education law, corporate reorganization, and merger negotiations. Attorneys concentrating their practice in these several fields draw upon an integrated data base that provides both institutions with an elevated overview and analysis of available merger options, near-term legal implications, and the ramifications of potential litigation and claims. Experienced counsel know the threshold questions that must be posed regarding applicable statutory authority, corporate articles of organization and amendment, internal bylaws, and related legal restrictions on the transferability of assets and the liquidation of outstanding liabilities. They are also familiar with merger documentation and its management.

A mutual-growth model works best with independent merger counsel with no direct or indirect conflict of interest in the business outcomes of the merger. This will require careful examination of each attorney's institutional affiliations and partnership relationships. Often, concerns in this area can be assuaged through prior disclosure of real or apparent interests and nonparticipation or total recusal in certain aspects of the merger consultations and negotiations.

Finally, each counsel needs to be familiar with and sensitive to the nuances of the legal cultures on both campuses. An awareness of current collegial governance processes, handbook provisions, collective bargaining agreements, and residence life regulations will provide the attorneys with information necessary to facilitate the merger process.

Compensation and billing options include hourly billable rates with maximum obligation caps and fixed-fee per diem, weekly, monthly, and annual compensation models. Merging institutions can share expenses through a structured combination of billable time and fixed-fee retainer based on the experience level of the attorneys and their work effort and results. When viewed in the context of what is to be gained, legal service expenditures should be considered as preventive planning costs that may avoid long-term financial disability and adverse consequences. In each case, a preliminary budget should be assembled reflecting anticipated premerger legal planning, negotiation, and closing costs. These preliminary projections also incorporate the costs associated with each attorney's time, cash disbursements, and other related expenditures.

Strategic Legal Planning

Whatever the merger model chosen by the chief executive officers and members of the Merger Task Force, from the first planning discussions legal counsel must be cognizant of and sensitive to the powers and limitations set forth in the corporate charter, special legislation, and contract provisions. In advising the trustees, counsel must be alert to the numerous restrictions placed on trustee authority, further circumscribed by such fiduciary responsibilities as preserving corporate assets consistent with the institution's chartered mission while maximizing income and strengthening educational offerings. Beyond a working familiarity with the chartered purposes, special legislative enabling provisions, and other legal restrictions, counsel must be conversant with the trustees' own bylaws that set the ground rules for corporate change, including mergers, consolidations, affiliations, and asset transfers.

Just as important, counsel must be aware of contractual covenants and stipulations restricting the powers and assignable rights of the college within the context of mergers and other corporate changes. These restrictions may range from employee contracts and collective bargaining agreements to service contracts and facility use agreements. In addition, vendors' claims to exclusivity of service, subsisting commission payback arrangements and licenses, permits, and other legal authorizations must now be scrutinized, inventoried, and cross-tabulated. This integrative legal preparation will help to prevent any hidden liability pitfalls that could restrict the merging partners' options in the future.[16]

Educational Complementarity

As well as conducting an evaluation of the merger partner's academic stature and reputation, each institution should assess the educational programs and activities the partner offers to help determine whether the institutions' degree programs both mesh appropriately and provide programs for the future capable of attracting the critical mass of students essential to fund full implementation of the planned merger.

The smaller institution must develop a sense of the larger institution's scale of operations and financial depth. Does the larger institutional partner have the depth of resources necessary to effectively integrate the other college's educational mission and role without wholesale program curtailments and faculty retrenchments? If not, one or both institutions may be properly guided to consider such alternatives as an interim affiliation, program assets transfer, transformation into an educational foundation, or discontinuance through voluntary dissolution.

Trustee Governance

Members of the Merger Task Force and both senior leadership teams must be mindful of the importance that trustee governance and control will play in the overall merger implementation. Both institutions will need to consider a variety of shared governance models, possibly involving addition of trustee member seats to represent the merged college or phased-in trustee integration over a longer period of time. Conversely, both partners must remain realistic in their demands for a voice on the postmerger board of trustees, given their relative positions in negotiations and giving due regard to the continuing obligations, if any, assumed by the larger institution for support of the other's educational programs and activities.

Postmerger Institutional Name Change

Inevitably, the merging colleges or universities must confront the sensitive issue of postmerger name identification, for the realities of competitive marketing and niche adjustment have become powerful forces in contemporary higher education. From the perspective of the less dominant college or university, institutional pride, distinctiveness, and a natural desire to continue its traditions will weigh heavily in the balance of considerations. For the larger and more powerful institution, any dilution of its single identity or ambiguity regarding its present institutional name identification may be enough to extinguish its appetite for merger.

Merger partners may opt for simply establishing a school, division, or program within the merging institution which preserves the former institution's name and identity. In other instances, the more dominant institution may be amenable to a hyphenated name, or, in circumstances of consolidation, a new name might evolve reflecting the diverse institutional cultures and traditions of the merger partners.

Good-Faith Cooperation

At this point, partner colleges will want to stipulate mutual covenants to exercise their best good-faith efforts to achieve mutual merger objectives. This objective can be met by memorializing mutual covenants for noninterference and noncompetition to take effect during the period leading up to and after the consummation of the merger. These mutually restrictive covenants ensure that no party will attempt to obstruct another should one partner develop second thoughts and attempt to revitalize its campus after disappointment with some aspect of the merger negotiation.

Dissolution poses another potential dilemma for merging partners, as a less dominant college or university will have legitimate concerns regarding the useful life of its practical leverage should it wind down its affairs in advance of completing the merger process, relying on future covenants and pledges. The schools may wish to enter into "exclusivity of bargaining status and relationships" for a finite period of time, insuring the legal and bargaining fidelity of the parties. In certain instances, it may be legally appropriate to establish a noninterference provision that would prohibit any partner institution from attempting to undermine the bargaining position of another by ex parte communications with its students, faculty, and other communities it serves.

For clarity and finality in bringing merger negotiations to closure in the contract document, the schools should stipulate an integration clause, making valid only those provisions contained in the written merger agreement and laying to rest in advance the possibility of rights or oral representations raised later which were not ratified by the partners in the formal contract process. To establish mutual trust and confidence, an open-book financial policy allows any partner to inspect and copy another's financial records and wards off unnecessary controversy regarding inadequate or incomplete financial data and analysis.

Residual Merger Liabilities

In most mergers, even those based on mutual-growth principles, the more dominant college or university often seeks to avoid the burden of residual liabilities from a smaller institutional partner by incorporating a nonassumption of liabilities provision in its bargaining proposals. It may also require a transfer of all assets, including conveyance of all land and buildings, endowments, trusts, gifts, grants, and other tangible and intangible property such as intellectual property rights, copyrights, trademarks, patents, and royalties.

Leaving aside the legal nuances of indemnification, it is not unusual for the institutions to agree on reciprocal indemnification for liabilities arising out of actions within their respective control and responsibility up to and from the effective date of the merger. Additionally, each partner needs to address the others' legitimate concerns about inheriting untoward liability from the failure or neglect to perform respective covenants and responsibilities effectively under the terms of the merger agreement.

The institutions also need to stipulate to the delivery of certified independent audits for the last several fiscal cycles, which will provide historical cost and revenue history and begin to ensure a necessary and desirable measure of objectivity and conformity with generally accepted legal and accounting practices. Firm yet realistic timelines for the completion of negotiations, exercising of options, and execution of letters of intent need to be established before the final contract consummation; our experience shows that timelines of this nature are most sensibly left on a flexible rather than date-certain basis.

Human Resources

Whether protected by board-approved personnel policy, collective bargaining agreement, or past practice, the human resources of the merger partners are now placed within a legal and contractual framework that must be carefully evaluated. Reassignments and relocations—patterns of broad retrenchment have not characterized the mutual-growth model—are often undesired but unavoidable results of implementing the merger plan on a timely and cost-effective basis.

Academic needs, fidelity to dedicated employees, and harmonious labor relations are mutually lauded objectives at the outset of each merger process. When various employee factions begin inevitably to compete for power and position, however, the labor force of the dominant institutional partner must be checked by fair and equitable stewardship, practical parity, and, most importantly, a shared view of serving the greater academic good. The members of the Merger Task Force must consistently review the postmerger staff and faculty personnel model sought and the labor force means necessary to achieve those results. Typically, this process requires a sensitive, resourceful balancing by the task force and key academic managers of the interests of academic achievement and productivity, administrative efficiency, and nonduplication of efforts.

Master lists of classified, professional, and faculty labor force segments must be developed with notations of salary, rank, title, pay classifications, and fringe benefit impact. Indirect cost factors must also be assembled and presented for consideration to the trustees, chief executives, chief academic and financial officers, and possibly a personnel subcommittee of the Merger Task Force. Once this inventory and assessment process has been completed in detail, members of the task force and senior academic managers and faculty members should confer with their legal representatives to assess the liability exposure in the two or three most probable faculty and staff planning scenarios.

Collective Bargaining Implications

The process of planning and negotiating the personnel components of a merger agreement are simplified if faculty and staff members are not represented by classified employee union organizations. Whatever the combination of bargaining unit organizations, merger managers need to remain mindful of both bargaining obligations and the need to preserve a cohesive community of scholars and supporting work force able to attain the merger's broadest academic objectives.

Several mutual-growth mergers I have observed were enhanced by the structure and predictability afforded by a collective bargaining environment. Issues involving academic program consolidation, personnel transfers, and seniority were carefully addressed in an objective, criteria-based manner. (The collective bargaining implications of merger models are discussed further in chapter 5.)

Premerger Legal Audit

Before concluding the final merger negotiations and deciding which merger structure can best serve the future needs of both institutions, it is wise to engage counsel to conduct a focused premerger legal audit.[17] In so doing, both institutions can develop a central repository and useful frame of reference to evaluate their present legal strengths and weaknesses as well as the overall legal health and stability of the combined institution.

Counsel evaluates the corporate underpinnings and structure of the new institution, including its dual charter history and emerging bylaws, policies, governance processes, endowment structure, contractual systems, litigation history, and other indices of legal health.[18] This audit collects merger-specific information through the completion of a merger documents inventory, an internal merger questionnaire and personal interview process, and the research of applicable law.

Closure of Merger Negotiations

Eventually, the moment will arrive for the members of the Merger Task Force, the chief executive officers, and legal counsel to identify outstanding issues, clarify lingering questions of prospective contract rights, and propose an honest best offer to close the merger negotiation. What emerged as a pivotal issue early on, such as a postmerger institutional name, often wanes in significance compared to, for example, the continued employment of members of one college's work force or the credit enfranchisement of its student body.

At this final stage of negotiations, merger managers on both campuses must be prepared to make clear and convincing arguments to support their respective planning model in order to persuade both the other institution and their own constituencies of the advantages to be gained in the new structure. Passing the twin tests of campus support and partner agreement increases the likelihood that the other leadership team will accept the growth merger concept as integral to their institution's new structure and expanded mission.

Merger Contract Consummation

Upon signing, most merger contract agreements include a force majeure provision relieving all partners from the performance of their respective obligations in the event of delays caused by circumstances beyond their control. Agreements also typically incorporate successor or survival provisions that bind the institutional successors to the covenants contained in the main agreement.

The agreement also needs to stipulate the legal framework for interpreting the applicability and effect of the contract provisions. In most instances, this technical consideration presents no difficulty, as the institutions will be located in the same state and will apply the laws of the same forum. Finally, authorizing resolutions and certifications need to be presented with authorized signatures of corporate officers as required by law.

Contractual Liability

When one institution transfers or assigns its contractual rights or delegates its responsibilities to another in the context of the merger process, account must be taken of the outstanding liabilities that arise from such assignments and delegations. Contracts for goods and services may be open-ended or finite in duration. They usually contain termination provisions that may contemplate the discontinued operation of the institution through merger or voluntary dissolution. In situations involving campus concessionary operations such as bookstores, cafeterias, or vending machines, outstanding commission or other offsets may need to be reconciled and collected during the merger process.

The emerging institution must address existing employment contracts with faculty and staff who carry expectations of continuing employment. Even contracts currently in effect may, under certain circumstances, be subject to cancellation or termination when triggered by the discontinuance of one institution within a merger. Whatever the merger model, residual contractual liabilities must be fully and accurately assessed and their costs estimated during the closure of negotiations.

Capital Outlay Financing and New Facilities Development

In many growth mergers or consolidations, the facilities of one campus are sold, leased, or otherwise disposed of, and a need arises for new campus facilities for classrooms, research laboratories, faculty and administrative offices, and residential life activities. In some merger plans, unanticipated enrollment growth and satellite campus opportunities also drive the facilities development process.

Such possibilities mean that each institution while still in the negotiation stage must research the credit history of its merger partner, including the size of its debt service obligations, schedule of mortgage retirement, mortgage payment history, and prospects for future financial stability. Further, each partner must make itself aware before the contract consummation of the restrictive covenants that bind any other partner in the discharge of its payment obligations.

Educational Consumer Claims

Although state and federal courts have been generally loath to interpose themselves in adjudicating the quality of academic offerings, state higher education regulatory agencies and attorneys general are inclined to take a closer look when institutions merge, consolidate, transfer, discontinue, or otherwise begin the process of substantive change.

The range of educational consumer complaints that can arise during even a mission-complementary merger process run the gamut from constricted educational access to interruption in educational offerings and typically include such standard concerns as diminution of academic quality, student credit disenfranchisement, and loss of financial aid eligibility. One of the institutional partners may have assumed a greater burden in these areas than it is able to address during the merger process, and students will logically need to look to the combined institution for answers to their consumer concerns. In mutual-growth mergers, in particular, when expectations of success rise higher than in traditional bankruptcy-bailout merger models, it is crucial for the members of the Merger Task Force to respond rapidly and sensitively to all educational consumer claims in order to maintain community confidence levels and commitment to the merger concept.

Student Financial Aid Implications

As any of the institutional partners discontinue regular operations or are otherwise materially affected by the merger process, the combined college or university can expect to undergo multiple student financial aid audits by the U.S. Department of Education, state scholarship agencies, and guaranteed loan corporations. These audit and financial aid authorities will require documentation of continuity of operations, due diligence, compliance with financial aid stewardship requirements, continuous state licensing, and national, regional, and specialty accreditation.[19]

One partner often seeks to disclaim residual liability as the legal successor by pointing to the nonassumption of liability clauses in the merger agreements. If that institution has not accepted or benefited from the financial aid portfolio of any other partner, such residual responsibility properly falls to those with any unliquidated liabilities and should be addressed in the process of concluding that partner's financial and corporate affairs.

Student Records and Privacy Law

Institutional partners are responsible for designating a common student records center for the merged college or university which is in compliance with applicable federal and state educational and privacy laws governing the establishment, maintenance, and disclosure of student records systems.

Merging institutions in the public sector must also be mindful of applicable provisions of state records conservation law requiring the maintenance of certain public records for periods of specified duration depending on the type of documentation and the production of public documents for inspection and copying upon citizen requests.

Licensure and Accreditation

State regulatory agencies and regional and specialized accreditation organizations demonstrate keen interest in the impact of merger transactions on the quality of the degrees awarded by the combined college or university. Attentive to a potential dilution of academic quality in all faculty ranks, to gaps in curriculum coherence, or to any curtailment of course offerings, these licensing and accrediting agencies are responsible for investigating the academic, financial, and human resource implications of merging and for assessing the combined institutions's overall preparedness to sustain and continue the programs and activities of the former enterprises. As a general rule, the scrutiny of these agencies intensifies to the degree an institutional change is irrevocable.

For the most part, licensing and accrediting agencies request and appreciate an effort by institutions to inform them before decisions are made; these agencies should be notified at the earliest practicable juncture once merger plans are clear and before consummation is imminent. State statutes and degree-granting regulation standards may require prior notice, and accrediting agencies may require several months or more prior written notification of these anticipated substantive changes.[20]

In the end, it pays for all merger partners to communicate openly and forthrightly with state licensure and accrediting agencies early on in the merger planning process. This early warning approach can help avoid rumor and assuage emergent licensure and accreditation concerns.

CHAPTER THREE

The Role of Trustees and Governing Boards in College and University Mergers

John F. Welsh

Making the decision to alter the basic identity and organizational form of any college or university through merging is never easy. Even when handled with prudence and creativity, mergers and consolidations place new, challenging, and unique responsibilities on trustees and governing boards.

Mergers do not occur without the approval of the governing boards of the participating institutions, which will typically retain the authority to execute mergers in their legal form. The active involvement of individual trustees and governing boards, however, is critical to growth mergers in ways that go far beyond the legal act of approving the proposal and contractual agreement to merge.

The prevailing literature on institutional mergers, although frequently addressed to governing boards, fails to address the distinctive role trustees and boards play in planning and implementing a mutual-growth merger. The purpose of this chapter is to provide educational leaders with a summary of the challenges board members will face and the tasks they must complete for a college or university merger to fulfill its mutual-growth potential. Successful consideration of these factors will enable board members of public and independent institutions to develop and articulate more effective approaches to debating, planning, and implementing mergers and consolidations, particularly under potentially difficult political, demographic, or fiscal circumstances. Three premises guide this analysis. First, mutual-growth mergers incorporate new forms of governance and administration which are positive developments in the life of an educational institution, providing opportunities for qualitative and quantitative academic growth. Second, trustees and boards are critical architects and advocates for these changes and the processes facilitating them. Finally, although they are highly variable human activities, growth mergers remain a social process with an understandable structure of opportunities, tasks, and challenges.

From the perspective of trustees and governing boards, mutual-growth mergers are best understood as a fluid process that includes several identifiable stages. The overall merger process is similar to a timetable containing a number of benchmarks that indicate to the various institutional constituencies, factually and intuitively, the extent of movement that has already occurred toward a merger, as well as the movements likely to follow. Each benchmark in the merger timetable indicates a resolution of the challenges and tasks pertinent to that stage and the emergence of a new set of necessary deliberations and decisions.

Common to most successful college or university mergers are four elements signifying the central role of the board:

1. Identification of merger as the best approach to support and enhance the mission of the institution in its achievement of academic excellence and other related organizational goals

2. Negotiation of a merger agreement or proposal with another institutional board and its internal constituencies

3. Approval of the merger proposal by board action

4. Implementation of the merger plan and assessment of its progress

This chapter presents the four benchmarks from the frame of reference of the governing board, suggesting the issues, challenges, and tasks confronting the board and its individual trustees. The merger timetable is likely to appear somewhat different to the governing board than to other constituencies because of the unique responsibilities and expectations placed upon trustees. For the board, the merger timetable is primarily shaped by the board's policy-making role and its concern that its power and credibility can quickly dissolve in a poorly managed attempt at organizational change.

A schematic outline for the discussion in this chapter is presented in figure 3.1, with the four benchmarks arranged in chronological order, although movement from one stage to the next cannot be predicted with complete certainty. Although the stages are presented as discrete, in fact considerable overlap among them is likely. Each benchmark represents an impending change in the status of the institution, however, and a signal that new issues and potential conflicts are emerging.

The specific challenges a governing board will confront at each benchmark, summarized in figure 3.1, will most likely be shaped by

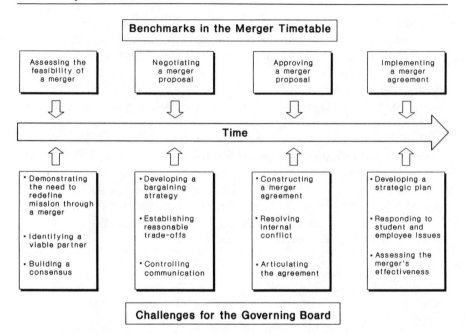

Figure 3.1. The Board's View of the Merger Timetable.

the board's historical role and the contemporary expectations the public has developed for governing boards.[1] These responsibilities can be subsumed under two categories. The first is the responsibility to advocate for the institution and to act as a buffer to intrusions from the external environment. Included under this heading are board activities in fund-raising and responding to pressures from licensing bodies, accreditation authorities, or other external organizations which may threaten the continuity and integrity of academic programs or support services. The second category is the responsibility to ensure that the institution is responsive to broader societal goals and is accountable to relevant constituent groups. Boards have responsibilities to ensure that budgets are reasonable, that institutions are cost efficient, and that academic programs maintain adequate levels of quality.

As simultaneous advocates for the institution and stewards responsible to external constituents, governing board members must continually mediate the tensions inherent in these sometimes conflicting expectations. On one side they must maintain the appropriate separation between their legislative and policy-making functions, and on the other, the executive functions assigned to the administration they collectively employ. In the context of a mission-complementary growth merger, the effectiveness of a board can be best judged by its ability to balance and integrate the roles of advocate and steward, and by its ability to articulate and maintain an appropriate separation between policy-making and policy administration.

In the 1990s, the higher education environment is characterized by unstable student pools, increased costs, declining federal revenue for research and student financial aid, and fiscal crises in state governments. Consequently, the stewardship aspect of higher education governance has significantly increased in importance. Boards have been impelled to expand the scope of their policy-making responsibilities. Under these volatile circumstances, boards often will consider dramatic resource reallocations, even internal reorganization, as a response for more effective governance, or, if necessary, to manage an institutional crisis.

In a mutual-growth college or university merger, even if the partners are not of equal strength, size, or reputation, each institution may still identify the merger strategy as a promising opportunity for academic enrichment, geographic expansion, broader educational marketing, and cultural diversification.[2] In some cases, the smaller or less dominant college may fear dramatic change, possibly significant loss, if a university or larger college simply acquires it. If the board of the smaller institution accepts major change as certain, however, it has an opportunity to shape more aggressively the reconfigured institution according to its evolving mission, priorities, values, and beliefs.[3] For the governing boards of participating institutions, mutual-growth mergers are a form of both board advocacy and stewardship, not only continuing the life of the original institution but expanding and enhancing its history and educational purposes.

Assessing the Feasibility of a Growth Merger

For any college or university, whether strong or struggling, the complex dynamics behind the decision to develop and approve even a mission-complementary merger plan can be unsettling and difficult. Once board members agree that a merger is feasible, members of the institutional community will be confronted by an emergent perspective that discourages business as usual. In fact, the decision to investigate the possibility of a growth merger is frequently and correctly interpreted to mean that the status quo is no longer acceptable to the governing body. Even in the mutual-growth context, the prospect of a merger typically reflects a need to improve, modernize, or stabilize a competitive position in the educational marketplace.

Board members soon appreciate that the decision to merge and the processes involved create a new source of institutional tension and conflict. If the mutual-growth strategy is managed properly, however, board activities preceding the decision to merge can substantially assuage initial anxieties and coordinate the development of a realistic strategy for the institution's future growth and increased competitiveness. The choice to merge proactively for institutional advancement still often occurs only after several more traditional strategies for academic reorganization have been considered and rejected through a comprehensive institutional planning process.

A useful and frequently employed approach to determine the feasibility of merger as a strategic institutional option is to create a special Merger Task Force responsible for a comprehensive review of the college or university's mission, including an environmental scan of its service area, its internal organization, the strength of its institutional competitors, and the impact of change on its educational programs and governance.[4] Two significant aspects of this type of mission review are the composition of the task force and the nature and extent of the review itself.

By assigning a comprehensive mission review and feasibility study to the Merger Task Force, the board (1) connects to this responsibility a sense of seriousness and visibility which transcends normal governance processes, (2) provides the task force with a genuine sense of independence from constituent groups that normally impact institutional governance, and (3) lays an early foundation for achieving consensus regarding the evolving merger model and eventual proposal.

The Merger Task Force can function most effectively when it is comprised of individuals who represent critical constituencies and who are oriented to substantive outcomes while remaining sensitive to issues of process and consensus building.[5] Members of the task force have dual roles: representing their specific constituent group on campus, and representing the task force to their constituent group. The composition of the Merger Task Force should be developed with this dual role as the predominant consideration.

Regarding the constituencies I have most often observed on a task force, senior faculty representation will be necessary, especially from degree programs that are critical and complementary to the degree programs of the partner institution. The faculty representatives should have achieved high visibility, respect, and influence at their institution based upon teaching ability, scholarship, and years of service. The role of senior faculty members on the Merger Task Force includes representing faculty concerns and perspectives as well as regularly communicating the concerns and perspectives of the task force to the faculties of both institutional partners.

The task force must also include representatives from several levels of both administrations, although the combined board leadership should ensure that the task force has an appropriate degree of autonomy from administrative control. Most importantly, the chief academic officers from each institution should be represented. The chief financial and business officers will also play a critical role in such a group, for they have a degree of autonomy from the political constraints imposed by academic constituencies and are uniquely capable of assembling interpretive data on organizational productivity, efficiency, and cost. A meaningful assessment of the feasibility of a merger cannot occur without the expertise of these administrators.

Representatives from businesses and organizations in the local community can provide invaluable perspectives on the political and economic realities beyond campus boundaries, as well as contribute current opinion on the applicability of new, emerging, and ongoing curricula.

Finally, two critically important though often overlooked constituencies should be represented: alumni and students. Alumni provide one of the deepest and most committed pools of human resources in a merger process, including executives who may have directed or participated in mergers themselves. The active participation of alumni ensures that board members are made aware of alumni concerns about program retrenchment or campus closure early in the planning process. If the merger study is effectively oriented toward institutional advocacy and the mutual growth of institutional missions, the chairs of each alumni association should be invited to participate on the task force or to appoint an alumni representative. Furthermore, alumni and institutional advancement staff can offer valuable insights into the role combined endowments can play in financing a mutual growth merger. Finally, alumni can help predict the impact a merger might have on the ability of the reconfigured institution to raise money. Board members are frequently concerned that alumni representatives in a group studying something as unusual and as dramatic as institutional merger will create roadblocks to decision making and eventual success. It is important to include representatives from alumni organizations in the planning, however, so that they may act as liaisons and interpreters to the larger alumni constituencies concerning the factors that influence the feasibility of merging.

To complete the process, the governing board must aggressively solicit student government representatives from both campuses to contribute to the planning activities of the task force. Student leaders can serve as the most persuasive advocates for the merger to other students.

Cultivating student support for the merger on both campuses is often perceived by board members as a daunting challenge; however, the level of student support can be a blunt but fair measure of the effectiveness of the decision to merge. The Merger Task Force should keep the student leadership continually apprised of its work and observations. It should also invite student testimony and response to its preliminary findings and recommendations. At various points in numerous merger processes, I have observed how helpful it can be for members of the task force to request face-to-face discussions with student leaders from both campuses. Like all forms of significant organizational change, growth mergers may dramatically impact the quality and the access of students to the educational opportunities offered by their institutions. Consequently, the task force must also be fully informed on issues of multiculturalism and institutional diversity. Student services personnel, along with members of both student bodies, can provide this valuable information as members of the task force.

By appointing one of their most respected, dedicated, and experienced members as the chair of the task force, boards can ensure that their mandate will be effectively carried out and that one constituency will not dominate the work of the entire membership. The board member assigned this responsibility must make the necessary commitments in time and preparation to support the decision to merge and to take the lead in advocating the proposed change to all levels of both institutions.

The methodology and final document produced by the Merger Task Force has significantly different purposes from a self-study required by accrediting agencies or in strategic planning activities. Accreditation self-studies typically focus on institutional process, centering on the policies and mechanisms of internal governance and curriculum development. A mission review that considers a form of reorganization as dramatic as a mutual-growth merger must be responsive to a set of larger realities. As the attention of the task force is directed beyond current curricular and academic policy reviews to developing an educational vision based on mutual growth through merging, the feasibility study is more likely to produce a prudent, specific plan for institutional advancement than a set of merger invitations to geographically proximate colleges.[6]

A focus on mission review thus provides the context in which all possible future scenarios can be examined, even those the board deems unlikely. A Merger Task Force with the visible participation and support of the board to develop a data-based recommendation can usually be trusted to reject unrealistic alternatives. A successful mutual-growth merger must build consensus on the foundation provided by the Merger

Task Force. Therefore, it becomes critical that all constituencies perceive the work of the task force as fair, objective, and dispassionate. To accomplish this image, one component of the board's oversight is to ensure that the task force is protected from unwarranted, external political pressures. Finally, because governing boards have often been more disposed toward mergers than other constituencies of the university, it should be emphasized that the decision to merge should ultimately flow from the work of the task force and not be imposed on it.[7]

Evidence gathered from both successful and unsuccessful attempts at institutional merger points to the critical importance of extensive, collegial premerger planning and of carefully assessing merger possibilities and mission development. Hugh Thompson describes an attempt to merge Wayne State University and the Detroit Institute of Technology in 1979 which failed largely as a result of the absence of "strategic planning" for a joint study of merging, as well as the absence of significant trustee participation in the process.[8]

Once representatives of the boards of Wayne State and the Detroit Institute of Technology met and agreed that a merger should be studied, administrative task forces were assigned to identify critical issues and make recommendations regarding their resolution. The responsibilities assigned to the task forces tended to follow normal higher education governance lines. For example, the chief academic officers met to study academic policies, programs, and personnel. Program consultants met with faculty to study and recommend solutions to the programmatic issues that arose with the possibility of the merger. At this early point in the process, the boards, faculty, staff, students, alumni, and external stakeholders were apprised of the intent to study a merger.

Despite eight months of study, the institutions decided to terminate the merger discussions, as they were adversely affecting student recruitment and the cultivation of philanthropic support, especially at the Detroit Institute of Technology. Thompson notes that, even though the staff and faculty at both institutions were willing to meet to consider significant issues, there was no joint Merger Task Force or standing committee to address the broader goals and concepts of the growth merger strategy or to provide the in-depth deliberation and analysis essential to anticipate larger problems and their resolution. Thompson concludes that the mechanisms for defining the possibility of a merger could have been effectively developed by a joint task force. At a minimum, members from both boards should have been appointed to one joint standing committee with the planning, time, staff resources, and visibility to coordinate a meaningful study.

A recent merger model that more successfully adhered to mutual-growth guidelines was the decision in 1990 by the Kansas Board of Regents to merge Kansas State University and Kansas College of Technology, a two-year institution in Salina, Kansas, offering associate-level programs in engineering technology and industrial technology. Although the situation was parallel in many ways to that in Detroit, a most significant difference was that the Kansas Board of Regents is a consolidated statewide governing board that controlled both schools.

Frustrated with continued enrollment problems, the failure of Kansas College of Technology to fully realize its mission, and previous unsuccessful attempts to reorganize the institution, the board charged a Merger Task Force in November 1989 with recommending a viable mission and organizational structure for the school. The board assigned one of its veteran members to chair the ten-person group, which was comprised of technology faculty members, influential community leaders, and industrial chief executives. The task force was provided with sufficient resources and professional staff support to explore the full range of issues related to new mission options. Equally critical, the board publicized the formation and agenda of the Merger Task Force in advance of media exposure, which enabled the board to clarify its objectives and frame the discussion.

Seven months later, in June 1990, the task force recommended a merger of Kansas State University and Kansas College of Technology, having reviewed extensive fiscal and programmatic data and constituent testimony, and having considered and rejected several organizational alternatives.[9] The board of regents and the Kansas legislature concurred with the analysis and the recommendation.

By including one of its members as the chair of the Merger Task Force, and by designating to one of its professional staff the responsibility for data collection and analysis, the regents publicly conveyed a commitment to develop the future of Kansas College of Technology in a positive direction. At the same time, they created an infrastructure for policy-making which proved adequate to the task of anticipating and overcoming political challenges. Most observers agree that it is doubtful the merger would have occurred without the board's activism and public commitment to the change.

Negotiating the Merger Agreement

Mutual-growth mergers require deliberate, disciplined, and sustained efforts by governing boards to negotiate a favorable reorganization with another institution. This process includes several tasks of significant concern from the board's perspective. To formulate a constructive bargaining proposal, the decision that merger is a feasible and advantageous goal must be made before entering the negotiations. In reality, these two tasks overlap, as the study of the merger's feasibility typically produces a general outline of objectives the board plans to achieve during merger negotiations. A merger feasibility study depends upon precise, comprehensive information and analysis regarding complementary institutional partners, and it will unavoidably generate attention and concern at other institutions.

Developing an effective bargaining approach requires each board to determine exactly what it wishes to accomplish in a mutual-growth merger. The goals of the process should be identified and ranked as board members develop a consistent and shared view of the institutional trade-offs they are willing to make. The board must reach agreement on what is important to retain and acceptable to relinquish from an educational perspective in the pending reorganization. The programs and traditions most central to each institution's academic mission and identity will have to be kept, as will the symbolic elements of an institution's identity.[10] A thoughtless and precipitous devaluing of an institution's logo, colors, name, or mascot can easily undermine the whole plan to merge and earn the board the enduring enmity of students, faculty, and alumni.

As it approaches the bargaining process, each board must candidly assess its own negotiating strengths and weaknesses and develop strategies to preserve the strength of their institution's mission and educational vision. Because the processes of a merger carry the threat of a schism between the board and members of the institutional administrations, this assessment must include a focused review of the capabilities and attitudes of the present executive, academic, and financial leadership of the institutions. Failure to resolve conflicts between the board and key administrators can discourage complementary merger partners and place the board in a weakened bargaining position.

Mutual-growth mergers offer greater advantages to certain groups on a campus than others—a school of nursing in one instance, an athletic department in another—and boards may face resistance from one or more constituent groups in early community discussions. In my experience with the model, achieving a credible level of support does not require unanimity or even a majority of advocates in the early stages of the process. Achieving critical mass refers to winning the cumulative advocacy of those who are best able to gather support and ensure final acceptance of the plan by a majority of other stakeholders.

Controlling communication about the current status of contemplated or ongoing merger negotiations is one of the most difficult tasks in the merger process for board members, for any event that significantly affects the mission of the institution attracts public scrutiny. On the one hand, public discourse about the details of merger negotiations can become an impediment if the reasons for merger are misinterpreted or the mutual-growth concept is misunderstood. On the other, when efforts to control communication are narrowly circumscribed by legal or ethical constraints on confidentiality, secrecy in negotiations can operate against the visibility that might otherwise build support for the mutual-growth strategy.[11] The overall communication process is significantly improved when members of the board are careful to use advance press releases and coordinated statements through official media channels to articulate specific merger topics under consideration. Experience dictates that formal and official media are the most effective mechanisms for preempting rumors, so planners and negotiators representing boards need to reach an overall agreement on the means and methods for disseminating information throughout the process.

One striking example of a poorly managed communication strategy, which provoked a citizens' opposition campaign and derailed a group of potential mergers, occurred in Texas in 1987. A commission appointed by the state legislature to study all governance issues of Texas higher education recommended three mergers: North Texas State and Texas Woman's University, Texas Southern University and the University of Houston's downtown campus, and Corpus Christi State and Texas A&I University. These recommendations were announced in the absence of any meaningful context or dialogue with the critical stakeholders—alumni, local business leaders, and politicians—who bitterly attacked them. Eventually, the plan was withdrawn in the middle of its negotiation with the state legislature. Some state education leaders lament a significant opportunity missed to improve the organization of educational governance in Texas.[12]

Although Texas had been experiencing severe fiscal problems at that time, the proposed mergers were intended to encompass the mutual-growth concepts of increasing access for minority students and achieving growth in complementary academic programs. The failure to cultivate stakeholder support by effectively communicating the rationale for the decision to restructure, however, killed most, if not all constituent support for the proposed mergers. Because the commission's findings were coupled with recommendations to close institutions, the commission unfortunately communicated to the public a strategy for reorganization framed as retrenchment, when it had wished to communicate precisely the opposite.

Approving the Merger Proposal

The final approval of the merger plan is achieved through each board's formal action to dissolve one or more institutions as freestanding entities and to approve their merger or consolidation. Because board meetings are not appropriate forums for ambiguity or conflict in decision making, final approval of the proposal will be predicated upon a clear and persuasive merger agreement along with the resolution or mitigation of opposition.

Merger agreements should also specify the responsibilities of boards, chief executive officers, academic managers, and the joint Merger Task Force during the implementation of the merger model and beyond, if appropriate. Each board member needs to be familiar with the principal elements of the pending merger process, including any contingencies placed on the agreement by the institutions or state government. A detailed report, preceded by an executive summary, is the most effective instrument to educate the members of both boards about the complementary goals achieved by merging, and how the organizational, curricular, programmatic, and fiscal elements of the agreement were developed.

Legal counsel should participate in all aspects of the negotiation process and assist in the development of the plan for implementation. It is critical for the board's counsel to provide, among other sources of authority, at least three sets of information before approval of the merger agreement: (1) requirements from state regulatory agencies affecting the legal agreement to merge; (2) statutes controlling mergers and specifying the procedures the board must follow to complete the merger transaction; and (3) a summary of the institution's charters, property deeds, assets and residual interests, and liabilities.[13]

The commitment of individual trustees and of the board collectively becomes paramount at this stage of the process. Having approved the merger concept and plan, the leadership of individual trustees is now essential in securing the final approval of each full board in a manner that does not create conflict, disrupt the process, or haunt the newly merged institution. V. L. Meek notes, "It is important to remember that the achievement of a successful merger requires skillful leaders, dedicated to the idea of change." The strength of the board's leadership is a factor that cannot be underestimated in the negotiation and approval processes. For both to be successful, Meek continues, "there must be a core of 'institutional elites' in the institutions involved who are committed to the proposal and prepared to push it through despite opposition."[14]

The approval of the merger agreement becomes the official statement of both boards on the future of the reconfigured institution. Therefore, it should be straightforward and should emphasize both the preservation and transformation of both institutional identities through a complementary model of mission enhancement. There have been examples of merger approvals involving contending institutional partners, however, thus complicating board judgments. In the decision by the Kansas Board of Regents to merge Kansas State University and the Kansas College of Technology, Pittsburg State University was being considered as a potential third partner up to the point of the board's formal decision. Located in Pittsburg, Kansas, it had been assigned a statewide mission in technology education by the board of regents. Its administration was genuinely enthused about the possibility of a merger with Kansas College of Technology and marketed its viability in a merger proposal grounded in its mission complementary with that school. Although the board of regents concurred with the analysis provided by Pittsburg State, it concluded that a merger with Kansas State would accomplish the same programmatic mesh, and the resources and name recognition of the larger land-grant institution would make the Salina campus more competitive in regard to student recruitment and program quality.

In this case, mission complementarity and an adequate financial resource base, in combination, proved to be the critical factors in the decision to approve a merger plan. The leadership of the board of regents expected each of the two contending institutions to provide a case for a compelling program fit in addition to a detailed plan for the legal, fiscal, and administrative dimensions of merger.

Implementing the Mutual-Growth Strategy

Implementation begins with the acceptance of the merger agreement by all parties and continues until the institutions are fully integrated. Although its design should be based upon a strategic plan drawn from the merger agreement, all details of the process cannot be specified in advance. The implementation plan must, however, be sufficiently specific for members of the Merger Task Force, key academic managers, and faculty committee members to understand how the merger *should* be implemented. The plan should also indicate the basic elements of the combined board's oversight of the merger itself. A number of recent models have used the board's executive committee and other standing and ad hoc committee structures as effective mechanisms to address academic, administrative, and facilities issues in their early stages.

The joint faculty committees and appropriate subcommittees of the overall task force provide an additional support structure critical during the implementation phase. Often, for example, a committee comprised of academic deans, department chairs, and personnel directors outlines necessary revisions to professional personnel policies and procedures. Additional task force subcommittees are typically formed in areas such as student life and services, library and learning resources, physical plant expansion, external affairs, legal issues, and alumni relations.

The general needs of both students and faculty may have been studied during the planning process, but more concrete short- and long-term objectives in these areas become critical during the implementation phase. Some employees must retrain to remain employed, and they need to know that resources for this retraining will be available as a component of the growth merger model. Students need advisory support to move into reconfigured degree programs in the merged college or university, perhaps through written guides to the requirements necessary. Many students need their financial aid packages restructured. Normally, board members do not intervene in this level of implementation and merger-related decision making; however, the board should request periodic reports on how these and other employee, faculty, and student issues are being resolved.

The new, expanded board needs to make a persuasive and visible effort to ensure that the missions and identities of both institutions will continue to exist and be educationally enhanced in the complementary model of merger. This may be achieved in a number of ways depending on the particular partners and agreement. Administrative restructuring may make retaining the names of both institutions possible and advisable, as in the instances of Case Western Reserve University, or, in London, Queen Mary and Westfield College. Another recommendation is that respected administrators and faculty members who have been prominent opinion leaders at both institutions be retained and elevated. A demonstrable effort by the combined board to protect the identity and union of *both* educational entities is critical to maintaining trust, confidence, and support from faculty, alumni, students, and external constituents in the postmerger environment.

Understandably, the implementation of mergers can rarely be predicted precisely from a design or a blueprint. The reality of the reconfigured institution will unfold during implementation, and board members, key academic managers, students, and alumni will rapidly discover the process to be a variable one yielding many outcomes unenvisioned at the outset.[15]

Thompson suggests that higher education mergers can take five years or more to complete, while Millett argues that mergers may re-

Tasks for Governing Boards in Mutual-Growth Mergers

Assessing the Feasibility of the Merger Concept

- Development of charge to merger task force to study mission enhancement through merger

  Consideration of options for mission enhancement
  Identification of date to receive report from the merger task force

- Development of composition and leadership of the merger task force
- Development of strategy to communicate with critical stakeholders
- Appointment of members of the task force
- Development of the public relations plan for the task force
- Development of background materials for task force, including data on:

  History and mission of partner institutions
  Cost, productivity, efficiency, by program and unit
  Enrollment by program, over time
  Growth and use of endowments
  Condition and utilization rates of facilities
  Marketability of programs and graduates
  Academic program mesh and duplication

- Development of strategy to receive testimony from conferees

Negotiating the Merger Agreement

- Identification of principle mutual-growth goals for the merger
- Identification of institutional assets and strengths
- Development of list of trade-offs and giveaway positions
- Assessment of negotiating strengths and weaknesses
- Identification of critical symbols of institutional identity
- Agreement on public relations regarding negotiations
- Development of strategy to build consensus for merger agreement

quire up to ten years for the wounds to heal and for benefits to begin to show.[16] The longer the merger's implementation, the greater the likelihood that the principal participants will change, including central members of the board, administrators, and faculty. Therefore, it is essential that the board collectively maintain a running journal of merger-related tasks, activities, and accomplishments. Especially important is a report that identifies the educational and organizational goals the board originally sought to achieve in proposing the growth merger concept.

Tasks for Governing Boards in Mutual-Growth Mergers (*cont'd*)

Approving the Merger Proposal

- Development of executive summary of merger plan

    Elements of merger agreement
    Discussion of methodology and process

- Education of board members about the merger plan
- Development of summary of legal requirements and contingencies for the merger
- Plan to address and mitigate residual conflicts
- Formal vote
- Communications and public relations about the agreement

Implementing the Final Agreement

- Appointment of ad hoc work groups to resolve issues regarding

    Curriculum
    Faculty personnel
    Administrative personnel
    Budgeting and financial planning
    Student services
    Institutional advancement
    Physical plant and facilities expansion

- Development of plan to monitor the progress of work groups
- Identification and cultivation of institutional opinion leaders
- Monitoring merger progress and effectiveness through outcomes assessments tied to original merger goals
- Effecting changes in board composition and leadership

Ideally, the board will record and approve at the outset what it intends to accomplish in the process and how it plans to measure the success of the mutual-growth strategy through a system of outcomes assessments. In reality, even the primary goals of the merger will be reshaped. This realization does not present a problem to board members if an official record is faithfully kept throughout the process identifying how goals evolved or were altered in response to new circumstances and perceptions of what is desirable and feasible.

For the board, the effectiveness of the merger will be gauged primarily in terms of the future health and viability of the reconfigured college or university. A meaningful assessment should thus include an examination of data that reflect the original feasibility study. This assessment can then be integrated into the new institution's long-term planning activities, particularly those related to mission development.

The primary role of governing boards in higher education mergers is to articulate the basic strategy for achieving each benchmark in the merger process. Specific growth merger models will typically also require many additional, more specific tasks and many permutations of those listed in table 3.1. Although many of these tasks will be accomplished by subcommittees of the task force and other joint committees, it is critical over time for the board to ensure that each task has been assigned and monitored to completion, and, in this way, to acknowledge that mergers affect every unit and constituency within the institution.

Included in its planning as well must be the strategy for the board's own transformation. Even in mutual-growth models, merging may result in the dissolution of a board. Boards may become integrated or consolidated, share governance temporarily, or send a cohort of members to the new entity. This prospect of significant change for the board itself must be pursued and accepted as dispassionately by its membership as all other merger efforts. Although the boards of public institutions may pursue the mutual-growth concept differently than the boards of independent institutions, due to statutory and constitutional limitations on their power and authority, the ability of any board to direct a growth merger to successful completion requires a core of members dedicated to the concept and to have sufficient collective experience to address the merger's curricular, personnel, student, and fiscal components with skill and confidence.

In this period of increasing social change and economic instability, strategic institutional reorganization is a necessary element of effective and responsible lay governance. Effective advocacy and stewardship by governing boards may now include proposing the merger of their institution for growth purposes with an academically complementary college or university, thus ensuring not only continuity but also the enhancement of the mission, traditions, and programs of their own institution.

CHAPTER FOUR

Presidential Leadership and the Mutual-Growth Concept

Bryan E. Carlson

A hero cannot be a hero unless in a heroic world. *Nathaniel Hawthorne*

The achievement of a mutual-growth merger requires a new vision of higher education management, and its ultimate success depends on the leadership provided by the overall chief executive officer. At the outset, the presidents involved must recognize and acknowledge to their communities that mergers in any industry are enormously complex transactions that represent a significant, even extreme, challenge to executive leadership. Harry J. Gray, the retired chair of United Technologies Corporation, shed light on how difficult mergers can be for chief executive officers when he stated that they require "fierce determination, considerable endurance, and thick-skinned aggressiveness." As a result of his advocacy of mergers as a growth strategy, Gray was depicted at various times during his career as King Kong, Dracula, and a buzzard.[1]

A mutual-growth merger, however, should also be viewed as an opportunity for chief executive officers to demonstrate their leadership capacity and as an opportunity for the participating institutions to achieve a level of educational quality unattainable under their present circumstances. With these positive prospects in mind, it would be prudent for the chief executive officer contemplating the mutual-growth strategy to review several practical considerations, based on my experience with this approach, before initiating any specific merger-related activities.

Recognize uniqueness. Every merger is organically unique. Although both this chapter and this book focus on the development and implementation of one merger type—the mission-complementary, mutual-growth model—no higher education merger replicates another. A merger can occur only when two or more organizations agree to relinquish some degree of their sovereignty to form a new entity with its own unique educational mission. Just as the institutional partners have developed idiosyncratic systems and structures, the processes that characterize their merger will be complex and intricate. Typically, the lesson for presidents is the unpredictability of the merger process and the need to expect the unexpected.

Designate a leader. Ideally, at the beginning of the merger process, one leader should be designated and acknowledged as the overall chief executive officer of the new institution for the postmerger period. That officer will then be in the appropriate position to conceptualize and direct the larger processes of the merger. Without an overall leader, the merger has a greater chance to flounder or even to fail. The chief executive officer has an extremely delicate role, typically functioning without confirmed authority over the other organization, at least during the early stages of implementation. This becomes especially challenging when it is necessary to work with the board of trustees of the other college or university, which may be in conflict over how to fulfill its own fiduciary responsibilities. The overall chief executive officer faces the extraordinary task of inspiring the leadership elements of two separate boards with a common vision and permanently shared future. Although never an easy task even for an experienced chief executive officer, it is an essential one in order to avoid discord and in order for the merger finally to achieve its mutual-growth objectives.

Avoid power struggles. When an overall chief executive officer cannot be immediately designated, for whatever reason, it is still essential, particularly for the members of the Merger Task Force, to avoid the perils of a dual leadership struggle. Experience suggests that the organizational synergies that characterize a mutual-growth merger will not occur until the leadership question is resolved. Although not always possible, it is easier to avoid a significant power struggle when the merger plan might coincide with retirement, reassignment, or logical subordination of one of the presidents involved. In our experience, if the two chief executive officers vie for superordinate authority, their respective constituencies are drawn into a struggle for power, which may in turn preempt the integrative, team-building activities that are delicate and arduous processes even under optimum circumstances.

Seize opportunities. In spite of the complexities of the process, a mutual-growth merger represents a rare opportunity in the life of an institution and its chief executive officer to achieve a quantum advance in institutional quality. In each merger plan, numerous opportunities occur to combine and concentrate human, physical, and financial resources with a clear mandate to achieve new levels of academic excellence. The combined institution also offers unprecedented chances for economies of scale and greater overall efficiency. The postmerger college or university can also reposition itself strategically, as the growth merger concept often brings the possibility of upward mobility within the larger regional and national academic community. All of these potentially positive merger outcomes must be scrutinized carefully by the presidents involved, as institutional success or failure at the completion of a project receives a good deal of public notice and often is attributed to the leadership performance of the overall chief executive officer.

These challenges to the leadership of a mission-complementary merger—understanding the unpredictability of the process, recognizing the importance of designating one chief executive officer at the earliest stage, accepting the imperative to avoid a power struggle, and recognizing the extraordinary opportunity for presidential leadership—provide an overview of the risks and rewards presidents confront with this institutional strategy. Any president contemplating a commitment to growth merger planning, however, would be wise to undertake a more intensive examination of the organizational and management theories pertinent to the mutual-growth concept.

The remainder of this chapter offers a step-by-step outline of the role and objectives of a chief executive officer in the growth merger process, focusing in detail on the higher education management strategy and broader entrepreneurial presidential leadership model essential to a successful mutual-growth merger.

The Context for Presidential Leadership

Any theory of management relevant to the organizational dynamics of a mutual-growth merger must account for external cultural factors that impact the process, and especially with regard to the element of leadership. It has often been asserted in recent years that American society is experiencing a "leadership crisis." George Roche, president of Hillsdale College, has claimed that antiheroic philosophies have gained force over the last six centuries and have reached "a malignant ascendance . . . that is destroying civilized life." As a result of this phenomenon, Roche believes, U.S. society has resigned itself to being shaped and determined by outside forces. He goes on to state that the prevalence of antiheroism in our culture "offers neither a new vision of good . . . nor the courage of leadership."[2]

Roche's perspective represents an extreme point of view, but a strong resistance to leadership often operates within our culture. This antileadership phenomenon has had an impact within American higher education in the serious constraints sometimes placed upon the leadership initiatives of college and university presidents. The critical consideration for chief executive officers in any review of the growth merger strategy will be the need to anticipate the obstacles to leadership inherent within the culture of their own college or university.

Barbara Kellerman, the dean of graduate studies and research at Fairleigh Dickinson University, has examined these constraints upon presidential leadership in detail in her identification of the "general antipathy to leadership" that can be traced to the country's original leaders and their aversion to monarchy.[3] In the context of this continuing resistance to and mistrust of bold initiatives, academic entrepreneurialism is often viewed as unacceptable or inappropriate in the academy. Hence, the leader of a higher education merger is viewed by many colleagues as a nonconformist and educational and organizational risk taker.

In spite of these deep-rooted constraints upon entrepreneurialism, however, the circumstances and implementation of a merger can actually be used to address many of the elements of institutional resistance. Once the decision to merge has been made on the corporate level, an extraordinary mandate for presidential leadership emerges, as every constituency in the institution facing the merger transition immediately recognizes and experiences anxiety concerning the prospect of significant institutional change. A skillful chief executive officer may capitalize on this dynamic situation by engaging the entire organization in goal-oriented assignments related to the merger plan. This move will relieve anxieties, but even more importantly, the true mutual growth of the institutions becomes fully dependent upon the involvement of all personnel constituencies in the processes of the merger plan.

As both institutions become engaged in the activities of the merger process, the organizational climate becomes much more receptive to presidential leadership. Although hundreds of decisions are coordinated by the Merger Task Force on many different institutional levels, the overall chief executive officer is at the center of most major decisions early in the discussions. In fact, these negotiations provide rare opportunities for a president to seize the moment and achieve a leadership stature increasingly uncommon in higher education management. A

Pew Higher Education Research Program report suggests that an understandable yearning has developed today for "effective decision-makers—in the old days . . . called men and women with vision and backbone—who feel empowered."[4]

Adapting Chief Executive Leadership Styles

Although it is important for the president to recognize the leadership opportunities inherent in the merger strategy, it is also critical for the chief executive to comprehend and adopt the leadership style that will be effective in completing the merger successfully. The presidents should understand at this point that they must perform a leadership role more transformational than transactional in nature. Estela Bensimon defines the difference between these two styles in an academic setting: "Transactional leaders are depicted as accepting and maintaining the culture of an organization as it exists—its belief system, language, and group norms. In contrast, transformational leaders change organizational culture by introducing new beliefs and goals and by changing how group members define their roles."[5]

In a mutual-growth merger the entire organizational context is altered as two or more institutions are transformed into a single, more powerful entity. The chief executive officer should remain aware, however, that the transformational leadership style most suited to managing a growth merger process is unlikely to be the norm in the current college and university administration. As George Keller has noted on several occasions, an incremental approach to significant institutional decision making is a deep-rooted phenomenon in higher education: "One of the reasons that management science had a hard time taking root in higher education was the thick, deep adherence by campus department chairmen, deans, vice-presidents, and presidents to incrementalism. While management science is rational—economic, incrementalism is partisan—political. Incrementalism holds that the world is not rational and people are often not rational."[6] Even though incrementalism can be a more reasonable approach than Keller acknowledges here, for the purposes of accomplishing a higher education merger it does not constitute the recommended alternative. In the mutual-growth model, the chief executive officer must be prepared to use management techniques to their fullest in order to effect dramatic changes coherently in a condensed period of time.

During merger implementation, the transformational leadership provided by the overall chief executive officer will redefine many if not all of the existing organizational norms. In many sometimes subtle ways, the will of the president can become what might be called the life force of the merger. In the corporate environment, David Ravenscroft has written, once the chief executive officer identifies the central reason for a particular merger, all kinds of striking synergies are suddenly discovered.[7] Experience shows that complementary missions and a desire, or need, for new kinds of growth on both campuses can stimulate this same leadership phenomenon in higher education mergers.

Presidential Involvement in the Merger Process

The success of the mutual-growth strategy depends upon effective entrepreneurial leadership by a president, and to be effective, the president must be able, as Robert Birnbaum suggests, "to provide leadership, direction, coherence, and progress in an organization with conflicting authority structures, multiple social systems, and contested goals."[8]

Put more simply, in order to achieve leadership success in the growth merger model, presidents must perform a macromanagerial role. The chief executive must become the conceptualizer for the entire organization, including the combined governing board and faculty. As Warren Bennis recently noted, however, performing as a conceptualizer means more than simply being the organization's idea person. Presidents as conceptualizers both possess entrepreneurial vision and take the time to consider carefully the forces that will affect the destiny of the institution.[9] In a mutual-growth merger, this role becomes even more fundamental, as the destiny of the institution must be redefined as well as all of the present agreements affected by this redefinition.

To manage successfully the mutual-growth strategy through the postmerger period and over the long term, the chief executive must delegate extensive authority and embrace the practice of consensus management. Every merger presents thousands of unforeseen questions, and effective presidents will foster multiple leadership initiatives to focus on each of these areas, no matter how small. The critical realization for presidents will be that, as Bennis states, "empowerment is the collective effect of leadership."[10] To cope with the overwhelming details of a merger activity, it is imperative for presidents to empower appropriately all of their subordinates.

A key point is that the empowerment of subordinates must be within the scope and bounds of the president's vision for the future of the institution, or conflicts deleterious both to the institution and to the merger may arise. It is particularly true in higher education that the president's responsibility for, and control of, the vision that guides and shapes that institution also serves as the crux of final authority within the organizational structure.[11] In a related sense, the degree to which presidents have mastered the role of conceptualizer determines the degree to which they will be secure in delegating authority and managing by consensus.

In sum, for an appropriate period of time, the goals of the growth merger and the mission of the combined institution become synonymous. In this manner, virtually all of the president's authority may be focused on the successful achievement of the merger model. The merger process is such an encompassing organizational activity that certain institutional functions may even be suspended temporarily before their redefinition and reemergence in the new institutional structure. In this way, merging institutions appropriately become what Pascarella and Frohman have described as "purpose-driven organizations" during the implementation phases. Such organizations are "driven by capturing the sense of purpose that a leader provides, institutionalizing it, and making it the driving force for all of the organization's activities, policies, and practices."[12] These factors, informed by an ongoing awareness that ideas drive institutions more often than do the personalities or charisma of their leaders, constitute the essential components of entrepreneurial leadership and macromanagerial style that shape the effective involvement of the president in a growth merger process.

Mergers as a New Approach to Higher Education Management

A mutual-growth merger may also be viewed from the perspective of an enormous management exercise, even while acknowledging the traditional distrust of what *management* connotes in American higher education. Robert Birnbaum, one of the most prolific contemporary writers on the subject of governance in higher education, has concluded that virtually all of the "management control systems" introduced in higher education have failed. Under that category he includes master planning, program budgeting, zero-based budgeting, management information systems, management by objectives, strategic planning, and entrepreneurship.[13]

Those who resist or oppose the entire concept of management in higher education, including Birnbaum, have taken an untenable position in my experience. Nationally, higher education can no longer afford to forestall the advantages of appropriate principles of contemporary management science. Institutional quality and, in some cases, institutional survival have become increasingly dependent upon managerial effectiveness. Reality has demonstrated that a lack of effective management in colleges and universities can be a source of embarrassment, not to mention lost students and revenues, described by Cohen, March, and Olsen as the "garbage can" model of management, a higher education decision-making framework characterized by unclear goals and a constantly shifting group of participants.[14]

In a merger, there is less time to address serious resistance and barriers to sound management practices. The chief executive officer consequently must devise a proven strategy to overcome any aspects of a traditional antimanagement syndrome. In a number of successful growth mergers, the strategy has been simple: *empower the faculty to manage rather than to be managed.* Legitimate faculty and staff empowerment thus becomes fundamental to a merger-based vision of higher education management. When the faculty members are authentically empowered in appropriate managerial roles, an accompanying element of accountability reinforces the leadership role of the president.

Once a college or university organizes itself and operates under a single hierarchy of authority and empowers the faculty into a position of central authority within that hierarchy, the entire organization becomes a more balanced entity. Under these conditions, higher education institutions can be more effectively focused toward goals such as merger when a complementary institutional partner has been identified. George Keller has envisioned the need for this kind of managerial revolution in colleges and universities and has offered the following definition of effective management: "While administration sees that things are done right, management sees that the right things are done. . . . Management is the entrepreneurial element. It works to make things better and appropriately different."[15]

The success of mutual-growth mergers up to the year 2000 and beyond will depend on new management structures and practices such as these. A growth merger is such a comprehensive management exercise that it cannot and should not be managed by administrators alone; faculty must be empowered to manage and collaborate in almost all merger activities, this empowerment must be responsive to the new institutional vision articulated by the president.

Organizational Dysfunction and the Potential for Failure

If the effective, single hierarchy of institutional authority critical to the successful merger cannot be established early on, presidents would be well advised to reconsider the larger mutual-growth objectives they are hoping to achieve. I have observed this type of struggle in more than one merger negotiation, and it often exerts a generally destabilizing force on the mutual-growth approach. Within the merger plan, however, the chief executive officer and members of the Merger Task Force must also acknowledge the legitimate distinctions between the realms of administrative and professional faculty authority, as the faculty will be asked to make significant contributions during the implementation process as an integral unit within the larger organizational hierarchy. Dysfunction occurs when the collective authority of the faculty operates in opposition to the merger concept and to the leadership team attempting to accomplish it.

Many experts have detailed these symptoms of organizational dysfunction in contemporary higher education. Austin and Gamson have asserted that "the coexistence of collegial and bureaucratic frameworks is anomalous" and have employed the terminology, "a workplace of two cultures." Birnbaum describes collegiate governance in the United States as "unique dualism," "dualism of controls," and "a loosely coupled system." But perhaps most apt is Keller's description of a dual hierarchy. Keller has also quite vividly articulated the impact of the dysfunction: "There is the authority problem. One does not have to be a political theorist to realize that dual leadership does not work or that little gets done when the king and the barons of the realm have equal power and different views of where to go or how to proceed. Yet many colleges and universities make little apparent effort to break out of their dual authority and stalemates."[16]

Hierarchical dysfunctions such as these can easily stalemate a mutual-growth merger regardless of its potential to enhance both institutions. As Joseph P. O'Neill points out, "Opposition from faculty . . . is one of the standard reasons why college mergers fail."[17] In the face of faculty resistance, presidential options are limited, as even mission-complementary colleges and universities cannot be transformed through merger without the participation and endorsement of the faculty. The most effective model to address this challenge has been to empower the faculty in appropriate areas as managers of the merger. Faculty may effectively exercise managerial authority within contemporary higher education systems, and the managerial empowerment of faculty members has the ability to reconcile and overcome a dual-hierarchy stalemate. As faculty authority is expanded, so too will be faculty responsibility to the corporate institutional body as well as to the goals of the mutual-growth concept.

The Mount Ida Model of Academic Management

Mount Ida College in Massachusetts during the late 1980s successfully completed four merger activities ranging from programmatic merger to institutional acquisition. Mount Ida had been experimenting with a faculty-based management system since the beginning of the decade, and the mergers provided an opportunity to test its efficacy.

Results have continued to be persuasively positive as, over a four-year period, faculty members have remolded the entire curriculum and enrollments have increased from 800 to 1,700 students. The college has also been restructured into eight constituent schools, while the first-year applicant pool has tripled, reaching an approximate total of 3,600. Necessarily, the physical plant has doubled in size, as the stature of the institution has increased throughout the northeast region.

In retrospect, Mount Ida's success was possible only because faculty members had the authority both to make decisions about merger-related activities and then to implement those decisions. Over two-thirds of the full-time faculty operate with decentralized, statutory decision-making authority in the forms of school, program, and curriculum directorships. Their authority further has actualized the standards adopted by the American Association of University Professors, which recognize the primary responsibility faculty members hold for curriculum, subject matter, methods of instruction, research, faculty status, and those aspects of student life most closely connected to the educational process. Additionally, these faculty members hold decision-making authority in departmental and programmatic personnel areas.

From an organizational perspective, this managerial model is predicated upon the belief that "effective presidents decentralize the decision-making process to the extent that decisions are made at the lowest possible organizational level."[18] Further, the consensus among both faculty and administration is that significant change is not exclusively a top-down phenomenon, but rather that successful curricular, personnel, and even fiscal initiatives can and will arise anywhere within the faculty-centered academic management structure, simultaneously expanding the opportunity for a consensus management approach. The great majority of academic management decisions at the college during the past ten years have been made within the peer context. In this more flattened organizational hierarchy, individual faculty managers use collaborative, participatory decision-making techniques, as well as being subject to the overview of the faculty senate, of which they all are members.

The managerial model now employed at Mount Ida and several other schools undertaking growth mergers exemplifies one of the new forms of academic management Ernest Boyer recently called for, as it assigns to all faculty members with academic administrative appointments, such as department chairs and program directors, a statutory authority along with the more traditional forms of authority common at higher education institutions.[19] Finally, faculty responsibility and faculty commitment are acknowledged as essential to institutional excellence. As Robert Greenleaf has noted, however, "What I identified as a crisis of leadership in colleges and universities eight years ago, after considerable involvement with academic institutions, I now see as a symptom of the failure of faculties to accept that the price of freedom everywhere, in their case academic freedom, is responsibility."[20] In this context, it is fair to add that the managerial model at Mount Ida challenges faculty members using it to accept new levels of responsibility and to achieve new levels of professional excellence within the flexibility of the mutual-growth approach.

Higher Education Mergers in a National Context

The president contemplating a mission-complementary growth merger would be wise to review the larger phenomenon of mergers and acquisitions as a contemporary corporate and societal trend. These transactions have certain typologies as well as universal characteristics, and presidents need to understand their implications while identifying the strategic opportunities that may be unique to a particular plan or approach.

Buono and Bowditch in *The Human Side of Mergers and Acquisitions* have pointed out that the terms *merger, acquisition,* and *consolidation* are often used interchangeably, but that these three transactions are distinct. The authors also identify four types of mergers categorized by the Federal Trade Commission: horizontal, vertical product extension, market extension, and unrelated. The chief executive officer needs to understand the basic differences among these types and approaches as well as, for example, the following phases of a hypothetical merger which the authors outline: precombination, combination planning, announced combination, initial combination process, formal physical-legal combination, combination aftermath, and psychological combination.[21] Experience suggests that foreknowledge of these stages and categories by the president and members of the Merger Task Force directly impacts the intricate transactions of the merger process and its chances for long-term success.

Another presidential responsibility prior to developing the merger model is to complete a candid assessment of the range of potential benefits. Here again, a thorough familiarity of the recent phenomenon of mergers and acquisitions is necessary. As an example, in "The 1980's Merger Wave," Ravenscroft identifies up to fifteen motives for a merger.[22] Research indicates that the opportunities to achieve growth, to accomplish diversification, to acquire assets, to expand human resources, and to achieve economies of scale have formed the basic elements of the new mutual-growth concept. As these potential benefits are perceived, it becomes easier to grasp how merging as a higher education management strategy has attracted a growing group of faculty members and academic administrators.

In retrospect, one of the most important lessons a chief executive officer can draw from a review of the new mutual-growth approach is that a percentage of these agreements may not achieve success when judged against original expectations. In the U.S. corporate sector a central question for chief executives has continued to be whether the financial and growth potentials of their merger plan, often based on a bankruptcy or bailout objective, can ever be fully achieved, and if not, what will prevent this. One of the overriding reasons for adopting a mutual-growth approach is that it provides an opportunity not only to realize financial stability and growth objectives, but also to achieve new levels of academic excellence through the involvement of faculty, students, and even alumni, in the enhancement of institutional mission, degree programs, and educational services.

The Advancement of the Mutual-Growth Concept

My conviction has grown during the past ten years that the mutual-growth merger model is a sound strategy to join proactively two healthy colleges or universities and, further, that this plan constitutes a new approach to academic management with far-reaching applications. Gail Chambers identified three higher education merger types several years ago: bankruptcy-bailout, mutual retrenchment of institutions with like academic programming, and mutual growth of institutions combining complementary offerings.[23] The third category, mutual-growth merger, appears to represent the best and only opportunity to achieve a level of educational excellence which significantly exceeds that of the separate institutions before the merger.

In a mutual-growth merger, the president's foremost challenge is to conceptualize and articulate an expanded mission that incorporates and enlarges the missions of the institutional partners into a new educational enterprise, as Harry Gray says, "in such a way that the whole [becomes] greater than the sum of the parts."[24] Beyond incorporating separate institutional missions, however, the chief executive officer and members of the Merger Task Force must also dedicate themselves to preserving the most important aspects of the constituent institutions' identities and educational legacies within the larger entity. In return, the institutional partners must accept some degree of fundamental change. Each institution, no matter how dominant the role of one partner may be, will need to relinquish a degree of sovereignty within the combined institution. Only through this process can the potential for authentic synergy within the mutual-growth strategy become possible.

In earlier decades, a number of prominent universities such as Oxford, Carnegie-Melon, and the Claremont colleges have incorporated elements of the mutual-growth concept in their master planning processes, yet perhaps one of the most overlooked examples of mutual-growth advancement nationally is Harvard University. In its present configuration, the Harvard University–Radcliffe College model represents a de facto mutual-growth merger despite no official corporate merging. The educational missions of Harvard and Radcliffe have been fundamentally transformed by the evolution of coeducational academic and residential functions, while Radcliffe women may still avail themselves of a wide range of special services and programs distinctive to their own institution. However, both Harvard and Radcliffe have relinquished various degrees of institutional sovereignty in order to transform and combine their basic academic missions into a larger, more integrated, and more relevant educational enterprise.

In the Mount Ida College mergers, the stated goal was "to distinguish rather than to extinguish" the traditions, legacies, and academic functions of the new institutional partners. The four involved institutions all had a certain degree of longevity: Mount Ida College, founded in 1899; Chamberlayne Junior College, founded in 1892; the Coyne School of Electricity, founded in 1896; and the New England Institute of Arts and Sciences—now Funeral Service Education—founded in 1907. The academic strategy that preserved and distinguished the last three institutions was their reorganization as schools within the expanded Mount Ida College. Simultaneously, the additional resources generated through the mergers allowed Mount Ida to upgrade its five ongoing academic divisions within the new schools structure of the expanded college. Each of the newly identified schools of the college retains its own admissions and recruiting focus, academic budgeting model, and appropriate student traditions and programs.

The merger activities at Mount Ida enabled the college to accelerate the achievement of several major goals envisioned by the chief executive officer in a series of strategic plans during the previous decade. Most importantly, the mergers expedited Mount Ida's evolution from a two-year college to a two-plus-two, associate's and bachelor's degree-granting academic structure and created the basis for the transition into a fully coeducational institution. During this transition, the institution's operating budget increased from $6 million to $14 million. Perhaps most startling, however, was the sustained expansion of the college's

---

Administrative Barriers to Postmerger Growth

- Passive resistance
- Overt resistance
- Decreased commitment
- Absenteeism

- Turnover
- Role ambiguity
- Persistent culture shock

---

student market base and applicant pool during the greatest demographic decline in New England in half a century. A concern before the mergers was that the college would be vulnerable to postmerger shrinkage after the initial infusion of new applications and students. In fact, the mutual growth has been actual and has facilitated an expansion of the enrollments of every institutional partner over premerger levels.

Barriers to Complementary Growth

The chief executive officer must also remain clearly focused on the dramatic impact of a growth merger upon the administrations and staffs involved. Significant internal struggles inevitably occur during most merger implementations. More than in the faculty area, the administrative personnel component of a higher education merger plan can simulate the dynamics of a merger in the corporate world. Each functional area in the institution has a unique set of difficulties with prominent problems that may include passive resistance, outright resistance, decreased commitment, absenteeism, turnover, role ambiguity, and persistent culture shock.[25]

Presidents may find it useful to view most of the personnel struggles and difficulties as barriers to complementary growth or, more simply, mergeritis. Members of the administration of the more dominant institution, to the degree this applies, are typically invested in the status quo and not predisposed to alter the basic structures and methodologies of their work. Conversely, administrators at the other college or university may propose specific changes to demonstrate their value and worth in the expanded organizational structure. These dynamics can lead to conflicts that require patient and skillful management by the chief executive officer and members of the Merger Task Force. Both constituencies are bound to suffer various forms of discomfort and dislocation until the new institutional synthesis has been articulated and accepted.

Strategically, the chief executive officer needs to understand and guide the merger process during this swiftly changing phase. As Price

Pritchett stated, "Top management cannot prevent the . . . shockwaves."[26] Presidents can, however, spare themselves much anguish if they recognize and accept that conflicts and struggles such as these accompany the merger process and can be creatively resolved. Buono and Bowditch suggest that it is often wiser to think in terms of coping with, rather than managing, the tensions and uncertainties that inevitably emerge.[27] In the mutual-growth model, the new administrative team and organizational structure are derived from the best that each institutional partner has to offer. Presidents cannot fully prescribe outcomes in the early stages of the process because new forms of productivity and commitment to the combined institution may take several years to develop, the product of sustained experimentation by the integrated administrative staff. Mutual growth can only occur in colleges and universities willing to experience the difficulties of the process as the new institutional culture evolves.

Some chief executive officers claim it is futile to attempt work-force integration during a merger transaction. A bank president who had recently completed a merger told me, "If I had to do it over again, I would fire all the employees of either Bank A or Bank B." Even accounting for the frustrations of directing a large merger process, this approach could never achieve success in higher education. The principle of collegiality grounds the entire U.S. higher education system, and, in part because of this tradition, colleges and universities are naturally more tolerant and creative toward internal cultural differences. Innovative chief executive officers assess and measure this tolerance as an indicator of their institution's capacity for growth—including mutual growth.

Ultimately, the merger plan achieves a stage of completion and equilibrium, and many of the symptoms discussed here fade and dissolve. Buono and Bowditch describe the conditions under which these tensions abate: "After the dissipation of the feeling that one's psychological contract has been violated, mutual understandings will stabilize as the organization takes on a new identity."[28] This new identity and enhanced mission can then be sustained by the new organizational culture, whose ongoing members understand the struggles and conflicts that made possible its creation.

From several different perspectives, I have here considered the mutual-growth concept as a form of heroic accomplishment in contemporary higher education. Although presidents must be prepared to overcome the so-called antiheroic or antileadership elements in their own institutional cultures, they should not envision or present themselves as the heroes of the merger process. In fact, presidents must prepare to reassign a good measure of the sovereignty of their college or university to a larger whole in order to achieve this transformation, and in this process they need to instill new beliefs and goals in all of their community members. Under normal conditions the position of campus president, according to Keller, "is arguably the toughest job in America."[29] Under merger conditions, the leadership challenge for presidents becomes even more extraordinary.

In the experience of many with the mutual-growth model, the basis for meeting this challenge is conveyed in the statement by Pascarella and Frohman: "Leadership largely involves the growth of others."[30] With this perspective in mind, the heroic elements of a mutual-growth merger are the combined faculty and administrative work forces who accomplish its thousands of fundamental, inevitable tasks.

This is not to deny in any way the necessity for presidents to provide leadership. Rather, the form this leadership should take is through inspiring others with a new institutional vision and serving as its principal conceptualizer and architect. Presidents will need to lead not by managing the faculty but rather by empowering faculty members to manage, not just during the merger process but in the life of the new institution. To the degree that faculty members accept appropriate managerial responsibilities in governing colleges and universities, mutual growth through merging can occur to new and dramatic extents. In exercising these new forms of authority and responsibility, the faculty will become invested in the postmerger structure naturally and authentically.

Heroes of the merger will also emerge from the administrative sector. Mutual growth, as a concept, mandates the preservation of the merging institutions, their missions, and their constituencies within the larger whole. In order to create this larger enterprise, there must be a period of experimentation. Presidents cannot be prescriptive during the experimentation stage without preempting growth. Conflicts and struggles will inevitably erupt, but a new organizational culture will eventually evolve which can be creatively shaped by the combined administrative leadership team.

At the completion of the growth merger process, the institution will achieve a new vision and equilibrium. If mutual growth has occurred in both the academic and administrative realms, the college or university will be prepared to enter an era of unprecedented excellence, and as such excellence is achieved, it will behoove the president to remain humble in the knowledge that, without the contributions of its faculty and administrators, the new institution would never have been possible.

CHAPTER FIVE

An Academic Action Plan for Faculty Involvement, Curriculum Revision, and Professional Development

James Martin

Premerger Academic Planning

At the 1987 Wingspread Conference, "Mergers and Acquisitions in Private Higher Education," speakers agreed that the compelling force behind almost every academic merger in the first half of this century had been financial necessity. However, in assessing the need to plan strategically and proactively for the future because of factors such as declining federal support, fluctuating student demographics, eroding consumer confidence in higher education, and declining student skill levels, the group created a model for an "ideal" merger, one that included geographic proximity, commonality of mission and heritage, greater enrollment size, increased fund-raising opportunities, and, most importantly for this study, academic and program complementarity.[1] In the mutual-growth merger model, definitive financial parameters are carefully determined and clearly communicated at the outset of the planning process by the joint leadership team. At that point executive and financial managers may begin to step back from control of many aspects of the merger process while faculty members and key academic administrators become its principal architects through a comprehensive plan for curriculum revision and professional development.

Lacking the severe fiscal limitations that characterize retrenchment and bankruptcy mergers, premerger planning in the mutual-growth model assumes a different role and importance. Beyond the senior officers who must be familiar with each level of the merger's planning, R. Kirby Godsey, president of Mercer University, which merged with Tift College in 1986, points out that "there must be a critical mass of institutional decision-makers (presidents, trustees, and opinion-makers)

A Summary Action Plan for Merger Implementation

- Develop premerger academic planning objectives
- Form joint committee to review and revise combined curriculum
- Form joint committee to review and redesign faculty staffing
- Form joint governance committee to integrate systems
- Consolidate personnel policies

  Faculty rank systems
  Tenure systems
  Compensation levels
  Benefits programs
  Faculty duties and responsibilities
  Reappointment criteria
  Retrenchment criteria
  Collective bargaining agreements
  Faculty handbook organization

- Provide uninterrupted professional development opportunities for combined faculties
- Form joint academic oversight committee to review success of new academic policies at one-, three-, and five-year check points

---

committed to the process of merger. Without this ingredient, even a clear understanding of what 'ought' to be done will not be sufficient. . . . The merger must have a cadre of persons who have examined the facts [and] . . . understand institutional heritage and purpose, and who possess the discipline to keep the larger perspective."[2]

In examining a merger that failed between the universities of Bridgeport and New Haven several years ago, one researcher wrote, "not only must all those who take part in the planning keenly anticipate how a new institution will be set in motion, but those who will move it must be brought into the planning process. At the very least, the presidents should have been in attendance at the crucial planning sessions."[3]

In 1975, Widener College in Chester, Pennsylvania, merged following the mutual-growth strategy with the Delaware Law School and with Brandywine College, a two-year institution combining liberal arts and professional studies. In 1979, Widener achieved full university status through eight constituent schools and colleges incorporated in Pennsylvania and Delaware. In the premerger planning process to join these three institutions, president Robert Bruce and his senior management team developed three cross-campus committees to address the major curricular, faculty, and student development aspects of their unusual college–junior college–law school structure. A Joint Academic Affairs Committee, a Joint Faculty Affairs Committee, and a Joint Student Life Committee were created with faculty and administrative representatives from all three institutions to serve both as the first symbols of the joined colleges and as working task forces to articulate institutional strategies for program diversification, human resource development, student activities, and land and space usage.

In the premerger planning stages of Mount Ida College's merger with Chamberlayne Junior College, a commercial art and design school in downtown Boston, the two deans of students developed a Joint Student Issues Committee and shared leadership and policy formulation responsibilities equally during the premerger period. In the financial planning area, the chief financial officer at Mount Ida was appointed acting executive director of the Chamberlayne campus for the year leading up to the merger to coordinate the development of a unified financial system for the new structure. In the principal academic planning areas of curriculum revision and personnel assessment, the colleges formed two task forces to develop working relationships among a wider range of colleagues as well as a new format for the sensitive discussions pending in these areas. A Joint Task Force on Curriculum Review and Revision and a smaller Joint Committee on Faculty Personnel Planning were also formed and charged with developing the principal curricular and staff planning recommendations.

During premerger planning to combine Queen Mary and Westfield Colleges within the University of London, a group of three deans was formed to direct the academic, financial, and student life dimensions of the transitional two-campus college. During the premerger and merger implementation periods, one dean took general responsibility for the combined academic planning on both campuses, the second was charged with developing an initial financial plan for the merged institution, and the third assumed overall leadership for student development issues.

As the merger's joint planning and leadership groups meet to articulate long-term objectives, and as the senior financial officer clarifies the fiscal considerations that must be observed, the combined admissions departments should attend planning meetings and be enlisted to produce student market studies to address the next five- and ten-year periods, as differences in institutional reputation can exert a disproportionate influence on formative planning discussions.[4] In a mutual-growth merger, when opportunity rather than survival is the primary objective, the new leadership team can use these studies to achieve an expanded market share in regional and national recruiting efforts. They may achieve a further benefit by sharing these documents with department and program chairs, who at this point can be incorporated fully into the broadened merger planning group.

The final component of premerger planning is a joint institutional academic needs assessment aimed at commonality of mission and, more specifically, at the structure of each program and department, which will provide the foundation for blending the goals and objectives of both institutions into one. The needs assessment brings closure to premerger activities, and from this point forward planning gives way to the collegial meeting and negotiating that are the merger's true implementation. Merging to enhance academic quality now shifts from being a rationale for discussion to the shaping force behind every staffing and curricular proposal approved by the Merger Task Force and its subcommittees.

Curriculum Review and Revision

By this point, tremendous paperwork has in most cases been generated by several study groups and committees, all with detailed, inclusive agendas—yet so far nothing has actually been merged. The Joint Committee on Curriculum Revision is the first step many institutions take as their transition into actual merger and as the cornerstone of their new institutional relationship. (See figure 5.1 for a full outline of the planning stages discussed in this chapter.)

In the Widener–Brandywine–Delaware Law School merger, a Joint Academic Affairs Committee was immediately formed to oversee the complex curricular issues involved in joining the degree programs of a professional school, a college, and a junior college. As well as coordinating these central curriculum revision issues for the three institutions throughout the implementation process, the committee was also charged with developing a strategic plan in curricular areas for these new schools of Widener University. One responsibility the group focused on initially was new degree development. Following the merger, professors from the university and the law school developed joint-degree programs in the areas of JD-MBA, JD-MPA, and JD-Psy.D. In each instance, curriculum development was employed as the authenticating process to unify three proximate colleges into a multipurpose regional university.

During the curriculum review process, for a variety of reasons, academic leaders may experience the first overt resistance to merger on one or both campuses. Territorial and seniority-based conflicts can be common early responses to the uncertainties and difficulties of joining separate institutional cultures. This reaction partly grows out of the perception that significant advantages should be gained by merging, yet the merger agreement, which must satisfy all institutional constituencies, has not yet been fully articulated and shared with them.[5] In this uncertain environment, senior faculty members and academic administrators have the main responsibility for determining the shape of the new institutional structure. Curriculum review and revision form the core of this shared responsibility.

Not surprisingly, however, curriculum revision appears to have produced only a small number of studies in the literature on academic mergers. One reason is that the process must become so individualized for each set of institutions. The academic deans, department chairs, and combined faculties form a good part of the identity of the new institution, and a carefully managed review process can yield numerous additional benefits for all involved. During the early planning stages, a large percentage of instructors inevitably experience confusion and anxiety. Meeting to revise the merged curriculum provides the most natural set of introductions for the two faculties and allows for a natural development of collegiality and cooperation among those now shaping the merger process.

Mount Ida College faculty members formed a two-year Task Force on Curriculum Review and Revision with members of the faculty from Chamberlayne Junior College and the Coyne School of Technical Electricity during their three-way merger in 1987. This joint committee coordinated the design of the new college's curricula by implementing a "schools" model of academic program and faculty organization in which the largest departments and divisions at Mount Ida and Chamberlayne were joined into six schools, maintaining their own admissions recruiters and academic identities. The combined art and design departments of the two colleges were renamed the Chamberlayne School of Design and Merchandising; the Coyne School of Electricity became an additional, seventh school of Mount Ida College. One year later, when the college merged with the New England Institute of Funeral Service Education, the institute became the eighth school of the expanded structure. While the Chamberlayne and Coyne schools and the New England Institute, along with five enlarged departments now designated as schools, maintain individual academic profiles, the faculties and students from the four campuses have been carefully combined in the new structure over a three-year period, through this curriculum-driven process.

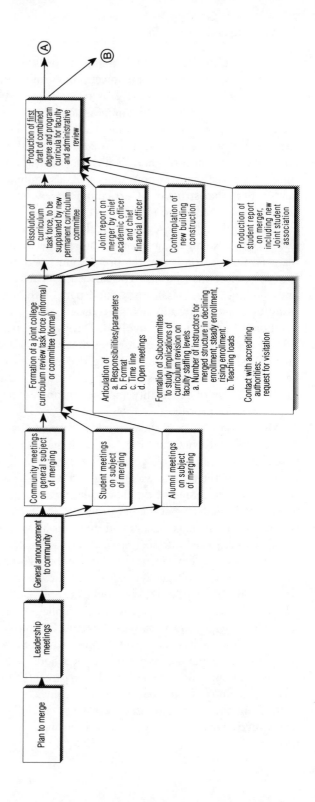

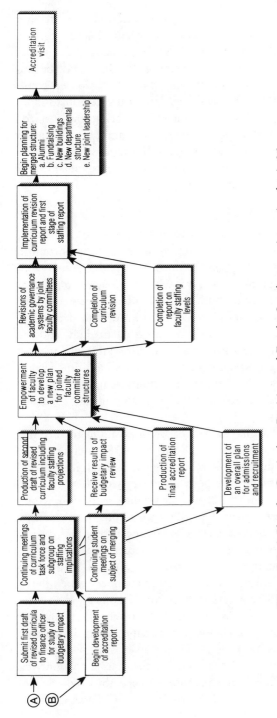

Figure 5.1. A Plan for Curriculum Revision and Faculty Involvement in an Academic Merger.

As the institutional goals of growth and academic quality are further refined and applied to each program and department of a new college, progress on two levels may be observed. On one level, issues such as increased course offerings and new degree authorities may be addressed. On a deeper level, two essential questions may be posed simultaneously for the first time: What is the culture of the new institution, and what were the true identities of the institutions being transformed? Questions such as these may appear to be luxuries amid the turmoil of closing a campus or balancing two budgets, but as answers to them are clarified and noted, the academic managers will learn much that is valuable about those whom they are to lead.[6]

Academic Staff Planning

Faculty staffing issues form the second major academic component of merger planning and implementation, and it has been important in our experience to conduct this planning process simultaneously with the joint review of curriculum. In fact, it is wise for a nucleus of Merger Task Force members to serve on both the curriculum review and staff planning committees. New colleagues come to know and depend on each other during the revision of the combined curriculum, and the next step is the design of a new personnel plan for staffing the merged structure. A growth merger does not guarantee that all full-time faculty positions will be preserved, and the assumption among rank-and-file faculty members that this should occur will pose a significant challenge to the project's managers.

Merger leadership teams have taken different positions toward this basic issue early in their discussions. During the 1986 merger of the College of St. Catherine and St. Mary's College in St. Paul, Minnesota, the announcement was made that both campuses would continue to operate and that faculty from St. Mary's, the smaller institution, would hold positions on the newly named St. Mary's Campus of the College of St. Catherine. No lay-offs or retrenchments occurred, and overall faculty numbers have grown steadily since the merger agreement. Similarly, during the 1989 merger of Gannon University and Villa Maria College in Pennsylvania, all Villa Maria faculty members were offered positions in the enlarged structure of Gannon University, then integrated into its rank and tenure systems as full participants. Tenure at Villa Maria became tenure at Gannon University; professional rank was transferred as rank within the larger university system.[7] Cumulative full-time faculty numbered sixty-four at the start of Mount Ida College's mergers with Chamberlayne Junior College, the Coyne School of Electrical Studies, and the New England Institute of Funeral Service

Education. Since the completion of the third merger, the combined institution has added eight full-time faculty positions to meet the needs of an enrollment that has grown by over 800 students to a total of 1,650.

Conversely, in the merger between Tift College and Mercer University, Tift faculty members understood that not all full-time positions would be preserved in the Mercer system, as degree programs and core curricula duplicated each other in several key areas. In actuality, almost every full-time Tift faculty member was eventually placed at Mercer or secured a teaching position at a comparable institution.[8] At Widener University, the merger design provided faculty members from partner institutions an appointment in one of Widener's eight newly formed schools rather than universitywide. This plan has served the rapidly expanding Widener structure well during the past decade, as faculty leaders have been encouraged to become more entrepreneurial in their outlooks while the university has been able to keep faculty positions proportional to school enrollments. As an example, when Delaware Law School merged with Widener in 1975, it brought seventeen full-time faculty positions. At the start of the 1992–93 academic year, its successor, the Widener University School of Law, offered full-time contracts to eighty-nine faculty members.

To address the range of sensitive personnel decisions mentioned here, leadership teams from all campuses had to develop candid working relationships. At the point that staff planning is to begin, senior academic administrators need to meet with the chief executives of both institutions to clarify the line of academic authority in the new structure. If rank, salary, and tenure are comparable, even though numbers of faculty on each campus may be significantly different, recommended staffing plans may emerge rapidly and coherently. If a common ground for unified decision making cannot be reached readily, senior academic officers must still establish the basis for cooperation and collegiality which will guide their subordinates. In the Mount Ida College staff planning model, broadened communication was achieved by inviting the chief financial officer of both campuses and a member of the board of trustees to serve on the Joint Committee on Faculty Personnel Planning, which offered academic managers a set of resources rarely accessible through their campus committee system. In the College of St. Catherine–St. Mary's merger, the chief executive officers of the respective campuses became active participants at periodic points in the meetings of the curriculum revision and personnel planning subcommittees of their task forces. In the Widener–Brandywine–Delaware Law School plan, the provost, academic deans, and faculty representatives from the campuses joined these subcommittees. This close involvement—with the staffing function in particular—helped build a strong foundation of understanding and trust among the merging faculties regarding their executive colleagues.

On the issue of faculty involvement in decision making, both researchers and merger participants have observed that faculty committees have been found to work most successfully when they are asked not about individual programs or people but about methods and criteria.[9] Administrators and faculty decision makers must also remain sensitive not only to issues such as seniority and benefits but also to deeper differences between campus cultures, as these will constitute a multitude of unwritten yet tangible factors governing employment relationships. Each merger reviewed in this chapter has developed a unique campus culture that must be acknowledged and supported both by the new academic leadership team and by staff members and classroom instructors at all levels of the combined organization. Examples of these special cultural factors include Villa Maria College's mission to support the educational needs of women beyond traditional college age within the Gannon University educational operation and the curricular tensions that could arise between associate's degree faculty in nursing at St. Mary's College and bachelor's degree instructors in nursing at the College of St. Catherine or between engineering faculty members at Kansas State University and engineering technology faculty at the Kansas College of Technology. Distinctions between academic cultures may also be more overt, such as those between religious orders like the Congregation of Christian Brothers and the Sisters of Charity, which joined recently in the merger of Iona and Elizabeth Seton colleges in New York, or the professional traditions of the U.S. funeral industry at the New England Institute addressed in its recent merger with Mount Ida College, an institution known for blending professional careers and the liberal arts.

Since even a growth merger may involve focused staff reductions resulting from duplication or the curtailment of program enrollments, the staff planning task force needs to publicize its criteria for decision making in its earliest discussions. At the least, criteria should include factors such as program coherence, affirmative action principles, and seniority issues—time in rank, time in institution, and age of program or department.

During the Tift-Mercer merger, with the understanding and announcement that it would not be possible to preserve all Tift positions, an internal task force of Tift representatives coordinated the personnel planning for all Tift full-time faculty members. Tenured Tift faculty retained their tenure on the Mercer faculty; remaining Tift faculty were given priority consideration for all new positions in their disciplines at Mercer. Through skillful planning on the part of the deans of Tift and Mercer, every full-time faculty member at Tift except one was placed in a new position within three years of the merger. In an alternative approach, the chief executive and academic officers of Gannon University and Villa Maria College retained KMPG–Peat Marwick as consultants during both the first and second stages of their planning, and Peat Marwick produced two comprehensive reports on a variety of planning decisions ranging from mission review to staffing and facilities needs.

The process of staff review should also incorporate factors such as the fit of each program with the mission of the new institution and whether a program's standards will articulate within its new academic environment. After reviewing projected decisions from an affirmative action perspective, a consideration often neglected in a merger, an equitable method must be devised to weigh the issue of seniority within the combined faculties. It is interesting to note that in the mergers of several large universities such as Kansas State and Widener, seniority was reviewed and incorporated in the new staffing plan without the apparent deference accorded it in the mergers of several smaller institutions such as Mount Ida–Chamberlayne and St. Mary's–College of St. Catherine.

This is the strategic time to let faculty members know that administrative positions are also being reviewed for duplication, consonance with mission, and seniority. In the St. Mary's–College of St. Catherine merger, it was announced that while no administrative lay-offs would occur, economies of scale would be accomplished by not replacing administrators who retired or left voluntarily. For smaller colleges, this strategy of early announcement, job preservation, and nonreplacement has proven to be effective and sensitive to the needs of a campus culture lacking some of the resources offered by a large university. In the Chamberlayne–Mount Ida merger, through creative staff realignment, it was possible to offer the Chamberlayne academic dean the directorship of the new, enlarged School of Liberal Arts.

Academic managers of the Kansas State–Kansas College of Technology merger plan faced an unusual circumstance in which the college, with less than one-twentieth as many students as the university, had four vice presidents to the university's three. A collaborative decision reduced the total number of vice presidents to three and redistributed their former duties on the college's campus among several individuals at the director level, enhancing their responsibilities and career growth. The savings accomplished in these significant administrative reductions increased the number of faculty on the college's campus to address course needs caused by the transfer of several university bachelor's degrees to that site. The preservation of both campuses in a merger, as in the plans for the College of St. Catherine–St. Mary's and Widener–Brandywine–Delaware Law School mergers, is one of the most significant factors impacting overall administrative staffing levels.

At this point in the merger's implementation, the Merger Task Force must confirm whether the proposals for staffing are to be recommendations from a joint faculty-administrative body directly to the president or whether the faculty members involved will offer their recommendations to the senior academic officers for their initial review and approval. (These new lines of authority will significantly influence the merger's next phase, governance review.) In the recent Kansas merger, the matter was clearly one of board of regents authority, demonstrated both in the formation of the Regents Task Force on the Future Direction of Kansas College of Technology and in the board's decision to upgrade the College of Technology campus through a planned $10 million renovation, although this was made possible through internal reallocation on the campus, a citywide sales tax that yielded more than $4 million, and gifts to the university. State funds were not used to support the merger. The recommendations of the St. Mary's–College of St. Catherine Curricular and Staffing Task Force were received for implementation by a joint committee of the college's chief executive, chief academic, and chief financial officers. In the Villa Maria–Gannon University merger process, curricular recommendations were submitted to the joint Deans' Council, and staffing recommendations were received by the university's president and vice presidents for academic and financial affairs. In the plan to join the New England Institute of Funeral Service Education and Mount Ida College, personnel recommendations for faculty and staff members were ultimately reviewed by a joint subcommittee of the two boards of trustees.

A key to success for each task force's personnel planning subcommittee will be to maintain realistic expectations from the outset, for "a danger exists that systems will overpromise the results that are likely to occur." Further, "it is difficult to persuade those in low-priority areas that they should be low priorities."[10]

Integrating Academic Governance

After devising the necessary curriculum revisions and submitting staffing proposals to support them, faculty members and administrators step back and focus the emerging organizational structure within a broader educational perspective by clarifying the new institution's model of collegial governance and documenting it in the first joint faculty handbook. For a growth merger to succeed both in fact and perception, a coherent, harmonious academic governance system must emerge from the institutional consolidation. If the new structure does not embody as strong a voice and support system for the combined faculties as their individual models had provided, the institution has suffered an avoidable loss.

Governance articulation has been addressed through a variety of approaches in recent mutual-growth mergers. Faculty senate leaders in the Gannon–Villa Maria and Tift-Mercer mergers immediately incorporated the merged faculty members from the smaller colleges, Villa Maria and Tift, into the representative senate systems of the universities. In the ongoing implementation of the Kansas College of Technology–Kansas State merger, the faculty senates of both schools have appointed a subcommittee of the whole specifically to address faculty senate consolidation, particularly with regard to new course approval and academic personnel policies. A general incorporation of the College of Technology's 40 senators into the 100-representative university senate has been planned; however, the university employs more than 1,500 faculty members, and the influence of the College of Technology's smaller senate will be further reviewed in the context of the larger body.[11]

In the Widener University mergers, the larger institution initially invited Brandywine College and Delaware Law School faculty representatives to join a large and, as it was discovered, cumbersome university council. As the new university matured, representatives from the three institutions acknowledged that its culture and purposes were clear and coherent enough to support increased degrees of governance self-definition for the teaching faculties of the three campuses. Approximately five years after the merger, leaders from the constituent campuses developed a more local approach to governance through the creation of separate faculty councils for each of the three campuses. These councils now conduct their own faculty business except in the areas of faculty personnel policy and all appeal procedures, which remain universitywide in their jurisdiction.[12]

For approximately 30 percent of the faculty members on a campus, the shape and nature of the academic governance system is of little consequence, according to a Carnegie Commission survey of over five thousand faculty members completed in the mid-1980s. For a greater proportion of faculty members, the impact and authenticity of governance, much more acutely than student evaluations or departmental rewards, is the significant barometer of an instructor's professional identity and sense of purpose. Without creatively and directly addressing the merger of the campus governance systems, administrators and faculty members hold the combined institution back from what it might accomplish. A body of scholarship is now beginning to accumulate which clarifies new faculty-administrative partnerships within a shared governance model.[13] The concept of shared governance has emerged as particularly significant to the mutual-growth strategy.

In response to the challenges provoked by the incorporation of three governance systems in four years, in 1991 merger planners at Mount Ida College used the resources of the newest school of the College, the Naples Institute Conference Center in Naples, Florida, to hold a national forum on new models of effective academic governance, especially in the context of mergers and consolidations. The consensus formulated by the participating presidents and senate chairs, as reported in the *Chronicle of Higher Education,* was that more information sharing between faculty senates and chief executive and financial officers must occur for shared governance to succeed. In the financial area most of all, they agreed, effective campus governance systems incorporate the vice president for financial affairs, who in turn shares increasing amounts of budgetary information and decision-making authority with faculty senators and senate subcommittees.[14]

Mission-complementary mergers can contribute to the development of new academic governance systems that are more flexible, subtle, and collaborative. Traditional models of academic governance have maintained more static relations between faculty and administrative leaders, and communication has occurred through slower, more formalized channels. In faculties combined through merger, innovations can be implemented and communication can become more open and interactive. Merger Task Force members at Mount Ida College and its three merger partners adopted an interactive approach to integrating academic governance structures by bringing faculty and administrators from the four institutions together to collaborate in developing a new governance structure. With four separate committee systems, methods of representation, and assembly formats, the new institution drew elements from every college in devising its comprehensive, merged model. In the new structure, the number of principal committees, by joint faculty consensus, was reduced from eleven to four: academic standards, curriculum, finance, and rank and promotion.

Contrary to much of the current literature on higher education management it is our observation that many faculty members who have successfully managed a growth merger possess more managerial skills than their governance systems may require. Rather, the systems themselves need review and further development. As many academic administrators acknowledge, they may more effectively guide than control systems, and as faculty representatives manage their emerging influence more persuasively even more meaningful and responsive forms of collegial governance will evolve from mutual-growth merger structures.[15]

Consolidating Personnel Policies

At this stage of each merger, it is necessary either to create an entirely new faculty handbook or to revise substantially and combine the handbooks of the partner institutions. Either approach will raise many labor relations questions and pose the challenge of codifying the shared understandings supporting the new institutional culture for both present and future faculty members.

The most significant personnel issues that must be resolved include faculty rank, tenure, compensation, benefits, faculty duties and responsibilities, reappointment and retrenchment policies, collective bargaining agreements, and the faculty handbook.

Faculty Rank

A coordination of the rank systems at both institutions should be based on a collaboratively devised method to rationalize the standards in each rank category of the combined structure. Similar to their plans for governance, several merging colleges have recently taken creative approaches to joining rank structures with differing criteria and promotion procedures. Kansas State–Kansas College of Technology merger planners agreed to spend two years from the point of merging to identify the greatest institutional needs in the area of rank. From the outset, they announced that no global rank agreements would be devised. Widener University developed with Brandywine College associate's degree faculty members a new rank system for Brandywine personnel with a different terminal degree requirement for all ranks except full professor, which reflected a universitywide standard. In the College of St. Catherine–St. Mary's merger, faculty members from both colleges also approved a different rank system for the faculty members from St. Mary's, with adjusted credentials and publications requirements to address and support their associate's degree heritage.[16]

Tenure

Although some have suggested that tenure is a deterrent to growth mergers, we have not observed this and would note from experience that tenure typically becomes the new standard in a successful mutual-growth plan unless neither institution previously employed it. If only one institution maintains a tenure system, as was the case in the Chamberlayne–Mount Ida merger, the combined college or university will confront one of its most significant merger-related decisions in determining tenure's status in the new academic structure. In this instance, the new institution chose to adopt tenure as a collegewide personnel policy. The American Association of University Professors has taken a clear stand in support of the stability provided by the preservation of tenure, and institutions have learned to weigh carefully any move to lessen or abolish its connection to the college's academic and legal identity.

At the same time, from a higher education legal point of view, it is false to presume that tenure routinely provides insulation from discontinued employment. The presence of tenure often has carried an implied moral as much as explicit legal obligation. In most current personnel handbooks and collective bargaining agreements, tenure and seniority are not protected through cause, financial exigency, or program discontinuance, a lack of protection that has sometimes been challenged in court. The concept of merging colleges for mutual growth, however, often includes tenure as an academic community-building instrument that enhances rather than dilutes the quality of the combined institution. Tenure provides a common foundation of definitions and trust through which academic administrators and Merger Task Force members may reward teaching effectiveness, research presentation and publication, and continuing professional development.

In some instances of institutional closure or mandated reductions in force, tenure has proven to be an extremely difficult managerial and financial hurdle, but within the context of a carefully conceptualized mutual-growth merger of complementary educational partners, tenure may be viewed as an effective academic support system that preserves the shape and identity of the collective faculty.

In every mutual-growth merger we have researched, preexistent tenure has been preserved. As one Gannon employee stated vis-à-vis the merger with Villa Maria, "Villa tenure meant Gannon tenure."[17] Similarly, Kansas State honored all cases of tenure for College of Technology professors who moved to its campus. A study was also commissioned on the College of Technology campus to determine after merger implementation whether a special tenure system would benefit its faculty in light of the differing standards on their original campus; the commitment has been made to serve the best interests of the combined institution while still respecting the separate histories of its faculties. In the Mercer-Tift merger, tenure existed and was respected on both campuses, with faculty members from Tift receiving full standing in the larger university system, whose requirements they would then observe.

Although a tenure system at any merging campus has often been perceived both by higher education researchers and chief executive officers as one of the greatest potential barriers to a successful college or university merger, an increasing number of academic managers and strategic planners have recently observed that a true mutual-growth, mission-complementary strategy does not involve a stream of faculty retrenchments within a reduced overall structure. Rather, a mutual-growth merger plan provides the human and financial resources for a natural expansion of the two enterprises into a single community whose mission is dedicated to the support and enhancement, rather than curtailment, of faculty strengths and teaching positions.

Similarly, while seniority is not a required criterion in implementing this type of merger, we continue to support it as an elementary governing factor. To the degree it is financially practicable and programmatically plausible, seniority effectively conveys the broader mutual-growth purpose of preserving the integrity of both institutional cultures. Even though a number of judicial opinions have released some presidents and chief academic officers from a strict adherence to seniority in cases of significant reductions in force, the mandates of a college or university closure including these major staff reductions differ from the strategic personnel planning in a mutual-growth merger. Observation suggests that, more than almost any other guideline, seniority can provide a foundation for the greatest degree of coherence and harmony during the extraordinary uncertainties of an institutional merger.

In implementing the overall academic action plan, Merger Task Force managers and members must identify and nurture the evolving community of scholars of the new institution, for it is most clearly out of this core of shared beliefs, professional research, and classroom commitment that the identity and academic reputation of the post-merger college or university will develop. Tenure and seniority, rather than being viewed as antagonists to mutual growth, might better be seen as systems that, with skillful implementation, can enhance the merged institution.[18]

Compensation

Salary and increment levels will differ in the two institutions, possibly to a marked degree, and administrators and senior faculty members may need to define early and often the differences between a decision to "equalize" salaries (by which faculty members from each college receive compensation according to a new, fully justified salary scale) and a plan to "adjust" salaries (so that those of faculty members from the lower-paying institutions are raised to the levels of the higher-paying schools on a case-by-case basis). As rapidly as possible, financial managers from all institutions will need to share budget plans and information to develop a common rationale for future salary and increment plans.

Two basic approaches—to equalize or not—emerge most often in a review of the compensation aspects of recent mutual-growth mergers. In the development of the models for the Mount Ida–Chamberlayne–New England Institute and Gannon–Villa Maria mergers, academic and financial managers agreed to equalize all salaries over a two- to three-year transition period. Thus, faculty members in the lower-paying salary structures in the Gannon–Villa Maria and Mount Ida–Chamberlayne–New England Institute mergers were assured of special increments through an equalization formula specific to the salary scales of the institutional partners. In the Mercer-Tift merger, Tift faculty entering the Mercer faculty automatically received comparable salaries.

In the College of St. Catherine–St. Mary's, Widener University–Brandywine College, and Kansas State–Kansas College of Technology mergers, faculty members on the lower scales received employment security but no equalization increment. Task Force members in the College of St. Catherine–St. Mary's and Widener-Brandywine mergers reviewed regional and national salary levels for faculty members at institutions comparable in size and mission to the smaller merger partner and found their present compensation levels to be competitive in each instance. Thus, by agreement, salaries were not equalized or significantly adjusted upward in these mergers on an institutionwide basis; however, all other elements of the improved benefits package at the larger institution were extended to the faculty members of the new partner.

Benefits

Although usually less charged and complex than tenure and salary compensation, the broader issue of benefits has dramatically risen in importance on many campuses as cost-of-living raises have failed to keep pace with inflation and as issues such as employee day-care and parenting leaves have taken on new value to increasing numbers of younger instructors starting careers and families simultaneously. Financial planners also need to distinguish between a faculty benefit (sabbatical, course-release time, travel support for paper presentations) and benefits typically awarded to staff members as well (leaves of absence, health insurance, pension contributions). Gannon University offered Villa Maria College faculty members the university's full range of benefit options upon merging; Mercer University extended their benefits package to both tenured and nontenured Tift faculty members in their merger. Widener University connected various benefits options to the particular school within the larger university the new faculty member was joining. Chamberlayne Junior College and the New England Institute contributed high-quality benefit options to their merger agreements with Mount Ida College; faculty members at the combined college are now offered an enhanced menu of health and professional development benefits including the options from two other institutions.

The complexities and swiftly rising costs of almost all aspects of university benefit structures cause this component of even a mission-complementary merger to require a set of negotiations specific to the needs and resources of the combined institutional culture.

Faculty Duties and Responsibilities

Often overlooked by strategic planners is the fact that institutions may present remarkably different parameters of what is expected from faculty members contractually. Faculty members at the more liberal arts–oriented College of St. Catherine, for instance, taught a six-course, twenty-four credit annual load; faculty at St. Mary's College taught a heavier contact hour–based annual load of technical courses. Some institutions address these differences by referencing explanations within the faculty handbook accompanying each annual contract, which does not resolve many of the unexpected issues the Merger Task Force and key administrators face. One school's handbook may stipulate two office hours per week while the other mandates a five-day work week for faculty members during the academic year. Discrepancies such as these reflect not only differences between duties and benefits but a core issue that most likely arose during curriculum and staffing reviews as well: What is the new mission of the merged institution now being shaped by dozens, even hundreds, of individuals?

Reappointment and Retrenchment Policies

Task force members and academic managers must ascertain whether there is notable variance in the two systems for reappointment and retrenchment of academic personnel. If common ground is minimal, those involved should consult jointly with legal counsel for both institutions to develop one plan for the reappointments—and, if appropriate, retrenchments—accompanying the merger. Devising a common, administration-supported grievance procedure as one component of this plan is an effective strategy to address the potential personnel challenges that can arise in any merger.

Collective Bargaining Agreements

Similar to tenure, collective bargaining concerns have routinely been viewed as major deterrents to successful growth mergers in higher education. While it can be said that collective bargaining agreements at any of the institutions rarely make the mutual-growth process easier, it is also fair to say that the presence of collective bargaining among faculty, staff, or both should be viewed by the members of the Merger Task Force, senior administrators, faculty leaders, and respective counsel not as a threat but as one of the special characteristics to be addressed and managed in their merger plan. To forgo the long-term benefits of a mission-complementary college or university merger because of concerns related to the prerogatives of collective bargaining units is to misjudge both the power and the flexibility of the mutual-growth approach as a strategy for academic management.

In the presence of one or more bargaining units, institutional chief executives and the members of the Merger Task Force must decide within the framework of their first discussions the position of the merged board and administration toward a faculty or staff union. While we have reviewed several basic models for growth mergers that include collective bargaining, in our observation, it is realistic to assume that if a unit exists on one campus (particularly the larger, more dominant campus, if there is one), bargaining will be an aspect of the new college or university. Only in instances in which the smaller institution was represented by a unit and the larger school, typically a university, was not have we observed an attempt to dissolve the union and rehire faculty members as employees of the new institution. This approach can be fraught with difficulties and requires strenuous attempts to maintain open, candid communication between faculty and administration throughout the planning process, even then without a guarantee of success. System-wide, we have noted a rise in the number of states now considering the merger of their state, community, and/or technical college programs, and in each instance, it will be critical for academic managers to address responsibly and creatively the factor of collective bargaining.

The mutual-growth strategy is dedicated to the support and enhancement of faculty personnel and resources. If collective bargaining is present, particularly at only one of the institutions, planners must skillfully gauge the degree to which a merger can occur between unionized and nonunionized faculties and staffs. In the independent colleges and universities discussed in this chapter, collective bargaining was typically not a factor during merger implementation. As noted, however, in each U.S. state college or university system, and in the state-supported British university model, collective bargaining need not be a barrier to an aggressive merger plan. Still, it must be approached as a factor that will not facilitate the process and that will require significant patience on the part of planners and candid communication between the new administration and the bargaining unit.

Five considerations in the development of a mutual-growth model including collective bargaining units on one or more campuses are to encourage candor, to avoid confrontation, to address union and non-union policy differences, to separate bargaining issues from governance issues, and to recognize union loyalty.

Encourage candor. Acknowledge that there will be no easy solutions institutionally but that there are options to consider and that a model will be developed collaboratively to suit the situation.

Avoid confrontation. A complementary growth merger is a rare opportunity for a faculty union legitimately to increase its membership. Administrations must grasp and acknowledge this and not be open to charges of unfairly breaking the union if it is the will of the combined faculty to enlarge its membership through incorporation of non-unionized members from the partner campus. In most institutional mergers, this move will come in the form of a new union election, which should not be viewed as a threat. In the cases of different bargaining units on the two campuses, the resolution would be to hold one coordinated election to determine the final representative.

Address differences between union and nonunion personnel policies. Whatever the final status of unit representation, the Merger Task Force needs to address and resolve the outstanding policy differences between the union-supported personnel system and that of a nonunionized partner institution. A good-faith effort by both institutions to incorporate the personnel gains achieved by the union into the structure of the merged institution, apart from the ongoing larger debate on unit representation, creates a positive foundation on which the new college or university may build after the unionization question has been resolved.

Coordinate and separate bargaining issues from governance issues. No effective standard or pattern exists for the complex relationship between the prerogatives of collective bargaining and academic governance systems. Prospective merger partners need to distinguish clearly and firmly throughout the merger planning and implementation processes between areas coordinated through the negotiation of a new union contract and the often significant breadth of academic and personnel policies subject to the collegial governance system. Whether academic governance representatives should be involved in annual salary and contract discussions is debatable. For growth mergers, it is most important to clarify at both institutions from the earliest merger discussions the areas that are to be handled on an ongoing basis by the faculty senate and those that, in the new structure, will need to be included within the parameters of the collective bargaining contract. On this issue, the American Association of University Professors and the National Education Association have both approved major statements acknowledging the role of academic governance on their campuses.

Recognize union loyalty. For the long-term stability and commitment of the merged faculty and staff, both the Merger Task Force and the combined senior leadership group must acknowledge and affirm the qualitative differences among three professional loyalties: to one's former institution, to the emerging college or university, and, to one's collective bargaining unit. While commitment to one's union has been viewed by some as one more deterrent to any form of merger success, official recognition of the significance of union loyalty creates a positive context within the mutual-growth process for faculty support of the merger's broader goals and sends a message to those in a bargaining unit that the nature of their contractual connection to their employer is taken seriously.[19]

Faculty Handbook

A task force subcommittee including members of both faculties and administrations, as well as counsel, would optimally be formed with the single, time-limited task of creating the first handbook for the merged institution. If appropriate, a consultant specializing in handbook design might be retained as a member of this planning group. The new handbook would eventually be issued to faculty members with their first annual contract from the combined institution. After reaching a clear agreement on the current policies and regulations of both institutions, the work might be divided into the sections discussed in this chapter, along with any additional items specific to the merger. With the timetable for completion coordinated with the issuance of new contracts, various sections could be submitted for review by the entire Merger Task Force and counsel before consideration and approval by the combined faculty.

Typically, sections are passed back and forth several times until they reach a final stage of faculty and legal approval. Both compromise and consensus are needed at this stage of the process, as it is a time for administrators and faculty members collectively to share new and ongoing concerns about workplace issues. After the final draft has been approved and cross-checked by the subcommittee, the Merger Task Force, and college counsel, most institutions complete the process through approval by the combined faculties and boards of trustees.[20]

Professional Development Opportunities for Faculty Members

As a rising proportion of academic administrators have relinquished their faculty status since the 1950s and become permanent in their positions, divisions of opinion have developed on many campuses regarding the concept of professional development, its value, and the best ways to implement it. During this same period, many contemporary institutions, especially those of small-to-medium size and second-tier reputation, have become trapped by pressures that would have seemed improbable just a few years earlier: the disappearance of many forms of institutional loyalty among younger faculty members, a shrinking student enrollment base, a reduction in the number of doctoral degrees awarded each year, the eroding viability of a two-year college degree even as enrollments rise among community colleges, consumer-oriented parents demanding for their children full-time instructors who hold terminal degrees, and students who forgo higher education to start families and businesses. Such pressures pit smaller institutions against each other for academic survival through competition for national and regional development grants and through higher salary scales and lower course loads for prominent young instructors, among other factors. In this context, mission-complementary, mutual-growth mergers provide increased resources to allow institutions to raise their levels of academic quality while increasing the faculty professional development opportunities that undergird this process.

Added to the above concerns is the realization that career paths at a college, even more than at a university, have short advancement ladders and flat salary curves. On a campus, professional growth often involves a new title and responsibilities rather than a promotion. Many faculty members have become stuck at stages of advancement below their skill levels because of a pyramid structure that allows for only a handful of senior officers.[21] For example, the number of vice presidents and senior administrative officers in the Kansas State–Kansas College of Technology merger was halved.

Merger planners from both the faculty and the administration must reward incumbents and recruit talented younger colleagues who will bring excellence to their campus. Older faculty members who continue to teach only adequately will inevitably feel the scrutiny both of their new peers, levels beneath them on the salary scale, and of their senior supervisors, who are attempting to raise standards and increase institutional competitiveness. As noted, merged faculty members from smaller institutions such as Brandywine, Villa Maria, Tift, and the Kansas College of Technology, notwithstanding earlier levels of skill and achievement, are presently teaching and conducting research within far more competitive regional or national universities.

A mutual-growth merger offers the chance to address these challenges directly. Every academic manager we interviewed spoke pointedly in support of the mutual-growth approach as an effective vehicle to raise academic quality while doubling or even tripling the quality and amount of individual professional development options for faculty members on their campuses. Mercer University, now approaching a $100 million annual budget, offers faculty members from Tift the full resources of its University Relations and Development Office as well as the research resources from its graduate schools of medicine, engineering, and law. In turn, Mercer has been enriched by the educational traditions and distinguished faculty of one of the South's most respected colleges of women's and teacher education.[22]

At the point of merging, faculty from Villa Maria College received salary increments equalizing them at university level and full participation in the founding and development of the new College of Health Studies at Gannon University. Gannon faculty members received the staff and curricular resources of a high-quality nursing school, a new education department, and quality academic programming in areas such as physical therapy, respiratory care, and physician's assistantship.[23]

Mount Ida College has been enriched by the incorporation of the faculty and laboratory resources of New England's only college of funeral service education and the studio component of one of the region's strongest colleges of art and design. Faculty members from Chamberlayne Junior College and the New England Institute gained a ninety-acre suburban campus accessible by Boston public transportation, residence accommodations for upwards of a thousand students, and two purpose-built classroom buildings providing the most advanced level of clinical embalming and design studio facilities.

Academic managers at Kansas State and Widener Universities have each gained new campuses for expanded academic programming, staff development, and revenue diversification purposes. In these merger models, Widener's new law school has quadrupled its size in a decade, and Kansas State will now have the personnel and physical resources to sustain one of the two premier colleges of engineering technology in the state. Faculty members joining the Kansas State and Widener systems through merger will have immediate access to significantly greater professional development options, such as funds for increased sabbaticals and release-time, seed money for grant opportunities, and individual support such as teaching fellows and research assistants.[24]

In the traditional view, no great college or university has ever been created through merger. The literature on mergers in higher education remains small, conservative in approach, dedicated to the standard topics of bankruptcy and retrenchment; indicatively, it has been fifteen years since the last book-length examination was published specifically on this topic. Growth mergers are not suggested for every institution, no matter how creative its leadership team may be. The educational traditions of Amherst, Duke, or Wellesley, along with the other 150 or so institutions in their select group nationally, serve as multipurpose role models as much as degree-granting operations for the large group of aspiring, midrange colleges and universities in this country. Although merger would most likely do little to enhance the mission of these influential schools, for a growing number of U.S. higher education institutions such as Kansas State, Mercer, Mount Ida, Saint Catherine's, and Widener, the academic development and quality improvement provided by the growth merger strategy make it a sound alternative to consider in the coming decades.

Three guidelines should guide the academic action plan in curricular and personnel areas. First, as one descends the links of academic leadership from board and chief executive to individual faculty and staff members, each level downward should be more proactively involved in the merger strategy's planning and implementation. After the presidents have reviewed the broad articulation of institutional mission and policy, academic and financial managers and faculty leaders need to interpret, define, and enact them. Second, the central purposes of the merger—the enhancement of educational quality in the combined institution and the mutual growth of the academic vision and will of each institutional partner—must be repeatedly referenced during each stage of discussion and implementation. The more familiar each administrator and faculty member becomes with a message that does not change, the greater the odds that the combined institution will move forward according to a coordinated, comprehensive agreement.[25] Finally, all, but especially the combined team of academic managers, must accept that a merger shapes not only the identities of the former institutions, but the commitment each employee holds to the new one.

II OPERATIONS

Financial Planning and

External Considerations

CHAPTER SIX

Strategic Planning for Growth Mergers

André Mayer

Strategic planning is the process that establishes the fundamental purposes of an organization and the general means by which it will achieve those purposes. For colleges and universities, the delineation of institutional mission, character, and culture—including philosophical and social commitments as well as broad considerations of scale, program scope, academic emphasis, and clientele—forms the core of the planning processes. Determining significant long-term goals and objectives and basic organizational structure are also matters of strategic policy. Finally, strategic planning addresses the acquisition and allocation of new resources to support an institution as it pursues its mission. These are, of course, the most important issues confronted in the course of a growth merger, whether it be through consolidation of the units within a university or the union of separate institutions.

Strategic planning gained popularity in American business during the 1960s and 1970s, especially in business schools and consulting firms, partly because of its supposed congruence with Japanese management practices. In businesses, the long-range component of planning tended to be exceedingly general, while the fundamental corporate goals it established were, despite some rather uncomfortable rhetoric about "values," explicitly quantitative. As this approach provided only a loose framework within which annual business plans could be formulated, it was sometimes, and rightly, referred to as "strategic management."

Although corporate executives adopted strategic planning to give direction to their managerial decisions, higher education leaders employed it as a flexible alternative to traditional master planning and comprehensive planning approaches. These planning modes, at once rigid and detailed, had served adequately during an era of sustained growth; however, in the turbulent environment of the 1970s, their lack of adaptability emerged as a serious, even dangerous, flaw. Entering a decade that was expected to be even more challenging, college and university administrators welcomed a method able to address the diffi-cult decisions imposed by limited and shrinking resources. Most of the basic writings on strategic planning in higher education appeared between 1978 and 1983, culminating in George Keller's influential syn-thesis, *Academic Strategy*.[1]

Since then, strategic planning has continued to evolve. Contrary to many planning projections, the 1980s turned out to be a surprisingly positive period for higher education in the United States, and attention shifted from prospects of retrenchment to more proactive strategies such as merging institutions for mutual growth. With the planning function within many institutions now integrated into its general ad-ministration, techniques developed in the corporate world have been adapted to the needs and conditions of academia, an environment gen-erally more amenable to long-range thinking and decision making. The most notable of these adaptations has been the realization that for academic institutions with multiple groups of stakeholders and a tradi-tion of shared governance the most important product of strategic plan-ning is usually not the plan itself but the broad consensus and "buy-in" developed through the planning process.

Of all the situations that arise in the life of a college or university, a merger for mutual growth is the quintessential occasion for strategic planning. First, it is a matter of choice—an opportunity, not a neces-sity—with the easy decision being not to merge. The decision to merge will lead to major changes in, even the transformation of, an institu-tion's character and mission. A new set of overall goals and objectives must be developed to move the newly merged institution forward. These goals must be endorsed and given life by a combined campus community and off-campus constituencies in the creation of the new institutional culture.[2]

The temptation may be to regard a merger as an immediate, short-term solution, as a matter to be addressed pragmatically through its nuts and bolts. This outlook can cause a senior leadership team or Merger Task Force to proceed in an operational planning mode and to treat the merger either as business as usual or by crisis management without due attention to its far-reaching implications. Pragmatism must be a keynote even in growth-merger planning, but approaches as nar-row as these represent false pragmatism. The more abstract issues are vitally important for the long-term success of a mutual-growth merger; they may also be critical to achieving sufficient support on both campuses to effect the merger in the first place.

Planning for Community

Merging colleges and universities for mutual growth involves strategic planning for at least three institutions. Each merger partner has its own values, culture, mission, resources, strengths, and weaknesses. No matter what its history, each carries its own potential future as an autonomous entity. Without a clear sense of their own positions and prospects, potential institutional partners cannot make an informed decision concerning the advantages of merger and will not commit themselves fully to the concept of mutual growth. Furthermore, the decisions and commitments made separately within the merging institutional cultures will affect the new college or university to be created by the merger.

In every merger situation, the plan for the new institution must be developed through a broad, participatory planning process. Unless this plan emerges in clear written form and is subjected to extensive discussion and explication, there is a risk that no shared understanding of the new institution's character and goals will be achieved. Equally important is the need for an inclusive plan for the merger process itself, allowing individuals and constituencies to see immediately when and how their specific concerns will be addressed.

This does not mean the decision to merge cannot be made, on any level, before the completion of the plan. It does imply, however, that the decision, on whatever level it is made, is only provisional until support for the merger is sufficiently broad and deep to implement it successfully. If the growth plan has not been adequately endorsed by faculty, students, and alumni—and each group will have its own reasons for opposition—the costs of merging will typically be prohibitive.

Formal strategic plans and planning processes for the original institutional partners are less critical than planning for the newly created structure, but they certainly have value in selling the merger to these same campus constituencies. The faculty in particular is far more likely to accept the idea of merger when it has a background of involvement in strategic planning. This reaction may be partly a matter of greater experience in planning processes, but it may also be the result of a deeper understanding of institutional complexity and of the imperatives for merger. Faculty members used to considering institutional dynamics over the long term will grasp more clearly considerations such as the financial constraints, competitive environment, and unrealized opportunities that can make merger an opportunity for institutional enhancement.

One particular advantage of an involved faculty is a realistic sense of the college's or university's standing in the academic world. Although a positive institutional self-image is an asset, an inflated valuation, particularly in relation to the institutional merger partner, can be a serious impediment. A lack of parity in institutional traditions and related self-images can prevent a mutually beneficial plan from taking root or cause abiding problems within the merged structure. When two branches of the University of Illinois were merged some years ago, an elaborate classification of all U.S. colleges and universities was required to demonstrate to one faculty that its campus was less distinguished than it imagined, and that the merger would place it in a more prestigious institutional peer group.[3]

Who should participate in merger planning? In one of the earliest works on strategic planning in higher education, Robert G. Cope in 1978 offered advice that still holds true: "The worst problems that administrators, trustees, faculty members, and planners get themselves into—misunderstandings, confusion, votes of no confidence, firings, and internecine warfare—are the results of spending too much time trying to decide on who decides what."[4] The nature of the decision to merge, and of the steps required to carry the merger through, is such that the firm commitment of trustees and chief executive officers is essential. The academic managers responsible for implementing the merger plan must also be involved in developing it, as the effectiveness of these leaders will be measured in terms of their success in enlisting others to the cause of merging.

From Analysis to Action

Strategic planning is a decision-oriented activity easily stalled by demands for more and more information—especially when the issues are large, the next steps uncertain, and the participants unused to management, as is sometimes the case with faculty members and others on merging campuses. At the same time, strategic planning is analytical in its approach to the future, which is one of the reasons it is applicable to situations of profound change such as higher education mergers. Task force members learn to cope skillfully with the fact that significant decisions will often be made on the basis of insufficient information.

Strategic planning analysis for a college or university covers three broad areas. The *external environment* in which the institution operates significantly influences the demand for its services, the nature or number of its potential clientele, the availability of resources to support its mission, and so on. The *internal capabilities* of the college determine, to a large extent, how it can respond to environmental forces by capitalizing on opportunities and developing fields of competitive advantage. The *goals and values of stakeholders* in the institution represent the key constituencies upon whom the college's future depends, whose support must be assured through its policies and priorities.

As compared to conventional operational planning, therefore, strategic planning imposes extraordinarily complex information demands. That orientation toward external conditions requires a far broader set of data and has given rise to sophisticated techniques of environmental scanning.[5] Concern for the values of stakeholders introduces issues that are not quantitative but qualitative, sometimes even irrational, and does so in a context that should be viewed as political. Even familiar internal institutional issues must be examined from unfamiliar perspectives in light of external considerations. Under such circumstances, the success of the planning effort will depend on the ability of the Merger Task Force overseeing the process to provide sufficient amounts of relevant, credible information and to avoid being trapped by unrealistic demands for additional data. Put differently, analytic support should be an integral part of the planning process and under the control of the academic managers as much as possible.

Classically, the strategic planning process begins with surveys of internal conditions (strengths and weaknesses) and the external environment (opportunities and threats), a phase often referred to as "SWOTS analysis." This is followed, in order, by review of the institutional mission statement, establishment of general goals derived from the overall mission, development of detailed objectives and action plans to achieve those goals, and analysis of resource requirements.[6] In a concise, operationally oriented planning document, this emerges as a mission statement, a set of global goals and objectives, specific work plans, deliverable products, assignments of responsibility, and a resource analysis.

A modified approach that has recently gained popularity reorders the traditional process by analyzing threats and opportunities before weaknesses and strengths, then using the identified environmental issues to establish goal areas in the development of the plan, with the formal mission statement adjusted as necessary.[7] By closely linking action plans within each goal area to broad external circumstances, this approach stresses the strategic function of accommodating the institution to its environment.

In a mutual-growth merger, an emphasis on externalities would set forth the rationale for merging, establish a common set of possibilities for the merging institutional communities, and provide a basis for assessing which internal conditions are, in fact, strengths and which are weaknesses. This approach requires strong academic management, for it allows administrative decisions on goals and strategies to shape the new mission statement. There is a trade-off, however, as the development of a mission statement as the general assertion of shared values for the new institution is also a significant opportunity for the executive leadership to forestall potential opposition among faculty, students, or alumni.

A truism of strategic planning is that not all decisions, even all important decisions, are strategic decisions. Physical design and planning priorities form a major component of institutional strategy, often involving immense expenditures and significant controversy, yet they do not typify strategic decision making. A unique aspect of merger planning is that many second-order decisions not considered strategic under normal circumstances take on heightened implications for institutional character and culture. Under these conditions, relatively straightforward planning objectives and administrative arrangements may have exaggerated effects on the direction of an institution's development and on its ability to complete its movement toward an intended goal rapidly and successfully.

The Elements of Strategic Merger Planning

The Basic Decision

The decision to pursue the possibility of a mission-complementary growth merger should precede the start of merger planning. The two key words in that sentence are *possibility* and *planning*. The decision at this stage is not to merge, but to consider its possibility. While much collective thought and discussion is likely to have occurred before such a decision is made, the decision nevertheless provides a basis for serious, structured, overt consideration of institutional merger through the strategic planning process.

Beyond this initial decision, there must be a general sense of what kind of merger is contemplated, and what kind of institution will emerge from it. A conglomerate merger, in which the institutions are under joint control but maintain separate identities and missions, requires a significantly different strategic process from melding two colleges into a single cultural unit. A measure of this difference will be demonstrated in the level of concern voiced over the name of the surviving institution. A merger intended to capture efficiencies within existing missions differs from one aimed primarily at creating new synergies in emerging areas of curricular opportunity. The issues to be faced in combining two relatively similar institutions differ from those raised by merging sharply contrasting campuses, though they are not necessarily easier to resolve.

The third aspect of the initial decision to proceed is the consideration of where in the emerging process, and by whom, specific resource and personnel decisions will be made. Merging, at this point, becomes for the involved academic managers and task force members a complicated, controversial undertaking. This realization carries two powerful implications. First, even growth merger talk can be disturbing and destabilizing to a campus, especially regarding employment security; thus, its degree of official sanction must be carefully explained and affirmed. Second, planning will not succeed without visible backing from the chief executive officers. If presidents and boards of trustees are not committed to serious investigation of the merger option, the planning process will not succeed. The process must be articulated to include a sense of how it will work and where it will end, and this includes a clear understanding of key decisions that will be taken at the highest level.

Information and Staffing

The two principal elements of support for a planning process are information and staffing. Often, the two are formally linked when staff responsibility for planning at a college or university is combined with the institutional research or budget functions. In practice, anyone staffing a planning process will devote most of her or his time to assembling, disseminating, and processing information.

As noted earlier, requisite aspects of an effective strategic process are providing relevant, credible information and avoiding open-ended information demands. Academic managers implementing a planning process, especially a participatory one, need to exercise forethought regarding what information will be provided and who will be responsible for providing it. Carefully selected information, synthesized and organized to answer anticipated questions and to respond to those that have arisen, will speed the planning effort. Quality, not volume, makes the difference. The goal is not to control the process by manipulating information; rather, the process must move forward at a manageable pace fueled by appropriate information at the appropriate time.[8]

Equally important to the success of the strategic plan is the proper staffing of the planning process. A single individual with merger experience can make a persuasive difference, whether working with senior management or with diverse constituencies. In normal strategic planning situations, planning consultants are valuable principally as advisers. Typically, it is a mistake for an institution to hire a consultant to write the actual plan, as many of the advantages arising from an inclusive planning process are thereby lost. In a merger, however, an outside consultant not linked to any of the merging institutions may have an unusual degree of credibility and value, as both neutral mediator and external change agent.

Structure and Process

The formal structures through which planning is conducted and the organization of a planning process are the subjects of an extensive literature, much of it useful but none directly applicable to the merger planning the institutions will face. In a merger situation, academic managers need to approach planning carefully, always aware that a merger, even one mission complementary in concept, requires reasoned improvisation.

A participative structure with special advantages in growth merger planning is a version of Keller's "Joint Big Decisions Committee."[9] JBDCs, which include highly respected individuals drawn from various campus constituencies (always faculty and administrators, frequently students and others), are charged with advising the president on institutionwide strategic issues. They have become increasingly prevalent in higher education over the past fifteen years, largely as a means of addressing the rifts that can develop between a faculty and administration. The advantages of JBDCs over traditional governance structures include, in addition to broader representation and a focus on decision making, a presumption of confidentiality. Although their existence, membership, and conclusions are public, their deliberations are usually secret. In a college or university merger, when traditional structures are placed in question, many of the objections to JBDCs lose their force, while the strengths of this approach take on increased importance. A high-powered planning group representing multiple constituencies at the merging institutions carries broad appeal and works well as a complement to the Merger Task Force or, in some mergers, as the task force itself.

Whichever formal planning structure is chosen, the process must be conveyed with the understanding that in merger situations operational decisions become strategic decisions. Most of the issues addressed in this book are, in this context, strategic issues, and the merger planning process should include mechanisms to incorporate and resolve them. Probably the most sensitive and complex of these implementation processes is the academic action plan described in chapter 5. Faculty involvement and endorsement is essential to the success of the planning process and of the mutual-growth concept, as those at all levels of the faculty rank system must be guaranteed that academic issues will be addressed at every stage of the process, that faculty will play an appropriate part, and that, in fact, mutual growth and mission complementarity can translate into academic excellence.

By outlining a clear and realistic schedule for the planning process, organizers may resist pressures to address all issues at once. This strategy allows for the deferral of various operational and structural decisions until points at which they can be made most effectively. In this context, an interim academic structure may be helpful or necessary to allow members of the merged communities to work together for a time before final dispositions are made. Examples of this are the curriculum revision and faculty personnel subcommittees of the Merger Task Force outlined in chapter 5.

An institutional case in point is the merger of the private Swain School of Art with the public Southeastern Massachusetts University (now the University of Massachusetts at Dartmouth) in 1989. This was in most respects a mutual-growth merger, although Swain had been under considerable financial pressure. Because Swain was a small specialty institution, the academic aspects of the merger were addressed primarily by the art faculties of the two institutions. The merger was implemented in an initial phase by placing all the Swain art faculty and programs, including its nationally known master's level artisanry program, within Southeastern Massachusetts University's visual arts department. Although the overall academic programs of the two merger partners were in many respects complementary, this initial step was taken on an interim basis because it was believed that the creation of a single department would unite the faculty more effectively and avert long-term identification of units as Swain or Southeastern Massachusetts University departments. The plan also allowed time and experience to shape the administrative structure and program array of the combined institution, a process that continues. This two-step merger, with the first stage more extreme than the second, was practicable because the faculty of the two merging institutions, in collaboration, saw themselves firmly in control of the implementation process. The same approach imposed by administrative fiat might have been met by serious resistance.

In organizing and conducting the strategic merger process, and in establishing its basic parameters, academic managers and institutional leaders must ask themselves the following questions:

1. What are the merger's intended benefits for students, faculty members, administrators, alumni, and the local community?

2. Is the primary goal a unified, organic institution or a looser confederation?

3. How much structural and cultural change will be needed? How much is feasible?

4. How can the process be designed so that stakeholders will be decision makers?

5. What are the key decisions the process must address?

6. What are the most significant challenges to the merger's success?

Answers will vary in each case and will imply differing approaches. At least one point remains constant: the merger plan is *not* the merger. It is rather an outline and guide to be used in shaping the development of the new institution.

Planning and Implementation: Lessons from Experience

An informal survey of recent mergers involving private institutions in several parts of the country suggests both the range of issues of which merger planning must take account, and the variety of possible approaches to planning and implementation.[10] These cases include some in which a small college was absorbed by a much larger university, and others where partners of more equal size joined to form a substantially new institution with a new (or combined) name. While in virtually all instances one or both campuses faced enrollment or other financial problems, few cases involved any imminent threat to actual institutional survival. All resulted in stronger, more effective institutions that were better able than their predecessors to fulfull traditional missions and explore new ones; and even when merger was undertaken with some reluctance on one side or both, the theme of mutual growth proved invaluable in assuaging any sense of defeat and emphasizing hopes for the future.

The movement toward merger generally began with members (often the chairs) of the two boards of trustees and was carried forward under the auspices of the presidents. Where it was not obvious who would head the united entity—usually in the more complex mergers—an early decision proved desirable, as key vice presidencies could then be filled on a permanent basis, and the work of creating a unified administration begun. (In one merger, the designation of the smaller institution's president to lead the new one visibly reinforced the commitment to equal partnership.) At this early stage planning consultants, who as outsiders are not identified with either institution, prove useful in assessing the strategic position of the nascent merged institution and developing a clearly defined mission built on the histories and strengths of both merger partners. In one of the more complex mergers the outside consultant actually prepared an overall merger plan that outlined decision points and processes in considerable detail, working primarily with top administration but also hearing multiple viewpoints from the two communities and circulating interim reports for comment.

While mergers often raise formal legal and academic issues involving assets, regulatory status, and accreditation that may have significant implications for planning, the larger problems of a merger process tend to be human. A key to merger planning is to "anticipate and manage the inevitable hostilities that will arise from the start, some of which will persist throughout," says one seasoned planner. There will be resentments on both sides, he adds; "just assume they're going to be there." Even in administrative areas such as business affairs, where merger may be relatively rapid and straightforward, there may be difficulties of adjustment to new positions or procedures; moreover, administrators of a college merging out of existence, or those who opposed a merger, are prone to a sense of personal failure. The most serious human issues, however, lie elsewhere.

Mergers of schools and departments, as might be expected, pose the greatest difficulties. No matter what provision is made for combining faculties, some individuals and groups will feel they are being treated unfairly. The problems that arise when professors accustomed to different standards and expectations are brought together are obvious, but similarity, which implies potential overlap, raises difficulties of its own. Departments or programs that are largely complementary may sometimes join readily because curriculum, courses, and individual roles can remain the same, but more than one merger of very similar departments has become snagged over where a single course will fit into the program, or who will teach it. Because of curricular variations, business programs are often relatively difficult to combine, especially when one is accredited and the other is not. Business is in fact the only field in which several of the mergers reportedly caused significant academic problems for students, who are surprisingly little affected by changes that to faculty and staff seem earthshaking.

One tested approach to merger planning in the academic and student services areas is a carefully designed decision-oriented process based on established structures and functions. This might involve an overall task force, chaired by a chief academic officer (or by those of both institutions), consisting of the next level of administrators (deans and division heads), who in turn chair committees addressing issues in their field of responsibility (student services, libraries, programs and curricula, and so forth). Additional groups might address issues that cut across administrative units, such as the needs of part-time students. Though this phase of the merger process is to a greater or lesser degree participatory, its structure and schedule nevertheless emphasize timely decision making and balance between the merging campus communities over democratic process. If it is implemented successfully, the experience of working together to shape new departments and programs will unite the participants in support of the newly merged institution.

Indeed, a very clear lesson learned from this group of mergers is the vital importance of openness—not so much of broad active participation as of a free flow of information about how the process is proceeding. Because of the human issues, because resentment and suspicion are inevitable, those planning a merger are perforce called upon to avoid making a difficult situation worse. The most dangerous moment comes early: if the first word of substantive merger discussions leaks out as rumor, the subsequent process will be shadowed by distrust and fear. Similarly, at each major step, key stakeholders (especially the faculty) should know beforehand, even if only in general terms, what is coming and how it was decided. Two of the cases were very similar except that in one the merger process was kept under wraps until a fairly advanced stage, then presented as a fait accompli, while the other was relatively open; both mergers were carried through, but the former was attended by much greater hostility, which is likely to have a long-term negative effect on the merged institution.

Each of the mergers that was examined raised idiosyncratic issues. In one, the planned abandonment of a cherished campus became a focus of opposition; in another, underlying cultural conflict between the two institutions surfaced in a battle over class schedules. A small college merging into a larger university negotiated the preservation of its most distinctive program, which helped reconcile its constituencies to the loss of their school. Mergers of institutions of shared religious heritage eased new partnerships, while joining women's colleges to predominantly male, or even co-educational, ones raised special opposition (and both factors were apparent in several cases involving Catholic institutions).

Yet while none of the mergers was painless, all were successes. Each one preserved valuable resources for higher education while improving student opportunities and employee security. At best they created new institutions that, compared to their predecessors, have higher, clearer profiles in their service areas; stronger financial and alumni bases, enhanced efficiency, and streamlined administration; and broader missions and program offerings affording opportunities for new synergies. These are the core principles of merging colleges for mutual growth. The merger processes that were followed provide object lessons on some major planning considerations, notably the importance of openness and, in more complex cases, of the "academic action plan." But there is no such thing as an ideal case, or a universally applicable lesson. Every merger is unique.

Guidance for Current Merger Planners

The combination of factors to be considered in higher education strategic planning differs in each merger plan, and the formal structures and informal relationships through which planning is carried out will vary as well. The strategy to merge colleges or universities for their mutual growth is only now gaining attention in the literature of higher education planning. No off-the-shelf process borrowed from another organization can satisfactorily meet the needs of planning a complementary growth merger. A number of books and articles do, however, provide valuable guidance to those who are now contemplating this strategic option.

A good starting point, offering a concise introduction to planning processes and an extensive bibliography, is *A Guide for New Planners* by Donald M. Norris and Nick L. Poulton (Ann Arbor: Society for College and University Planning, 1991) or the section by the same authors in Marvin W. Peterson and Lisa A. Mets, eds., *Key Resources on Higher Education Governance, Management, and Leadership* (San Francisco: Jossey-Bass, 1987). Robert G. Cope, a pioneer of strategic planning, remains perhaps its clearest expositor, although his approach has grown more complex over the years. His recent *Opportunity from Strength: Strategic Planning Clarified with Case Examples* (Washington, D.C.: American Association for Higher Education, 1987) presents it as "direction finding for the whole enterprise in relation to the ecosystem." A series of articles by Robert C. Shirley, notably "Identifying the Levels of Strategy for a College or University" (*Long Range Planning* 16, 3 [1983]: 92–98), stresses the logic and structure of strategic planning as a decision-oriented process.

Beyond the specifics of planning practice, three publications offer valuable general insights about several elusive issues that must be addressed in planning a mutual-growth merger. Richard Morrill, president of the University of Richmond, explains the tension between academic values and management decision making in a pair of brief articles in KMPG–Peat Marwick's newsletter, *Management Issues for Colleges and Universities:* "Values and Decision Making within Higher Education" (August 1990) and "How To Manage Value Conflict" (September 1990). Institutional culture, a subject that has drawn much attention in recent years, is discussed in Ellen Earle Chaffee and William G. Tierney's *Collegiate Culture and Leadership Strategies* (New York: Macmillan, 1988). George Keller's *Academic Strategy: The Management Revolution in American Higher Education* (Baltimore: Johns Hopkins University Press, 1983), overtaken by events in some respects, has proved prescient in others. Its breadth of focus and emphasis on institutional character make it especially helpful in thinking about the mutual-growth approach.

All of these writings can provide valuable techniques and insights for academic managers now considering a strategic planning effort in higher education; but they can do no more. In merger planning each societal environment, each institution, and each set of issues is different, and so must each process be.

What distinguishes strategic planning from other forms of planning is its focus on matters of values, culture, character, and institutional mission. The uniqueness of merger planning derives, above all, from the fact that in a merger context an unusually broad range of issues assume strategic significance. The basic purpose of strategic merger planning, therefore, is to establish a process that can lead the multiple constituencies of the emerging institution, respecting their different cultures and identities, to shared goals and values. It is sometimes said of strategic planning that the activity, not the plan, is what matters, that the participation of individuals and groups in a common cause ultimately means more than the document they produce. This is another way of saying that the true product of strategic planning is not a written plan, but the decision of participants to commit themselves to a common vision of their institution's future. In a mutual-growth merger, no outcome can be more important.

CHAPTER SEVEN

The Implications of a Public Institutional Merger

Donald L. Zekan

Is the alternative to merger the status quo? In many state educational systems, academic planners and managers view the possibility of merger as something that may be discussed, even in detail, but that will never finally occur. Opinions throughout many public systems may vary, but eventually most researchers have agreed that mergers of public colleges and universities cannot easily be generalized because of their political contexts. This observation is purposely broad, but it does reveal several important policy aspects of mergers in U.S. public higher education.

For a deeper understanding of the issue, one needs to identify the impetus behind each decision to merge. Is the plan being proposed as at the level of public policy with institutional considerations secondary, or at the institutional level with political action focused on validating the design? This dichotomy between public policy and institutional prerogatives is useful as a first distinction in planning and then assessing public college and university mergers.

This distinction also represents a shift in focus from traditional wisdom on mergers in public systems. Most merger analyses focus on institutional priorities, often missing the broader context that informs both public policy and the organization and structure of higher education in that political jurisdiction. Public universities and colleges exist in two environments and must always strike a difficult balance between the purposes of higher education and of government. When the prospect of mutual institutional growth is added to the strategic approach, the larger complexities confronting both merger planners and the state educational bureaucracy grow significantly. Yet several proven growth-oriented planning solutions are now available to creative chief executive, academic, and financial officers.

117

Complementary-mission, mutual-growth mergers in public higher education are ultimately matters both of public policy and of providing enhanced educational opportunity to constituents. At the institutional level, this fundamental fact is often overlooked in the focus on relatively narrow matters of organizational structure, while the makers of public policy are concentrating on larger issues of public service. This disparity in perspective often blinds institutional leaders to the larger public policy context of the merger process.

The small literature on mergers in public higher education with an institution-oriented focus can be divided into two categories: how-to essays that provide a laundry list of issues to be considered by institutions facing the prospect of merger, and more general studies that summarize specific merger agreements. Lacking in both approaches is an overall theoretical perspective for mergers as a dynamic, growth-oriented strategy. I believe that the most appropriate focus for public sector mergers is away from institutional organizational characteristics and toward the complex relationship between institutional mission and public policy. In this context, a crucial factor for the success of public sector mergers becomes the interplay of public policy and institutional mission within local and regional political structures.

Gail Chambers, whose research principally concerns independent college mergers, has suggested that in private sector mergers institutional self-interest ultimately gives way to identification with the general public welfare.[1] She suggests that the overall merger process and the colleges implementing it are working toward the fulfillment of a public trust. Joseph O'Neill and Samuel Barnett, in their analysis of the merger issues involved in the legal change of corporate status, have reached a similar conclusion: "Trustees are, above all else, holders in trust of an estate provided by others for the benefit of society. Consequently, their first obligation in law is to that estate and to the successful completion of the institution's mission."[1] Chambers and O'Neill and Barnett indicate that boards of trustees primarily focus on institutional mission in a manner consistent with their public trust as their ultimate responsibility in merging private colleges and universities.

John Millett's 1976 study, *Mergers in Higher Education: An Analysis of Ten Case Studies,* was an effort to find commonalities among ten merger situations. Millett attempted to identify common precipitating characteristics in the ten cases but made little attempt to place mergers in a larger public or societal context. In his determination that financial issues, geographic proximity, and reputational matters were important in each decision to merge, as well as a variety of broader issues such as complementary programming and qualitative considerations, he finally suggests that these characteristics appear in specific institutional instances and are not generalizable.[2] With regard to public sector mergers, Millett stresses political interests as well as financial considerations. He acknowledges the importance of governmental action, and, hence, political action, but he seems to consider political action only as a step in resolving financial problems and does not address the larger issues of public policy in the merger of public institutions.

While influential, Millett's study remains essentially institution oriented. As so many colleges and universities now considering merger for mutual-growth reasons are public in mission and structure, it is this broader context of public higher education policy that will now be considered in more detail.

Merger Initiatives from the Public Sector

Corporate enterprises considering merger analyze the broader economic issues behind the prospective institutional change. Attention is focused on financial and economic factors such as equities, markets, interest rates, and stock values as well as numerous interlocking organizational outcomes. The traditional environment in which businesses operate defines the boundaries within which the merger must be considered.

Institutions of public higher education in the United States are participants in a political economy. In this light, it is important to recall Robert L. Curry and Larry L. Wade's observation that one of the fundamental properties of modern democracy is the direct, authoritative allocation, by government, of benefits and costs among individuals in the society. Public higher education reflects this democratic circumstance, according to Christopher Jencks and David Riesman: "In particular, low tuition and low admissions requirements are generally presumed to make public institutions more socially heterogeneous than private ones."[3] In considering mergers within the public sector, one ultimately must incorporate the fact that public higher education exists to distribute particular benefits and costs among the polity.

In recent years, many public institution educational managers have become aware of a tendency to view political action with disdain and as peripheral to the real purposes of the academy. This deprecation of politics, however, consistently has reflected more a lack of support for its processes than a true attack on the primacy of public policy. The ultimate authority in public sector mergers rests with the legislature and the executive, but public policy can be significantly influenced by educational leaders who join the political process.

The merger of Boston State College with the University of Massachusetts at Boston in 1982 is a regional example that demonstrates the hegemony of the political process in producing public policy. The merger was accomplished within an era of massive tax-reduction initiatives nationally and locally, during a controversial reorganization of the system of governance of public higher education in the state of Massachusetts. Viewing the merger eight years later, one may assess it as logical and successful, for the system has gained a strong and growing research university in place of two overlapping institutions in an ambiguous, uneasy relationship. Yet this consolidation was also characterized by the dominance of a legislature and executive and by distinctly separate institutional responses to the prospect of merging, both characteristics that imprinted the new institution.

Boston State College started as the Boston Normal School in 1852 to prepare young women to become teachers in the grammar schools of the city; it was later named the Teachers College of the City of Boston. In 1948, men were admitted to the institution, and in 1952 it became a part of the state system of higher education, severing its formal ties to city government. Through the 1950s, Boston State was subject to the same pressures for changes in curriculum as other state colleges both in the region and the nation. Academic programs were diversified from the traditional training of teachers to a broader emphasis on the liberal arts. In the 1970s, Boston State began adding degree programs in the professions.

As John Moon, a former Boston State faculty member, observed, through this long period of evolutionary change from normal school to state college to liberal arts college and then to professional college, no commitment was made to a common purpose similar to that which had existed at the institution in its earlier, clearer identity as a normal school. Those at the college saw a succession of presidents fail to gain the confidence of the faculty, as each neglected to define and articulate the identity of the evolving institution.

> Despite its long existence, therefore, the college had failed to develop a recognizable or respected presence through two decades of tumultuous change, faculty revolt, faculty quarrels, and student protest. Instead, still partly tarnished with a slur of "Huntington High," its reputation was further stained by the educational experiments of the 1960s and 1970s. Its achievements, in becoming an urban college, and steadily upgrading its faculty, in providing low-cost education and flexible hours to working class students, were ignored.[4]

The decades before the merger were difficult ones for Boston State. The institution had not made a clear, persuasive transition to a liberal arts and professional college structure, and its reputation had eroded. Further, it compared poorly to a new public university in the city of Boston.

The University of Massachusetts at Boston was founded in 1965 with a mission to serve the people of eastern Massachusetts, primarily those within the greater Boston area, by providing a full range of educational opportunities and postsecondary education common to those of other state universities. Faculty were recruited based on terminal degrees, and research and publication were emphasized. Through the 1970s, the university developed liberal arts and professional baccalaureate degrees as well as graduate level programs. The university moved from temporary quarters downtown to a permanent campus on Boston harbor in 1974. By 1982, it had achieved growing national recognition, and organizationally it reflected the prevailing form of other universities throughout the country, lacking only an extensive offering of doctoral programs.

The merger of Boston State College with the University of Massachusetts at Boston can be best understood in the context of the stresses on a public system of higher education in the 1970s in a state moving from an industrial to a service- and technology-based economy. The Massachusetts public higher education system consisted of five separate boards of trustees for the University of Massachusetts, Southeastern Massachusetts University, the University of Lowell, ten state colleges, and fifteen community colleges. In addition to the five boards was a central board of higher education that had little real authority, although its assigned responsibility was to review budgets and establish master plans. This segmented system gave rise to conflicting responsibilities and resulted in little overall coordination of public higher education in the state. A financial crisis in the middle of the decade finally called the entire system into question.

A special commission was convened to consider the reorganization of Massachusetts higher education. One commission subcommittee considered the overall governance of higher education in the state system, and the other focused on the reorganization of public higher education in the Boston area. The commission could not achieve consensus concerning the strength of the central governing board or the form reorganization should take within the city of Boston. Representatives of Boston State College and the university both opposed merging at this early stage, and their negative votes received support on the commission sufficient to continue the deadlock.

In April 1980, the Massachusetts House Ways and Means Committee released the fiscal year 1981 budget. The outside section of this budget proposed the creation of a fifteen-member Board of Regents of Higher Education to replace the separate boards. Although the senate did not go along with this proposal, agreement was reached to create a board of regents through an outside section of the final document. During the debate regarding the overall governance of public higher education in Massachusetts, issues connected to education in the city of Boston were temporarily deferred. The newly formed board of regents, however, which assumed statutory responsibility in March 1981, was granted the authority to terminate colleges and institutions.

The first substantive policy issue addressed by the board of regents was the organization of public higher education in Boston. It is not seen as coincidental that the first policy act of a newly created board of regents, consisting of fifteen individuals from disparate backgrounds, was the consolidation of the 130-year-old state college with the 17-year-old university.

Proposals to merge Boston State and the University of Massachusetts at Boston were consistently opposed by Boston State faculty and staff, who believed that there was no mandate to merge the two as equal institutions. Continuation of the existing structures was assumed to be the only acceptable alternative. The board of regents was considering the possibility of a three-year merger agreement when Massachusetts voters enacted a much-debated revenue-restraining referendum, Proposition 2½, capping local taxing authority. In the face of this drastic limitation on local revenue-raising capacity, the legislature proposed a substantial increase in funds for local aid for fiscal year 1982.

The budget enacted for that year was designed to force to a conclusion the issue of funding for public higher education in the city of Boston. Instead of separate appropriations for each institution, the budget clustered in one appropriation all public higher education in the city, including the University of Massachusetts at Boston, Boston State College, and three other institutions. The funding for this Boston cluster was $6 million short of level funding. In the face of this reduction, a plan was set in motion by the board of regents accelerating the process of merger from three years to barely a month. In August 1981, the board of regents decided to discontinue funding to Boston State College as an individual institution immediately.

The faculty union took the decision to court and obtained a restraining order that permitted the college to operate for the fall 1981 semester. Shortly thereafter, however, the board of regents declared a financial exigency as required by the union contract: the entire budget shortfall was to be assumed by Boston State College. An act of the legislature in January 1982 ratified this action and discontinued Boston State College as of January 24, 1982. The students and the academic programs became the responsibility of the university.

Ultimately, the University of Massachusetts at Boston retained Boston State faculty members with university level teaching credentials. Other state colleges in the system were reluctant to hire the remaining Boston State faculty members, however, because many would be senior to their own professors. Concerns also arose that these individuals would be placed in low-enrollment departments at other colleges in the system and in time would displace resident faculty members.

This was the sequence of events leading to the merger of Boston State College and the University of Massachusetts at Boston, yet a chronological perspective merely establishes the frame for understanding the issues that precipitated the merger and influenced the process of implementation.[5] In retrospect, one truth has become clear regarding this merger: the power of the political process prevailed. Whether the agreement by politicians occurred informally or in the committee rooms of the statehouse, the evidence overwhelmingly suggests that such an agreement existed and that it resulted in the reorganization of public higher education in Massachusetts.

Robert Quinn, former speaker of the Massachusetts House of Representatives and chair of the university's board of trustees, felt the merger was inevitable, especially after the significant reorganization of the public higher education system. Although it was not the university's decision to merge the two institutions, the senior leadership team and academic managers of the younger, larger institution took the issue of merger seriously and attempted to make decisions that would strengthen the resulting structure. Quinn suggests in retrospect that those lobbying on behalf of the state college obfuscated educational issues within the merger which the university had considered to be primary.[6]

Former representative Michael Creedon, then chair of the state house Committee on Ways and Means, believes the fiscal year 1982 budget process was the precipitating action causing the merger. The budget crisis was a result of Proposition 2½ and the state's effort to provide a substantial increase in local aid to cities and towns. Creedon suggests that there was a general understanding among all involved that the university was the appropriate provider of urban public baccalaureate education. Maintaining both institutions was perceived as redundant, particularly as Boston State had a poor location, aging facilities, and fewer credentialed faculty members. The board of regents did not create the merger; rather the real decision was made by the legislature, and underfunding the Boston cluster was the vehicle to accomplish it.[7]

Franklin Patterson, a professor at the University of Massachusetts at Boston at the time of the merger and formerly interim president of the University of Massachusetts, noted that although the university had no interest in the merger, once it was perceived as inevitable, the strategy became one of enabling the overall institution to emerge from the process stronger and enhanced in mission and vision. As the merger was being implemented, the sense developed among the participants that their primary responsibility was to see that the university improved itself.[8]

John Moon, then professor of history at Boston State College and president of its faculty association, led the fight to halt the internal reorganization caused by the merger. In "The Boston State Fiasco: A Personal View," he writes:

> The question that confronted the Regents when they assumed authority on March 1, 1981, was the question of public higher education in the Metropolitan Boston area. For a number of years a conviction had grown among the legislative leadership, a conviction shared by the Governor, that there were too many institutions of public higher education in the Boston area. Long before March 1, 1981, this conviction had hardened to dogma.
>
> Many Boston State College students and faculty are convinced that the destruction of BSC was a culmination of the sinister, well-coordinated conspiracy between leaders in state government, the high technology lobby, the private colleges and universities and the University of Massachusetts. A few men of power had decided that Boston State College must be eliminated.[9]

A pattern emerges in reviewing the sequence of events and comments by principal participants in the merger plan. The decision was an overt act of public policy, even though the intentions behind the policy development may have been hidden. Boston State College's representatives believed the alternative to merger was the status quo. Throughout the process, they continued to exercise a negative vote, attempting to stop the legislative momentum toward consolidation. Conversely, the university's leadership recognized that merger was inevitable and that the priorities were to maintain institutional integrity and to strengthen the overall educational process where possible.

The political process of merging Boston State College into the University of Massachusetts at Boston may appear labyrinthine, yet the steps toward merging are not unusual in the development of public policy. In the merger discussion, institutional issues became subsumed under the larger rubric of educational opportunity. Community needs were changing, and Boston State College was not adequately responding to the citizenry. On one hand, the new Bunker Hill and Roxbury community colleges were providing an open-access environment to the nontraditional population in the city, previously a segment of the population from which Boston State drew its students. On the other, the University of Massachusetts at Boston laid claim to the more traditional university offerings in its baccalaureate and master's programs. Boston State College found itself without a viable mission.

The alternative to merger was not the status quo. The alternative to merger with the University of Massachusetts at Boston could only have been developed by considering the revised policy issue of public higher education in the city. The impetus for merger appears to have been environmental, academically speaking. All four Boston institutions were part of a system of higher education in the city, and their relationship to each other precipitated merger. The plan and its timing were aspects of the development of public policy and the availability of public higher education opportunity.

As Millett pointed out, geographic proximity and the geographical nature of political jurisdictions are important matters to consider when merger is in prospect. The city of Boston represented both a geographical and political entity, and, as long as the separate institutions had distinct missions, it was appropriate for them to draw separately on public financial support. As the missions of these institutions began to converge, however, the issue of public expenditures became tied to the larger question of support for higher education. At this point the circumstance of geographical proximity became important. Why should the public support separate but complementary institutions of higher education several miles apart? The three public mergers examined in Millett's study reflect a similar pattern.

One of these, the combining of Lowell State College and the Lowell Technical Institute into Massachusett's University of Lowell, occurred in 1975. The two institutions were founded in the 1890s with distinct missions—teacher and textile industry training—only one mile apart in the city of Lowell. Over the years, Lowell State College became more liberal arts oriented, and the Lowell Technological Institute developed a strong science and technology curriculum. A single university with a variety of programs would offer greater opportunity to area citizens than two specialized institutions could provide, and a public policy rationale of expanded opportunity for area residents came at a time of expanding public higher education in Massachusetts and was sufficient to accomplish the merger.

Two other mergers in Millett's study represent the policy of expansion in public higher education through corporate change: the University of Buffalo with the State University of New York and the University of Kansas City with the State University of Missouri. In both instances existing institutions joined a larger public system, with merger representing a change from private individual entity to membership in a public multicampus system. Millett notes that "both institutions decided they could better perform their urban mission under the auspices of state government rather than to continue as independent institutions."[10] Writing almost twenty years ago during a period of expansion for public higher education, Millett would not have been alone in assuming the merits of state funding for the urban mission of an institution, as more funds then existed to support this worthy cause. In retrospect, the weight of public policy, not the readiness of institutions to merge, was paramount, although the institutions themselves participated in and influenced the process of relevant public policy development.

The University of Massachusetts at Boston and the University of Lowell mergers represent a model of top-down policy development with the impetus for merger occurring at state level. The mergers of the University of Buffalo and the University of Kansas City with their state systems were locally initiated actions that eventually influenced public policy.

Institution-based Merger Initiatives

The Massachusetts merger of Massasoit Community College in Brockton with the Blue Hills Technical Institute in Canton in 1985 was accomplished with the enactment of the state's fiscal 1986 budget, which included the legislative authorization for the merger. Although this merger was similar to the earlier merger of Boston State College and the University of Massachusetts at Boston because both were products of legislative action, significant differences lay in the process by which the legislation for each was created.

The merger that produced the expanded University of Massachusetts at Boston was the result of initiatives at the executive and legislative levels. The legislation that created the new Massasoit Community College was the culmination of a series of actions initiated at local levels which eventually resulted in approval by the legislature and the executive. In the latter instance, it was the responsibility of the institutions proposing merger to verify that the plan made sense both institutionally and with regard to the broader system of public higher education in Massachusetts.

The immediate precipitating factor in the merger of Massasoit and Blue Hills was the enactment of the Proposition 2½ tax-capping referendum, which had been a dominant factor in the earlier merger as well. The Blue Hills Technical Institute was operated by a regional school district that retained responsibility for vocational education for grades nine through twelve. Since the tax-capping referendum required a limitation on local expenditures, the seven-member town school district eliminated local tax support for the postsecondary activities of the regional school. Since the technical institute could not maintain an adequate level of performance without this local subsidy, the leadership of the institute sought alternative methods to finance its academic programs, including a separate state appropriation, an increase in tuition charges and, finally, a merger with Massasoit Community College.

Massasoit Community College is one of fifteen community colleges in the Massachusetts system, which has been planned geographically to reach 95 percent of the state population. College operations are overseen by a local board of trustees responsible to the Board of Regents of Higher Education. The institution enrolls students in curricula designed to meet the comprehensive community college mission of providing liberal arts transfer as well as occupational degree programs. Occupational degrees are in areas such as secretarial studies, accounting, and merchandising, which remain nonintensive in terms of equipment and capital outlay. Massasoit awards the associate in arts or associate in science in fourteen programs, as well as certificates in three one-year programs.

The Blue Hills Technical Institute operated under the auspices of the Blue Hills Regional School District, a district with a vocational education mission supported by seven area towns. The technical institute emphasized programs in which students learned manual and technical skills directly related to a vocation. The institution's avowed purpose was to develop technically confident individuals immediately ready to enter the job market. One of the reasons the institute had pursued postsecondary technical programs was the direct avoidance of such programs by public community colleges, a policy that left a void in the range of two-year programs available to state students.

As a consequence of the mandate to become self-supporting, tuition at the technical institute increased from $500 in 1980–81 to nearly $2,500 in 1984–85. At the same time the tuition increases were levied, the institute began an active effort to recruit and enroll students from outside the seven towns of the district to enlarge its student base. Ironically, the state formula-funding mechanism for regional school districts did not weigh funds from local appropriated sources but factored tuition into the computation. The result was a decrease in the relative level of state aid as tuition rose. The combination of no local funding for annual operations, increased tuition, and decreased state support during a period of declining enrollment made it clear that the technical institute could not survive as it was structured. Attempts to secure additional state support outside of the regional formula-funding mechanism failed.

Leaders of the school district first sought separate state support to preserve the institute but eventually found the concept of merger acceptable. Because the institute was publicly supported and awarded an associate's degree, merger with a state community college seemed most appropriate; as most of the towns in the regional school district were in the Massasoit Community College primary service area, it became the most logical partner. Massasoit's academic leaders considered the technical programs complementary to its comprehensive mission, and the additional building provided room for expansion, as its present campus in Brockton was near capacity.

Representatives of the technical institute and the community college planned the merger with a mutual-growth, complementary-mission goal. It remained for the two institutions to negotiate an agreement for approval by the legislature. Both administrations and faculties rapidly realized it was in their best interests to devise an amicable settlement before the matter entered the political process. Significantly, the president of Massasoit Community College had been an employee of Boston State College at the time of its merger with the University of Massachusetts at Boston. A particular emphasis in this later merger was thus to preserve the integrity of the personnel review and evaluation process. Massasoit chose to maintain all programs for at least one year after the consolidation and to continue the employment of all who chose to stay at the newly merged college. Institutional objectives and faculty union goals were similar because of this approach and were collaboratively achieved. With this guarantee of continued employment and the continuation of existing academic programs, other interinstitutional issues were resolved according to a coordinated, coherent pattern formulated at the local level.

This local agreement facilitated the political process that followed. The local legislative delegation to both the senate and the house vigorously supported the plan because of its expansion of educational opportunity to area residents; thus, while the college and the institute were resolving personnel and programming issues along with assessing the value of real estate and equipment, the legislative delegation emphasized service to constituents. It is important to note that the public policy issue was not institutional integrity or enhancement of the community college mission, but rather the expanded availability of educational opportunities to the citizens of the area. With a dedicated reconciliation of both the public policy and interinstitutional challenges, the progress toward merger accelerated.

In a twenty-seven-institution state system of public higher education, the chancellor of the board of regents must consider the precedent-setting nature of each merger decision because other colleges and universities may immediately choose to expand in the same manner. The major concern in Massachusetts at the time was the establishment of satellite campuses by other public institutions. Because the Blue Hills–Massasoit merger created no satellite campus, no precedent was set that would create difficulties for a specific public college or university or for the system. The regents saw local interest united behind the concept of merger along with the benefit of eliminating duplicate associate's degree programs competing in the same local area. Ultimately, the board of regents supported the merger, and no opposition was recorded to the action approving the plan.[11]

The consolidation of the Blue Hills Technical Institute and Massasoit Community College was amicably accomplished on August 2, 1985. The impetus for merger was local, and institutional issues related to the process were resolved before the proposition was brought before the executive and legislative branches holding final authority. A powerful negative vote could have been exercised by any of the factions involved during the process, yet even student groups from both institutions favored the plan because of the cost reductions that would accrue to them.

Leadership in a Public Merger

In this discussion of public higher education mergers, the initial challenge was to locate the true impetus behind the strategy to merge. For a clear assessment of a public sector merger, it is crucial to determine whether its initiation lies in the arena of public policy or in local institutional prerogatives. A significant factor as well is the role of institutional leadership. The examples in this chapter show that presidents and chancellors in the public sector are, by the nature of their positions, institutional chief executives as well as participants in a complex political process.

The relationship between state government and higher education is a dynamic partnership with imprecise boundaries. "The dynamic quality of the relationship occurs because the environment for government and higher education is shifting and turbulent. The relationship is reciprocal because each entity depends on the other; higher education, for example, has a vested interest in the health of the state's economy, and the state benefits from the knowledge, technology, and the graduates of colleges and universities."[12] One must also add this perspective to any assessment of mergers in the public sector.

Is the alternative to merger the status quo? The answer is a matter of strategy and leadership. Planners at the University of Massachusetts at Boston, Boston State College, Blue Hills Technical Institute, and Massasoit Community College all had to consider not only the institutional impact of merger but also its political probability and consequences. Growth mergers require new levels of institutional leadership in the manner proposed by Michael D. Cohen and James G. March in their study *Leadership and Ambiguity:* "We believe effective top executives are heroic; but their heroism lies not in their ability to lead their institutions to a pre-chosen destiny, nor in their responsibility for the major successes and failures realized by their institutions, but in their willingness to try to do better in the world where neither the meaning of 'better' nor the route toward realization is clear."[13]

Academic managers must consider not only the immediate institutional advantages in a merger proposal but also the broader context of public higher education in which the strategy has been developed. Institutional autonomy and self-interest are important as operating assumptions, but they do not constitute the framework for public debate on institutional mergers. Leaders must realize that merger in the public sector is an area where collegiate institutional autonomy confronts the complex issues of state government. The state holds final authority regarding approval, but the merging institutions can advance the model and pose the central questions.

What can be said of the future of public mutual-growth mergers? The prevailing trend in the literature on mergers in public higher education almost exclusively toward a focus on institutional issues. Yet this same evidence could be used to make a compelling argument for a shift in focus toward the development of public policy and the institution's role in accomplishing the ends of that policy. Clearly, any plan to merge public colleges or universities is an aspect of public policy, but it is increasingly important to recognize that institutional leaders must fully participate in the development of that policy if mutual growth and academic excellence are to be achieved.

Chambers and O'Neill and Barnett observed that private college mergers are accomplished in a manner consistent with their public trust. Although many public institutions may assume they are meeting the test of public trust merely by continuing to receive revenue support for their operations, the relationship between political and academic circumstances can change rapidly, provoking pointed debate concerning levels of government funding for proposed changes in structure or mission.

Conversely, public support for higher education may change for reasons independent of the prevailing mission of existing institutions. In the early 1990s, a contraction of public higher education systems is occurring in many states, as diminished state tax revenues provide less support for new public-sector initiatives. In this context, the mutual-growth merger strategy becomes even more attractive. A cost-effective, consensus-based approach to achieving academic excellence on two or more campuses, it also remains sensitive to the connections between institutions and their political jurisdictions as well as to the impact those connections will have on the success of future mergers in public higher education.

The Business Aspects of College and University Mergers: a Plan for Merger Financing and Resource Sharing

James E. Samels and Donald L. Zekan

The prevailing literature on growth mergers in higher education clearly indicates that financial considerations are at the core of the premerger planning process. There is little hope of effectively accomplishing a merger without a great deal of preliminary, yet detailed, financial analysis. Although the business end of a college or university merger must be carefully weighed by trustees, chief executives, campus finance officers, and the members of the Merger Task Force, little exists in print outlining a plan for proactive, premerger financial analysis and projection.

In this chapter, we address the financial bottom line of merger transactions beginning with basic premerger financial analysis and covering the range of debt structuring, merger financing ratios, independent audits of books of account and enrollments, consolidation of financial and managerial accounting systems, and alternative financing strategies for consummating merger transactions. We review pertinent collegiate accounting principles to construct a common frame of reference for undertaking a clear yet comprehensive premerger financial analysis of the assets, liabilities, fund balances, and potential economic consequences of the proposed merger transaction.

Financial and Accounting Reference Tools

Journal articles regarding business sector mergers abound, and consistent financial reporting in the corporate sector has been the norm, whereas higher education mergers have a much shorter and less uniform history of financial reporting. A meaningful analysis of financial information requires the consistent application of accounting prac-

---

Elements of a Merger Business Plan

- Use contemporary accounting conventions
- Analyze premerger financial condition

  Assets
  Liabilities
  Debt structures
  Fund balances
  Endowments
  Equity

- Develop an effective accounting plan for combinations
- Match financial model and objectives to merger strategy and structure

---

tices so that financial ratios and trends may be fully evaluated before a merger transaction is actually executed.

Even some chief financial officers are surprised to learn that accounting conventions for colleges and universities are of recent vintage. The first text on accounting for colleges and universities appeared in the 1930s, and it was not until 1952 that volume 1 of *College and University Business Administration* was issued. In 1968, a revised edition was published and widely acknowledged as the authoritative text by the American Institute of Certified Public Accountants (AICPA). The National Association of Colleges and University Business Officers (NACUBO) in 1990 published the *Financial Accounting and Reporting Manual for Higher Education* (Washington, D.C.), the most recent compilation of accounting standards for higher education. This manual also includes a discussion of emerging accounting issues. In 1980, NACUBO published a manual by Nathan Dickmeyer and K. Scott Hughes (and eventually developed a computerized program) for analyzing an institution's financial assets, *Financial Self-Assessment: A Workbook for Colleges* (Washington, D.C.). These publications serve as the organization's primary reference documents on financial accounting analysis and reporting in higher education.

The publication of these manuals indicates the profession's interest in the continuing development of useful and consistent financial reporting at colleges and universities. This dimension is important in evaluating the financial aspects of a prospective merger, even if the institutions considering merger are subject to the separate jurisdictions of the Financial Accounting Standards Board (FASB) and the Governmental Accounting Standards Board (GASB), both segments of the Financial Accounting Foundation, an independent nonprofit organization responsible for establishing accounting standards (referred to as generally accepted accounting principles, GAAP. FASB is responsible for not-for-profit organizations, including colleges and universities, that are not a part of state or local governments. GASB sets the standards for not-for-profit organizations under the auspices of state and local government.

The AICPA in 1975 published a second edition of its industry audit guide for colleges and universities, *Audits of Colleges and Universities.* Other references for interpreting financial ratios and trends that will prove useful as starting points to guide and inform the financial analysis of a prospective merger include: section 7 of NACUBO's *Financial Accounting and Reporting Manual for Higher Education,* KMPG–Peat Marwick's *Ratio Analysis in Higher Education* (1980), and NACUBO's 1988 *Handbook on Debt Management for Colleges and Universities* by Robert T. Forrester. These works include, among other subjects, ratios and trend analyses typical of a variety of college users of financial statements.

Higher Education Accounting Standards

Uniformity, detail, accuracy, and completeness are the hallmarks of financially well-planned higher education mergers. Consistently applied and uniformly designed financial analysis and reporting systems provide the necessary foundation for realistic, achievable growth merger goals. The business aspects of a college or university merger must contain, among other elements, independently audited financial statements. It is only through the use of independent third-party review that institutions can assure themselves of this consistent accounting treatment in connection with statements of financial condition. Lacking this neutral evaluation, participants in a merger agreement may become inadvertent victims of innocent misinterpretations of accounting standards.

In addition to the NACUBO financial manuals and the AICPA audit guide, the AICPA Statement of Position (SOP) 7408, *Financial Accounting and Reporting by Colleges and Universities,* was issued by a joint accounting group consisting of members from AICPA, NACUBO, and the National Center for Higher Education Management Systems. This 1974 SOP explains specific accounting elements and has been included in the AICPA audit guide since its issuance. Both FASB and GASB have ruled that accounting and reporting standards applicable to colleges and universities are established by *Audits of Colleges and*

Universities and AICPA SOP 7408, until new pronouncements are made by FASB or GASB.

Those still learning facets of the process of financial accounting and reporting come to realize that a working knowledge of these parameters is fundamental to a meaningful understanding of how and why to prepare financial statements on a consistent basis for merging institutions. This consistency contributes to both the comparability of premerger financial statements and to the analysis of elements within those statements.

Analysis of Premerger Financial Condition

As previously suggested, audited financial statements are essential for the analysis of institutional financial condition *before* the consummation of the merger. An audit by an independent third party will assure that the premerger statements are prepared in accordance with GAAP, and that the records upon which the statements are built are reliable.

The basic merger financial statements for external users are the balance sheet, the statement of changes in fund balances, and the statement of current funds, revenues, expenditures and other changes. Those involved in the premerger analysis of financial ratios and trends must balance both the content and the intent of these statements, as the rather simple nature of analytical computations may hide the significant interrelationship of the elements being compared.

Assets, Debt, and Liquidity

Financial ratios and trends can be quite revealing, and the outcomes of such analyses could be a significant element for determining the economic viability of a successful merger. More specifically, debt- and liquidity-related ratios are centrally important in the assessment of financial condition.

As the structuring and accounting treatment of college and university debt is becoming increasingly sophisticated, debt instrument analysis should accompany an evaluation of debt ratios. Among the major debt instruments for these purposes are zero coupon and deferred interest bonds, bonds collateralized with unrestricted endowment fund assets, and fixed and variable rate debt. In addition, pooled financings have become increasingly popular; in these arrangements, public and private borrowing and lending authorities issue bonds and reissue the proceeds to participating colleges and universities. In the latter instance, a dedicated revenue pledge is likely to be required, as is bond insurance or other third-party guarantees and credit enhancements. Care must be taken to detail the nature of each debt instrument, for accounting accommodations may include the consolidation or assumption of all liabilities, depending on the unique circumstances of the merger transaction.[1]

One ratio customarily used to evaluate long-term debt is that of expandable fund balances to long-term debt. Most qualified accounting professionals would concur that a one-to-one ratio is good and a two-to-one ratio excellent. A somewhat broader measure would be the ratio of total current fund balance to long-term debt, about which most expert observers would agree that .8 to 1 is acceptable and 1.08 to 1 is preferable.

A college or university seeking merger for financial reasons is unlikely to fall within the ratios noted above, but the prevailing standards provide for a full and accurate evaluation of the depth of any material financial problems. These ratios explore the relationship of accumulated funds to long-term debt, which is roughly analogous to debt-to-equity ratio in private industry. In most higher education mergers, these measures of capital structure are related to long-term sources of financing and will indicate additional opportunity or burden for the merged institution.

The ratios provided here are from the creditor point of view, in which safety of investment is the primary concern. All of these ratios should be considered within the context of the institution's postmerger capital structure, particularly in terms of long-term financing capacity. When postmerger capital formation is an issue, reference can be made to works by NACUBO and the state higher education executive officers.[2]

Liquidity analysis also assumes greater importance in a merger situation because of the many uncertainties surrounding the accomplishment of postmerger objectives within constraints of preliminary spending plans and revenue projections. The common liquidity measure is the quick-ratio, short-term assets divided by the short-term liabilities. This analysis determines the level of current resources available to meet short-term debt. In a merger a higher margin of near-term debt-paying capacity may be appropriate because of the many unknowns that emerge as the merger objectives are accomplished.

Return on Investment

Prospective assessment of financial condition in addition to an evaluation of capital structure and liquidity is critical. Return on investment (ROI) analysis is a basic but somewhat difficult computation in higher education, as the definition of return is somewhat problematic. Some form of trade-off analysis of the investment would be appropriate once a decision is reached on the expected level of the return. The return (outcome) must be defined as clearly as possible and might be measured as, for example, increased student market share, expanded enrollment, degree elevation, program diversification, strengthened faculty credentialing, improved library holdings, or renovated campus infrastructure.

Once this definitional step is completed, the ROI analysis compares the anticipated return against the investment to be made in the start-up and completion of the merger. Before an institution locks into the merger process, it must candidly ask whether its prospective investment in the merger, reduced to a dollar amount, is a viable financing transaction based on a projected yield of return. Once this question is answered, the institution should also ask whether alternative uses for the funds would provide the same or greater return on investment without the degree of risk inherent in a merger. Could the same return be gained, for example, by building a new facility on site or self-financing new academic program initiatives? This inquiry must, of necessity, consider less tangible factors such as reasonably anticipated economies of scale, efficiencies of operation through nonduplication, and, of course, economic synergies derived from the merger of economically competitive but complementary institutions.

Although the term *return on investment* is commonly used in the analysis of financial condition to evaluate earnings potential in prospective higher education mergers, much of the return expected will likely be nonfinancial. Hence, the ROI is a complex form of performance analysis using both financial and nonfinancial data, while keeping in mind that some of the major returns sought through the merger process could be intangible.

Care must be taken to be as specific as possible in determining this nonfinancial data, including analysis of enrollment, both historical and prospective (evaluations of both potential applicant inquiries and actual applications for admission); retention rates; full-time equivalent faculty; faculty credentialing costs for professional development; and ratio of tenured to nontenured faculty. Consideration should also be given to having *other* than conventional financial data audited prior to merger. Enrollments and library and equipment acquisitions should also be relatively easy additions to a financial audit and will add to the institutional reliability and comfort level of the analyses being performed.[3]

Other analytical issues to consider include asset valuation (including endowments, trusts, gifts, and grants) and market-related issues such as demographic and enrollment trends, student preference polling, and job market analyses. Although a broad range of academic program studies will be conducted in the development of each merger model, a correlative analysis of these critical items linked with the pertinent financial data becomes essential in the later, comprehensive evaluation of the overall merger plan and agreement.

Accounting for Combinations

There is a paucity of specific authoritative guidance in the area of accounting for colleges and universities combined by merger. In correspondence to the authors, Robert Forrester of the accounting firm of Coopers and Lybrand has outlined some of the issues involved in accounts for these combinations.[4]

Business combinations are accounted for under the terms of Accounting Principals Board (APB) 16. APB 16 primarily applies to companies where stockholder interests are considered. The *Financial Accounting and Reporting Manual* from NACUBO does not include guidance regarding the combination of accounts in a college merger situation. FASB Technical Bulletin 85-5 confirms the applicability of APB 16 to nonstock enterprises in discussing the pooling of mutual and cooperative enterprises, and therefore APB 16 would apply to the merger of colleges and universities.

APB 16 provides two methods for a business combination that occurs when one entity combines its resources with all or part of the resources of another entity—purchase and pooling of interest. The purchase method reflects the acquisition of one entity by another. In a purchase acquisition, cash customarily changes hands. An acquiring college or university records as its cost the required assets less any liabilities assumed. Operating results for the institutions are combined at the time of the acquisition. APB 16 provides that "accounting for a business combination by the purchase method follows principles normally applicable under historical costs accounting to record acquisitions of assets and issuances of stock and to accounting for assets and liabilities after acquisition."

Pooling-of-interest accounting carries forward the assets and liabilities of each entity at their recorded amount to the combined corporation. In higher education mergers to which the pooling-of-interest approach applies, assets, liabilities, and fund balances are combined on a balance sheet. The pooling-of-interest method is not an alternative to the purchase method. APB 16 provides that if a combination meets the criteria of pooling of interest, it is the method that should be used; otherwise the combination is a purchase. Ten rather strict criteria are established in paragraph 47 of APB 16, all of which must be met in order to apply the pooling-of-interest method.

Applying APB 16 to accounting for combinations of colleges and universities appears to be the controlling method at this time. Although stockholder interests are usually not an issue in such mergers, the accounts must still be combined to be consistent with GAAP. Other users of financial statements, including creditors and auditors, expect that the combination will be handled appropriately. By way of example, if a state legislature directed a state university and a public community college in the same city to be combined, the transaction would likely represent a "uniting of interest" and of ownership. Assets, liabilities, and fund balances would be combined at their book values and adjusted only to resolve inconsistencies in accounting methods.

When a private university absorbs another private institution in financial difficulty, one might expect the surviving institution to assume the liabilities of the other. This assumption of liability would be considered the cost of the acquisition. If a deficit existed and liabilities exceeded assets, then the combined enterprise would write the long-lived assets plan up to the value of the debt. Although in a commercial combination this difference would be accounted for as goodwill, in the case of a college or university one could simply assign the value to plant assets, not in excess of those reflected in an appraisal. If the debt assumed (cost) in an acquisition is less than the cost of the assets, the value assigned to the long-lived assets should be reduced proportionately.

In managing the issues associated with accounting for institutional combinations, one should not lose sight of the ultimate objective: to provide detailed, accurate, and complete financial reports for the new entity which are consistent with GAAP. These combined reports must provide for interinstitutional comparability and the analysis of performance with prior corresponding periods. A small investment at this stage that can produce long-term rewards is the engagement of an accounting firm familiar with the issues and procedures of institutional combinations.

Financial Options

For colleges and universities considering merger as a strategic plan, a variety of financial models are available to fund the transaction. The following financing options are described in relation to the corresponding legal category of merger structure.

For *pure mergers* (Institution A is merged into Institution B) A generally transfers its unencumbered assets to B in consideration for B's assumption of outstanding liabilities and agreement to carry on certain of A's educational programs and activities. The unique circumstances of each merger will define the scope of assets to be transferred and liabilities assumed. It is not uncommon for B to limit its assumption of liabilities to those outstanding liquidated debts, claims, and actions capable of finite calculation. To do otherwise would have the effect of making an unbridled pledge of the merging institution's credit. This assumption of liability points up the critical importance of an independent audit and comprehensive inventory of assets and liabilities prior to consummation of the merger contract. In addition, the leadership team at Institution A will want to ensure that Institution B's finance officers execute necessary and appropriate affidavits documenting the agreed-upon assumption of liabilities. Assets in these instances vary in form, ranging from pure cash-equivalent consideration invested in short- and long-term endowments, gifts, grants, trusts, and real property to intellectual property rights in curriculum, courses, research, and publication licenses. Similarly, liabilities can include a range of campus creditor claims, subsisting contract obligations, and pending litigation.

A second option is the wide range of modified merger transactions that provide for the phased *transfer* of certain *tangible* and *intangible* *assets* over time in conjunction with the sequenced merger of campus operations. This phased implementation of merger activities can extend over several academic years, with corresponding payment of consideration through partial transfer of assets and off-setting assumption of liability based on a fixed dollar amount, aggregate percentage, or other funding formula.

Consolidations present a third financing option, with both assets and liabilities transferred and assumed respectively by a new entity (A and B transfer assets to newly constituted Institution C, which assumes liabilities). In most consolidations, the new college or university is a reconstitution of the subsisting institution, often assuming a new corporate and campus name but incorporating existing faculty, staff, and facilities from the consolidating partners.

Fourth, and with increasing frequency, we are witnessing a series of *educational affiliations* and *joint ventures* predicated on flexible revenue and expense-sharing arrangements. These affiliation transactions set parameters for identifying costs of development, start-up, recruitment, advertising, management, and administrative overhead which may later be matched against tuition, fees, and charges from revenue. The net sum produced after deducting these contractually stipulated overhead expenses yields a measurable surplus for subsequent disposition based on fixed percentage shares, on variable rates tied to enrollments, or on other pro-rata share performance. A fixed dollar amount or sliding scale net surplus may be dedicated for program enhancement, professional development, and other necessary educational improvements required for effectively carrying out the mutual affiliation objectives.

Finally, a number of *program transfers* embrace courses, curriculum, and entire undergraduate or graduate programs. Typically, these transfers provide for a combination of assets to be conveyed, including voluntary faculty and curricular transfer, and even shifts in clinical affiliations and practicum sites.

The necessary business aspects of a higher education merger, although technical, should be one element in a larger appraisal of the merits of the mutual-growth model. As with financial reporting in general, the analyses required for this planning should help colleges and universities realistically evaluate their institutional objectives *before* they sign the merger agreement. Properly prepared, these analyses focus on the financial dimensions of how the merger makes economic sense, how its mutual financial objectives are to be accomplished, and whether the proposed model will produce the expected economic returns on investment critical to long-term success and stability. In a mutual-growth plan, the goal is a transaction that is propitious financially *and* educationally, furthering the educational goals and objectives of both institutional partners. The merger's financial plan remains a pivotal factor in raising academic quality.

A proactive approach to merger planning involves a thorough analysis of the merging institutions' assets, liabilities, fund balances, endowments, equity, and debt structures. Even assuming the institutions have prepared adequately from a financial point of view, there remains the complex, arduous task of consolidating books of account, financial reporting formats, and economic forecasting models.

While all institutions seek partners with enduring financial strengths in endowments, capital facilities, and other tangible assets, senior leadership teams and Merger Task Force members must also serve as educational stewards to identify partners that can produce the most advantageous mix of degree programs, students, and faculty to carry on the mission and vision of their institution. Whatever merger model is selected, the centrality of financial stability remains constant.

CHAPTER NINE

Merger Licensure and Accreditation

James E. Samels

In the context of the mutual-growth approach, academic managers need to know that the basic act of merging, even in a growth model, does not guarantee either the transfer or the continuity of each institution's accreditation and licensure. Carefully conceived merger plans, however, can produce increased academic stature and higher levels of degree-granting authority within the new institution's licensing and accreditation relationships.

Experienced state and regional regulators seek early and open disclosure of merger plans and ongoing positive relationships with both licensing and accreditation authorities. They further expect each merging institution to be familiar with academic quality control standards and available adjudicatory and appellate procedures and, most importantly, to pay meticulous attention to the preparation of required documentation. Merger documentation focuses on central regulatory issues such as institutional preparedness; financial depth; maturity of governance; administrative stability; academic program strength; curriculum coherence; instructional effectiveness; faculty credentials; research and publishing capacities; library and learning resource support; extent of educational and scientific equipment; student enrollments; student retention, attrition, and transfer; and condition of campus and facilities.

Extensive strategic planning and a realistic, consensus-driven timetable for implementation are trademarks of successful growth merger licensure and accreditation processes.[1] Licensing and accrediting agencies recognize the sensitivities surrounding premature disclosure of merger plans and the importance of strict confidentiality. In return, merging institutions must approach the licensing and accreditation processes with serious attention to detail, candid self-analysis, and honest predictions, minus any economic or political rationalizations that may have spurred the merger.[2]

The Legal Significance of Accreditation and Licensure

Accreditation and licensure are critical factors to the success, actual and perceived, of mutual-growth mergers because they determine the faculty and students the combined institution will attract, its student transfer options, its faculty scholarship and research focus, and its professional development and student placement resources.

Accreditation and licensure also directly impact the financial viability of the new institution, as federal financial aid to education statutes specify approval by a nationally recognized accrediting agency and state licensing authority as prerequisite to funding eligibility.[3] Typically, postsecondary institutions attain eligibility for such federal student financial aid by obtaining, first, state licensure, and second, accreditation from one of the national, regional, or specialty accrediting bodies recognized by the U.S. Department of Education. In some past mergers, institutional partners misperceived that continued accreditation and licensed status could be taken for granted as basic elements of their merger plan. In each instance, members of the Merger Task Force quickly learned that licensing and accreditation issues would require major commitments of personnel and planning on the part of the merger managers.

The Need for Adequate Preparation

For the members of the Merger Task Force and the higher education attorneys, there can be no substitute for acquiring a thorough familiarity with the full range of academic quality control standards promulgated by accrediting organizations and licensing agencies. Although the reading is voluminous, the first step in this learning process is to identify the pertinent statutory provisions establishing and governing the regulatory authority of the state's postsecondary degree-granting agency. This research should focus on provisions of law that detail the requirements and degree-granting standards the licensing agency must apply to degree petitions that come before it. In general, these legislative provisions address requirements relating to educational consumer protection, financial stability, corporate status, resident agent requirements, proprietary operations, notice, disclosure, nomenclature, governance, authority to operate degree programs, academic quality control standards, records conservation, admissions and transfer policies, adjudicatory rights, and appellate remedies.

In addition to the statutory requirements imposed by the agency's enabling legislation, most licensing entities also exercise the power to promulgate more specific degree-granting academic quality control criteria. These criteria typically include standards that outline rules governing the establishment and operation of postsecondary degree programs, informational and filing requirements, and other details relating to the composition of visiting committees, visiting committee reports, staff investigations, the rights of petitioning institutions for review and public hearing, and the final process for disposition and appeal. Obviously, timelines associated with multi-institutional merger filing requirements, campus visitations, and committee investigations and reports are significantly impacted by the factual and legal consequences of the impending merger transaction.

Most states maintain a central postsecondary degree-granting board, commission, or authority empowered to hear and decide matters involving the licensure of merging institutions. This jurisdictional authority applies whether the transaction involves pure merger, consolidation, joint-venture affiliation, transfer of program assets, or another form of substantive institutional change. In some states, the licensing agency's enabling legislation addresses specific requirements for notification, informational filings, regulatory review, and transaction approval. Other jurisdictions may only make general reference to "material" or "substantive" changes in institutional circumstances, thereby triggering a fact-finding review or follow-up investigation. In such cases, it is best to seek definitional guidance from the licensing agency at the first stage of merger discussions.

Whatever level of specificity may obtain, the licensing agency's legislation, when read together with its regulations, is virtually certain to require early and full disclosure of merger plans when final consummation and execution will impact the educational consumer interests of students, individually or collectively. As this will be the case in almost every merger model, legal representatives of merging institutions must be mindful of these regulatory concerns as well as of the broader educational consumer protection issues.

Accreditation guidelines and criteria must also be considered in postmerger implementation. As a rule, U.S. accrediting agencies require early notification of a proposed change of status. This notification in most instances constitutes a substantive change in the institution's nomenclature, program offerings, educational focus and scale, and complexity of operations. Obviously, as safeguards of educational consumer protection, accreditation agencies are concerned with raw academic quality such as faculty credentials, standardized admission test results, transferability, and graduate school acceptance rates as well as with each institution's stability, maturity, and financial resources to sustain its subsisting and newly proposed programs. Overall, merger preparedness must be gauged against the institutions' representations to their prospective student consumers, who are bound to be affected by the strategic plan's level of academic quality.

As an example, the Commission on Institutions of Higher Education of the New England Association of Schools and Colleges classifies any change in legal status, including a merger, as a "substantive change." Consequently, institutions involved in mergers are subject to the association's accreditation procedures for substantive changes. Under these procedures, an institution is required to notify the association at the inception of the planning stage of the proposed change; provide a report at least ninety days prior to the date of implementation, and be subject to evaluation by the association.[4] Only after a thorough evaluation of the merger plans by the accrediting agency can the determination be made that the merger will not adversely impact subsisting institutional accreditation.

Student Financial Assistance

During merger deliberations, the institutional partners' student financial aid portfolios are always evaluated. These reviews address standard federally sponsored scholarship and loan programs; state, quasi-public, and privately guaranteed loans; scholarships and veterans assistance; and other scholarship aid organizations and benefactors. Each of these programs, authorities, and organizations requires, as a matter of threshold eligibility, proof of fully licensed and accredited status.

When a merging institution has proposed an elevation of degree offerings, newly enrolled upper division students should only be recruited with full disclosure of the current status of license and accreditation petitions pending. Federal student financial aid officials will customarily await final licensing and accreditation findings before acting on student financial aid disbursements and reimbursement claims. As long as the postmerger entity is continuously licensed and accredited before the issuance of any new degrees, concerns regarding accreditation and licensing continuity should be assuaged.

Postmerger Accreditation and Licensure Investigation

Once the appropriately involved licensing agency has been notified of the impending merger transaction, it typically requests certain preliminary documentation pertaining to the details of the proposed transaction, merger implementation plans, reasonably anticipated postmerger outcomes, degree program offerings proposed for continuation, and, in the case of new degree programs, implications of initiating these changes after the merger is consummated. This review gives special focus to such issues as program-specific financial resources, faculty credentials, library collections, and research emphasis and will frame the licensing agency's initial reference for further investigation of the merger's mutual-growth design. Licensing officials also review forms of trustee governance and faculty involvement in the collegial dialogue preceding the merger transaction. In the course of this review, licensing agencies request a list of certified independent audits, consolidated and separate financial statements, endowment portfolios, and financial planning and program budgeting documents for all merging institutions. When the merger discussions move to their implementation stage, licensing agencies want to be sure the postmerger resource allocation plan preserves and enhances academic quality, both through its human resource dimensions (faculty credentials, work load distribution new hirings, and professional development) and through expanded curricular and program support (facilities, equipment, and library resources). Experience dictates that accrediting agencies analyze all of these factors, with special emphasis on the logic and depth of postmerger course and degree offerings to ensure a necessary level of curriculum coherence and mission complementarity.

In the best situations, a mutual-growth proposal comes as no surprise to the appropriate licensing and accreditation organizations, as the prospects for selecting a complementary institutional partner, developing effective joint mission statements, and assessing postmerger program viability will have already been broached with staff members at those agencies. This proactive collaboration should not be interpreted to mean that the combined board of trustees has abdicated any degree of its stewardship responsibilities. Rather, approaching these agencies at the start of the merger planning process should be viewed as an indicator of careful planning and institutional self-confidence. Institutional partners will avoid both surprise and negative reaction by establishing open, forthright licensing and accreditation dialogues.

Although standards will vary, most state and regional agencies review the following factors to determine the continuation of accreditation:

1. The purpose of the merger and its implications for the combined institutions' complementary growth and development

2. Descriptions of degree program changes arising from the proposed merger

3. Personnel changes in faculty and staff areas required

4. Faculty qualifications, library materials, and other learning resource and educational facilities required

5. Physical plant expansion and new instructional equipment required

6. Availability of combined financial support and projections of combined institutional needs, including estimates of all new additional costs resulting from the substantive change

7. The new institution's projection of future development goals

8. A feasibility assessment of postmerger strengths and long-range plans

In assessing these changes, most agencies will choose to perform on-site evaluations of the institutions before approving the change, with or without conditions, or disapproving the proposed model.

The overriding concern in higher education mergers is the impact of the transaction on the academic quality of the new institution for the educational consumer. As long as the combined college or university has proven it has committed sufficient resources to implement a growth plan in a responsible manner without diminution of academic quality, as well as demonstrated an available student market share or other predictable revenue sources to provide continuing financial stability, the regulatory agency will typically grant it licensure or accreditation.

Accreditation Visitation and Report

When campus visitations are recommended for accreditation purposes, visiting team members are drawn from the ranks of chief executive and senior financial officers, academic deans, and department chairs with expertise in areas of special relevance to the mission and academic emphasis of the new college or university. As a general rule, team members are selected from institutions outside the immediate geographic area of the petitioner and, in some instances, outside the student market competition region of the merging institutions. These several qualifications tend to ensure confidence in the committee's objectivity and neutrality.

Accreditation organizations will be concerned that their investigations be based on a close and careful inspection of the relevant facts presented by the merger and will therefore subsume these deliberations within either specific focused visits or regularly-scheduled plenary re-accreditation visitations during the period following the consummation of the merger agreement.

Whatever the timing and form of these potential visitations, it is clear that special attention will be given both to overall and program specific impacts the merger design will have on the combined institution. Should plans for a substantive change be disapproved by an accrediting agency, the institutions have the right to proceed with this change, but the plan will not carry accredited status and the institution will have to state this in its catalogues and other advertising literature. In cases such as this, additional institutional review and response would be necessary, including new documentation, to address the matter of continuation of accredited status.

Licensing Standards and Appellate Procedures

In situations when a licensing agency has a working familiarity and clear regulatory record with the merging institutions, a formal visitation can be dispensed with in favor of a staff evaluation predicated on documentation submitted in a previous stage of the merger planning process. Whether a visiting team is used or not, most state regulatory statutes and degree standards mandate that the agency review copies of a standard series of documents for both institutions:[5]

1. A copy of the existing institutional charter and references to previous petitions for substantive amendments of similar intent

2. A list of the members of the corporation and a copy of the institution's constitution and bylaws

3. Evidence of organizational stability, including a certified audit for the last two years

4. Information regarding tax status

5. A general statement regarding the institution's endowment funds

6. A list of the institution's physical properties

7. Copies of health and building certificates as well as appropriate licenses

8. A statement of current educational objectives and their relationship to the proposed merger plan

9. The most recent catalogue or bulletin

10. A list of faculty and administrative staff members

11. An inventory of instructional equipment

12. A comprehensive description of library facilities

13. Present admissions procedures and entrance requirements

14. Total enrollment for the current year

15. Graduation requirements for current courses and proposed requirements for new courses

16. A description of guidance and counseling programs

17. A description of health care provisions

18. A list of tuition charges plus any additional fees or charges

19. The total dollar value of financial aid funds

20. A list of accredited institutions that have accepted graduates during the past three years, including amounts of credit

21. A summary of types of positions obtained by graduates during the past three years

22. A list of accrediting associations that have approved the institution

23. A copy of the institution's affirmative action program

In most states, an institution that chooses to merge must amend its charter to reflect this structural corporate change. As indicated, the filing of such an amendment usually triggers an investigation by staff regulators, including a visiting committee. When the merging institution enjoys a legislative charter, a curative amendment may need to be filed with the state legislature, and appropriately involved legislative education committee staff members may refer the proposed amendment to the state licensing agency for review, comment, and recommendation.

Following investigation, a report is issued and the combined institution has an opportunity for review and comment. Thereafter, a public hearing is conducted, and the licensing agency makes a determination regarding the merger articles, which typically have been forwarded to the agency by the corporation division of the state secretary. If the impact of the proposed merger on degree-granting status is not approved, the agency states its reasons for such denial and an appeal may be made to a designated adjudicatory authority.

Educational Consumer Protection

From the start of Merger Task Force discussions, both accrediting and licensing agencies want to be informed regarding the net assets available in the postmerger institution for allocation to educational improvements. Their inquiries generally include an analysis of the operating and capital budget process with a regulatory focus aimed at developing a full and accurate picture of the new institutional resource allocation system that will distribute available funding and assets for the purposes designated by the successor board of trustees.

Differing academic standards of national, regional, and specialty accreditation agencies and state licensing authorities may sometimes give rise to an unexpected set of postmerger accreditation and licensing challenges. Leaving aside the inevitable differences between specialty accreditation agencies, the authors have observed in the mutual-growth mergers outlined in this book a clear pattern of regulatory reciprocity and administrative comity among and between regional accrediting and state licensing agencies. State licensing standards often incorporate by reference a presumption of overall institutional preparedness for purposes of licensing, provided each institution's regional accreditation is in good standing.

Accrediting and licensing agencies also need to be assured the educational interests of the student consumer are not being disenfranchised. Students expect full faith and credit within the combined institution's degree-granting system. Accreditation and licensing agencies carefully and independently review the new sequences of available course offerings to assure a timely completion of graduation requirements for earned degrees. Transfer students are equally entitled to receive full credit, giving due consideration to accreditation and licensing status.

Students are entitled to reasonable expectations of a quality campus experience from both educational and residential life aspects. Libraries require expanded shelf space, software programs, and distance learning opportunities, as well as other educational materials essential to an enhanced learning experience. Adequate common study areas and student union space conducive to learning must be made available so that the merged campus can invite educational inquiry consistent with the mission-complementary, mutual-growth approach.

Expectations such as these require adequate resources and flexible, creative planning systems. Accreditation and licensing agencies must have confidence in the ability of the postmerger institution's governing board and academic management team to lead the new college or university forward on an educationally and fiscally sound basis. Premerger planning and self-study documents should reflect this sensitivity to the postmerger educational consumer protection interests of students, faculty, and the larger community the combined institution will serve. In my experience, this may be achieved most effectively through an independent educational consumer interest evaluation at each stage of the process, including impact analyses by outside experts on the major components of the postmerger organization. Typically, these analyses will include an educational needs assessment and feasibility study, a student preference polling instrument, and an economic impact study. Although an assessment process this thorough is time-consuming, it has come to signify one of the emerging strategic differences between merging colleges for mutual growth and, as in earlier days, bailing them out of bankruptcy.

Characterized by their dedication to protecting the best educational interests of student consumers, accrediting and licensing agencies will continue to seek confirmation that the postmerger educational culture will be as vital, supportive, and enriching as that on both campuses before the merger implementation.

Forearmed with knowledge of and trust in pertinent regulatory requirements, colleges and universities contemplating complementary mergers experience smoother transitions to their new structures and continued accreditation and licensure. This continuity can be facilitated by early communication with the appropriately involved agencies, a shared, realistic vision that justifies the merger design, careful premerger strategic planning, and prudent institutional resource commitments.

III CONSTITUENTS

Campus Relations and Quality Service

Merging Diverse Student Cultures

Sheila Murphy

Although students should be viewed as central stakeholders and potentially powerful allies in the development of a college or university mutual-growth merger strategy, they are often considered junior partners in both its planning and implementation.[1] Even though among the goals of the merger plan are enhanced curricular opportunities and an increase in the perceived value of the degree, the process of merging two institutions represents significant disjuncture for all involved students and must be sensitively managed by an informed student affairs staff. The two or more merging student cultures need not be on a collision course; rather, the values, habits, traditions, and nuances of each culture can be incorporated into a new, more inclusive model in which all students benefit. It is up to the senior leadership team, the members of the Merger Task Force, and possibly its student affairs subcommittee to take a public prostudent position from the earliest joint discussions.

At the same time, merger planners should not expect students immediately to grasp and endorse the benefits of the mutual-growth strategy. Similar to faculty members and middle-level administrators, students may initially experience a distance and alienation from the key decision-making processes and react predictably with suspicion, fear, or anger. The traditional challenges of adolescent development typically play a role in students' responses to the announcement of merger planning. Late adolescents often view the uncertainties of merging as negatives and, to the degree they identify with their college or university, may experience the merger as a threat to their developing identities. Students may also feel a loss of control as they view their institution beginning to change. Worried about their futures, they may feel betrayed by the college or university that recruited them with the promise of a particular set of experiences within a specific environment. Students who believe that only colleges in financial trouble consider merging need to be reeducated. An additional factor is the healthy skepticism contemporary students feel toward a university's administration. Although many students may require extra time and attention to build their understanding of the benefits of the mutual-growth concept, planners and task force members need to acknowledge that students who appear difficult regarding their acceptance of change are engaging in age-appropriate behavior.

Other factors can play a role in students' initial responses, one of them being whether a student attends an institution initiating a merger and perceived as the more powerful, or a school that views itself as being consolidated and less powerful. Anthony Buono and James Bowditch quote H. Levinson, who "compares the merger process to the forming of a new family, particularly the arrival of a step-parent to replace a lost parent. In addition to the fear associated with such change, the child involved also experiences a range of negative feelings associated with the loss of a part of the family and past life. Moreover, the child may also react to what is perceived as controlling behavior by the new parent with feelings of betrayal and anger and may even leave home."[2] Awareness of these phenomena in advance of exploring even a mission-complementary merger will assist the deans of students and student affairs staffs, as well as Merger Task Force members, to anticipate and understand student objections and to plan effective strategies to incorporate and empower student constituents.

Reviewing Existing Policies and Practices

The joint student affairs staffs should review the combined policies and practices of both institutions as their initial contribution to the merger planning process. Many staffs have observed that premerger planning offers an opportunity to refine and refocus an existing mission in light of the challenges in integrating two or more student cultures. A student affairs task force including staff and students from both campuses and reporting to the overall Merger Task Force or steering committee has been the most effective model in several recent merger implementations.

The broad set of issues that follows can shape the initial planning sessions. Specific responses in each area, taken from institutions that have recently implemented the mutual-growth model, are provided in the second half of the chapter.

Operational Checklist for Merging Student Affairs Programs

- Academic advising systems
- Alumni affairs programming for students
- Learning assistance support
- Athletic programs
- Career services advising programs
- Career placement systems
- Codes of conduct
  Alcohol policies
  Harassment and discrimination policies
  Campus civility expectations

- Financial aid policies
- Fraternity and sorority policies
- Communication with parents
- Residential life and off-campus housing policies
- Student governance structures
- Student activities programming
- Volunteer and community service programs

Academic advising and learning assistance. The challenges a merger poses to the areas of academic services are reviewed more fully in the discussions in chapter 5 which focus on merging faculty and curricular structures. The impact on advising, however, especially for students who have declared a major and still have departmental or programmatic requirements to complete, must be considered by the larger Merger Task Force. The opportunity for a transcript review by a well-informed faculty member should be offered to each student, particularly in program areas that will be altered in the new structure. Careful advising of an enhanced course selection completed well in advance of the merging process demonstrates the realistic academic benefits of the mutual-growth approach for students.

Athletics. Many students and alumni experience their institution's personality most clearly and directly through its athletic teams and programs. The highly regulated environment of intercollegiate athletics contributes its own set of challenges to the mutual-growth model in the form of National Collegiate Athletic Association, National Junior College Athletic Association, and other conference-specific guidelines. Minimal disruptions in eligibility and clear and early notice of changes in program direction, if applicable, must be an acknowledged commitment by the academic managers on both campuses. Will the combined college or university support all of the intercollegiate teams that were supported by the individual institutions? If teams competed in different NCAA or NJCAA divisions, are eligibility guidelines clear? When the merger involves both two-year and four-year institutions, have the differing restrictions on participation been defined and acknowledged? Will access to practice facilities, equipment, and budgets be equitably distributed by the combined staff of the new institution? Are the structures that govern intramural activities flexible enough to accommodate new students with new interests?

Career services and placement. Consumers of education are increasingly looking to placement records and the ability to attract corporate recruiters to the campus as indices of an institution's perceived value in the marketplace. In mergers in which the incoming degrees offered and employment opportunities for new graduates vary more than minimally, how will the new college or university insure access to employers appropriate to all students? How will career services and placement offices insure representation of alumni from both institutions in its programs? How can the new institution assure its combined market of employers that the degree from the combined institution will be of enhanced value? How will individual alumni credentials and records be preserved in the new institutional structure?

Codes of conduct, including alcohol policies. Students immediately question how day-to-day policy differences will affect their lives in the merged environment. Have institutional policies on visitation, discipline systems, and other matters of student conduct been comparable? One of the most repeated questions pertains to alcohol policies. If one campus was dry and the other permitted the use of alcohol by students over twenty-one, how will these policies necessarily be reconciled? How do procedures for handling alcohol-related infractions compare, and what is the form of student participation in the judicial processes of each institution?

Financial aid. Typically, although the differential in tuition and fee structures is addressed in premerger planning, institutions also are likely to maintain differing internal policies governing the packaging of financial aid. In the new institution, how will parity among these financial aid packages be achieved? Regarding student employment, will jobs be lost, especially if the merger involves the closure of one or more campuses? What common factors will determine which students retain their campus jobs?

Fraternities and sororities. The appropriate role of fraternities and sororities is the topic of one of the most significant student-centered debates in contemporary U.S. higher education. Campuses without a Greek system are likely to be appropriately concerned about acquiring one through their merger partner. Campuses involved in sorority and fraternity life may view merging as an opportunity to dismantle their systems. If properties are owned by the national affiliates, will one institution wish to bear the implicit responsibilities that accompany fraternity life, even without property management? Are policies on recruitment and membership, such as co-ed or single sex, compatible? Are the chapters' governance structures through participation in Panhellenic or intra-fraternity councils consistent? How can national and local chapters be brought together? Are the financial policies for housing revenue consistent? Finally, what if the same national fraternity or sorority exists on both campuses?

Residential life. If a campus consolidation or closure may occur, the Merger Task Force needs to assess precisely the strain on residential capacity a growth merger is likely to cause. If all students cannot be accommodated on the single campus, initially or in the long term, policy questions regarding housing guarantees, typically offered newly enrolled students, must be addressed. Assuming adequate residential space is available, the task force subcommittee on student affairs needs to develop a compatible system for managing the student residential program, including its postmerger costs. Can room and board charges be separated? Is the quality of the facilities similar? Are single rooms and apartment-type suites both available? Merging two or more residential programs provides an unusual opportunity to join students from separate campus cultures and to incorporate their judgments in the formation of an enhanced plan for residential life. The mutual-growth approach, unlike former higher education merger models, can emphasize the value of student affairs prerogatives in the new institution rather than treat them as the minor feature they have traditionally been in bankruptcy-bailout merger planning.

Student governance and activities. As questions of governance are addressed, students should be given high levels of autonomy in determining the structure of their representative government for the new institution. Are the models of elected or appointed representation compatible? Are positions, terms of office, and practices compatible? Should a single governance structure be established initially, or might parallel structures be advantageous in the early stages of implementation? How can college-sponsored activities be planned to represent the traditions of both institutions? Can the goals of a growth merger be integrated into the plans for orientation, parents' weekend, homecoming, and other traditional activities? Furthermore, how can the experiences of the new and emerging student culture be most effectively transmitted through these events?

In cases where a student activities fee is collected and disbursed, how can the priorities of the student governance structures from both institutions most effectively be addressed? Discussions of whether to attempt to merge campus newspapers, yearbooks, and commencements may be useful barometers of the general level of student acceptance of the mutual-growth strategy. When it is logistically or financially possible to maintain a short-term distinction in ceremonial occasions such as student convocations or honors and awards presentations, some colleges have found it symbolically important to do so and to demonstrate support for a slow, gradual transition to fully merged status.

Recent Growth-Merger Implementations from the Student Affairs Perspective

The size, structure, and culture of the institutions implementing a higher education merger are significant determinants in planning the mutual-growth strategy from the perspective of the office of student affairs. In the recent Mercer University–Tift College merger in Georgia, a plan was created to preserve important Tift traditions and incorporate them into the life of Mercer University "through a lot of patient conversation with Tift students and alumnae," according to Dr. Barry Jenkins, Mercer's dean of student affairs in 1991. In Minneapolis–St. Paul, in the merger between the College of St. Catherine and St. Mary's College, "No one really noticed it," said Dr. Colleen Hegranes, dean of student affairs. Conversations with key student affairs staff members who have led merger task forces and implementation teams confirm that the college or university that experiences itself as being merged is greatly helped by a strategic effort to highlight the benefits, particularly the mutual benefits, of the growth strategy.[3]

In the 1989 merger between Iona College and Elizabeth Seton College in New York, Elizabeth Seton students viewed their institution as being "swallowed up" by the stronger and more stable Iona, according to Paul Lamontia, Iona's associate dean of students in 1991. The former Seton campus currently houses all associate's degree programs for the combined institution, and candidates who apply for admission to Iona are typically referred for admission to the new Elizabeth Seton School of Associate Degree Programs if this level of work initially seems more appropriate to their credentials. This revised academic structure, which is sensible and educationally advantageous to students, nevertheless can contribute to a perception of the Seton campus as the stepchild of Iona College. A systematic effort is being made to include students from the Seton campus, located four miles from the Iona campus, in that campus's programs and activities. The college provides transportation to both campuses, and, according to the associate dean, from the student life perspective, the merger is gradually being described as a success. In its postmerger phase, deans of students on each campus report to a vice president for student affairs on the Iona campus. The new institution has implemented the transition to a combined student newspaper and student government system and for the first time in 1991 introduced a single commencement and joint yearbook.[4]

The student affairs component of the late 1980s merger of Gannon University and Villa Maria College in Pennsylvania underscores the critical role staff members on the smaller campus can play. The Villa Maria president emerged as an advocate for the merger and, in assuming this role, exercised the greatest impact, both real and symbolic, in support of the mutual-growth concept. The president assumed the position of vice president of Gannon University and dean of Villa Maria College in the new institution. The deans of students positions were consolidated, with the dean from Gannon directing a combined Office of Student Affairs. According to Rev. Charles Drexler, in 1993 the acting dean of students for the combined institution, both the Gannon and Villa Maria administrations were sensitive to the merger-related concerns and anxieties of the students and staffs. The acting dean connected student responses to the stages of grief articulated in the work of Elisabeth Kubler-Ross: shock, denial, anger, and finally a healthy period of grieving for what has been lost.[5] Campuswide "listening sessions," in which members of the new combined administration made themselves available to the Villa Maria community, helped students address their own concerns about the losses associated with merger. Separate from these sessions was a series of meetings designed to provide students with factual information about how the mutual-growth strategy could dramatically expand the resources, support, and activities of the student life component of their college experience. These meetings were also a chance to discuss a collaborative design for implementation in student development areas. Leaders at Gannon and Villa agreed that these two kinds of meetings were usefully kept separate, and that their different agendas implicitly indicated to students the level of awareness and acceptance in their institutions regarding the legitimate need for attention to the student life content and process of a mutual-growth merger.

The merged university continues to operate both campuses, which are three miles apart. In 1990–91, the first year of merger implementation, the focus was on restructuring to balance the delivery of student services on both campuses. Shared programming constitutes the second phase of student affairs implementation. The acting dean acknowledges that Gannon was a stronger, more visible institution and is working with Villa Maria students to involve them in a university now enhanced by the addition of Villa's educational history and traditions. The university's first joint program will occur with the Founder's Awards Ceremony, honoring the outstanding scholarship and leadership of students on both campuses.[6]

The ability of an alumni association to rally student support and to mobilize student opinion is well documented throughout the history of modern higher education. Wilson College's 1974 attempt to close was successfully thwarted by alumnae effort, as was Mills College's 1990 attempt at coeducation. Resistance to the elimination of fraternities at Amherst, Colby, and Williams colleges in the 1980s was vehemently expressed and highly politicized through the well-coordinated efforts of their alumni. In growth-merger planning, the role of alumni must be increasingly considered, and a strategy to incorporate their full involvement must be formulated before antimerger sentiment becomes predominant.

Alumni resistance added an element of struggle to the merger of Mercer University and Tift College. Tift alumnae saw their unique identity as a southern teaching and women's college facing potential elimination and organized themselves and the students in opposition to the merger. The "Campaign to Save Tift" attempted to define and organize a group opposing the merger. With promises to increase financial support to the college and to increase assistance in recruiting students through more alumnae support, group organizers assumed the merger would become unnecessary. In response, teams of Mercer administrators visited the Tift campus on an ongoing basis to reassure the concerned group that the unique role of Tift in the history of higher education in Georgia would not only be preserved but enhanced by merging. Mercer redesigned significant space in a prominent campus building to serve as the new Tift College Alumnae Center and archives to house all of that college's records. A key focus of resistance to merging became the large Tift Bell, a central element of the annual May Festival at Tift. Wisely recognizing the importance of symbols in a major institutional transition, members of the Mercer administration reassured Tift students that the bell, and the traditions that accompanied it, would be significant additions to campus life at Mercer University and incorporated the May Festival into the new combined calendar.

Mercer also offered preferred housing in suite-style apartments to the Tift students who made the transition to the Macon campus. The Tift campus, eventually to be sold, has been designated as a continuing education site for the overall university during the transition period. Mercer also honored the Tift tuition rate at the point of merging for the remainder of each Tift student's time at the combined institution. These students, the last of whom graduated in 1990, received diplomas that read "Tift College of Mercer University" upon completion of their degrees.

The Merger Task Force developed a flexible plan to accommodate the Tift student body from the first merger planning discussions, and their careful systems for budgeting and programming activities eventually resulted in a smooth merger implementation. "It was really quite remarkable," according to Mercer's dean of students. "The desire to retain a unique Tift identity in the midst of Mercer student life quickly gave way to an even stronger desire to assimilate into the landscape at Mercer. The enthusiasm for the traditions disappeared. The reserved seat on the student government board was unoccupied, and Tift women were quickly accepted into the mainstream of academic and campus life at the university."[7] The students, in the dean's opinion, were able to recognize and grasp the benefits of their attendance at Mercer soon after arrival. The strong faculty and quality of academic life, the expanded facilities, the depth of resources available, and the enthusiasm for a larger, coeducational student body all appear to have contributed to the sense of acceptance on the part of Tift students. In the future, alumnae will be asked to designate on their annual fund contribution whether they wish to contribute to a special Tift College Foundation within the university fund-raising program or to contribute to the university as a whole. Proceeds from the sale of the Tift campus will support a scholarship endowment to provide assistance for Baptist women from Georgia to attend Mercer University.

Similar to the need for a small but effective group of key academic managers as outlined in the academic action plan in chapter 5, a senior member of the Tift leadership team, highly regarded by the Tift student community, proved to be an invaluable change agent in the traditional period. The Tift dean of students joined the career planning and placement staff at the university and maintained relationships with Tift students in the process. Identifying an advocate for students from the campus undergoing the greater transition has proven to be a successful component of several recent mutual-growth merger implementations.[8]

From a student affairs perspective, the transition to merged status has been more slow and steady on the campuses of St. Mary's College and the College of St. Catherine in Minnesota. The two institutions share many features, and the decision to operate both college sites has been a confirmation of mutual-growth potential while simultaneously avoiding the dislocation of numerous employees and students through the closing of one campus. The first stage of the plan was an administrative consolidation, and by 1991, the third year of the merger, both the faculty and staff had devised collaborative plans of implementation for their areas.

As St. Mary's College did not have an office of student affairs, as such, administrators at the College of St. Catherine confronted a more difficult challenge in creating a new structure on a partner campus five miles away. The St. Mary's campus now has its first director of student services, along with a residence staff who receive training in conjunction with St. Catherine's staff members, and increased support for on-campus programming. The current St. Mary's student population of nine hundred has an average age of 26.5 years, contrasted with a majority of students of traditional college age on the College of St. Catherine campus. The combined college provides transportation between the campuses for special events. In athletics, the institution has insured that the NCAA Women's Division recognizes the new College of St. Catherine as a single entity and that athletes from both campuses are eligible to participate on all intercollegiate teams.

All student affairs policies were reviewed as part of the merger plan, and residential life policies as well as codes of conduct and alcohol policies have been updated for consistency. Although St. Mary's did not have a formal student government association, a Weekend College Advisory Board advocates on behalf of all students of nontraditional college age. New policies on tuition and fee structures are also being developed to insure parity in the awarding of financial aid.

The Trustee Committee on Student Affairs coordinates funding and resource support for student needs as the merger implementation process draws to a close and the postmerger period begins. This slow, more gradual approach to consolidation has provided greater opportunities for acceptance and consensus to build on both campuses. The administrative philosophy at the College of St. Catherine has been to emphasize the process elements of the merging and therefore to incorporate a series of sequential modifications to current practice rather than radical transformations in the new institution. The dean of students has stated that "there will always be some separateness, and as long as there is cooperation, retaining some elements of separate identity is fine." A representative example of healthy separateness has been the decision to hold a separate commencement for the women of the St. Mary's campus. As all of these students graduate in allied health fields, and as many are returning students who work significant hours while raising children, commencement is a particularly powerful moment in their lives. "The path to this day is, in many cases, quite remarkable," observed the dean, "and we wanted to do whatever we could to retain the intimacy and emotion of the traditional St. Mary's commencement. It [has been] an important message to send to our St. Mary's campus students."[9]

Is a merger ever finally completed? From the student affairs perspective, the answer is yes, according to Dr. Noel Cartwright, director of the Counseling Center at the University of Massachusetts–Lowell, a 14,000-student comprehensive public university in Massachusetts. In 1975, Lowell State College merged with the Lowell Technical Institute to form the University of Lowell, now the University of Massachusetts–Lowell, one of the three largest institutions in the state's public system. The clusters of related academic disciplines now grouped on each campus initially provided both logistical and academic challenges to the members of the Merger Task Force. The departments of engineering, computer science, and the physical sciences are now located on the original institute campus, while the liberal arts, fine arts, and health sciences have been consolidated on the former state college campus. Partially in response to this restructuring, the new leadership team appointed the institute's dean of engineering to the newly created post of vice president for academic affairs. This individual was subsequently appointed president of the university with the backing of the combined faculty and staffs, who noted his sensitivity to the two traditions that formed their university's unique history. In this instance as well, the significance of even one familiar administrative change agent to the long-term success of a merger plan was acknowledged.

At the point of merging, Dr. Cartwright organized a set of straightforward discussions with students from both campuses, who quickly grasped the benefits of the mutual-growth strategy at the core of the Lowell model. There was immediate consensus that a university degree was preferable to either a state college or technical institute degree, and, with the initial logistical details resolved, students have been pleased by the results over the long term. Dr. Cartwright observed that one key to the success of the Lowell merger was the appointment of a president with experience on both campuses, as this persuasively "affirmed our new merged identity."[10]

Patience, an openness to new staffing and programming models, well-timed planning meetings with key alumni, and the use of familiar, effective staff members in merger implementation roles contribute most significantly to the ability of the Merger Task Force and its subcommittees to create and sustain an authentic responsiveness to the legitimate concerns of students on the merging campuses. In the midst of competing pressures for time and the need for steady progress toward the goal, the student affairs subcommittee must be in regular contact with key student leaders and opinion makers to keep student communities well informed of the plan. Some schools have found it useful to invite a reporter from the campus newspaper to attend task force discussions; others have chosen to assign one member of the task force to serve as liaison to the student press. Even during periods when there is no news to report, every available opportunity should be used to educate students about the concept of merging colleges for growth purposes.

Parents should also be viewed as constituents with a legitimate interest in the postmerger institution. If the college or university has a routine vehicle for communication with parents such as newsletters or periodic mailings, this should include an article that explains the mutual-growth model along with a time line for the merger process. If no such vehicle exists, an in-depth letter from the president or chief academic officer should be sent at least semiannually, perhaps along with other institutional news of interest to parents. Students who are uneasy with the merger strategy may consider transferring to another institution out of frustration or anger or because they believe their programs of study may no longer exist. Well-informed parents can be helpful in echoing the message of the beneficial effects of this merger model if they have been provided relevant information early in the planning process.

All institutions that consider the mutual-growth process need to address and overcome rumor-driven communication patterns on their campuses. One of the overlooked challenges of managing a merger is to maintain a steady flow of accurate information moving across and between campuses. This is particularly critical in student life areas where access to senior administrators may not be perceived as readily available. Several institutions that completed successful mergers responded to this concern with such strategies as a brochure entitled "Myths and Facts About the Proposed Merger," a question-and-answer column in the campus newspaper, regular appearances by task force members at student government and residence hall government meetings, and informational poster campaigns in heavily trafficked student areas.

Although the circumstances of each merger plan are complex and unique, efforts to incorporate student decision making not only represent good student development work but also contribute an integral element to the larger success of the mutual-growth approach to higher education management.

CHAPTER ELEVEN

Consolidating Library Collections and Learning-Resource Technologies

Patricia Sacks

In this chapter are outlined the most significant learning-resource-related challenges in a mutual-growth merger of colleges or universities and the short- and long-term planning processes the academic libraries involved may use to their greatest advantage in shaping the postmerger institution, processes that will provide the library facility and its staff members the most effective means to manage the dramatic environmental changes that accompany even a mission-complementary merger model. In particular, this chapter offers directors of libraries practical guidelines for the procedural aspects of merging, such as collections development policies, budget strategies, expansion planning, lending service issues, and, most importantly, human resources. The planning model outlined includes both the short-term and long-term decisions that, in my experience, determine the difference between a successful and failed library merger.

There is no one best approach to merging college and university libraries. Cultures and resources differ with each design. Critical for the staffs of library and learning-resource facilities involved in a merger, however, is the recognition that the force of change will always be external and beyond their control, which poses increased uncertainties for all internal conditions. Historically, library facilities have adjusted with little foreknowledge to external factors such as shifting budget constraints, rising journal prices, and rapidly evolving computer technologies. These situations continually exert pressures on most campuses for libraries to adjust their basic strategic plans. Internal pressures for change also arise within ongoing personnel structures, communication systems, and work-flow organization, as well as in the skills, attitudes, and aspirations of individual staff members, particularly those at the beginning of their careers. A successful mutual-growth merger in the library and learning-resource environment involves flexible, adaptive responses to all of these pressures both by a unified staff and by the members of the Merger Task Force, including its subcommittee on learning resources. These groups need to unite and affirm the centrality of library facilities to the merged institution's educational goals. Although the following discussion outlines elements most responsible for positive change in the merger strategy, the director and combined staffs must exercise firm control over these factors to take full advantage of the opportunities a growth merger can provide.

Strategic Planning in the Learning-Resource Context

As an introduction to the model, it should be useful to list the broader planning principles that have emerged in several recent growth-oriented library mergers, affiliations, and consolidations:

1. Institutional mergers alter accustomed practices and styles in the libraries and learning-resource centers involved and demand new attitudes to resolve difficulties both anticipated and unanticipated.

2. The successful library director encourages participation, shares power and information, and enhances the self-worth of the newly combined staff. Successfully accomplishing the transformation of the staff's institutional identities and self-interests to the new facility, including a central concern for its academic mission, is an essential leadership task.

3. Mergers involve an enormous amount of adjustment to change in a dramatically short period of time. There are limits to the amount and rate of change library staff members may be able to assimilate, and a series of in-service educational programs and activities, even over a multiyear period, should be scheduled to address this concern.

4. A period of staff experimentation should be planned before significant changes are implemented. Pilot library programs can outline proposed accommodations and enable both users and staff members to react to pending structures and services while reminding all involved that achieving acceptance in the later stages of a project can be equally as complex a challenge.

5. Experienced directors view the inevitable crises that occur during the merger process as opportunities for the new team of staff members to prove itself.

6. As the merger begins to alter or dissolve various traditions, the director needs to convince both staffs that participating in the comfort-

able network of their former facility will become progressively less important than how they adapt to and perform within the merged structure.

7. Library directors may sometimes overestimate their ability to manage a larger system that is experiencing conflict. They, along with other academic managers and the members of the Merger Task Force, need to acknowledge that this environment can be unsettling, even to an experienced professional, while remaining open to new solutions and ways of thinking.

The two highest priorities in the merger process from the director's point of view are developing a coherent overall planning strategy and meeting staff needs. At every level of the personnel structure, significant discomfort and tension are likely to arise when merger implementation begins, as staff members' frames of reference and expectation levels have been formed by their prior experiences and their shared library life. Although staff members may appear to be focusing on the merged operating system the new computers will use, for example, their planning discussion may sometimes be more accurately characterized by a defensiveness toward one system or the other. Experience indicates that collegial efforts to draft new policies can be resisted, even sabotaged, because of threats to the organizational culture.

It should be acknowledged that each merging library is continuing to respond to its community's needs. Each may still interpret its responsibility to be to its community, that is, the former community to which it continues to feel it belongs and which continues to seek its services. The institutional partner may still be seen by these staff members as "the other library," an intrusive, unwanted entity rather than a coequal enterprise with its own valued traditions. Directors need to remember in addressing this staff discomfort and disruption that the leadership challenge lies in their ability to recognize, understand, and ultimately resolve these differences on a one-to-one basis. In my experience, leaders who use the power of participation and information sharing among workers as methods to secure commitment to the new library's goals have been the most effective in achieving their mutual-growth objectives.

Rather than simply fulfilling an annual budget cycle, learning resource planning in a growth merger is fundamentally a process of consolidating and coordinating the budgets and programs of the library units—technical services, lending services, information services, media services—to determine the most effective allocation of resources among them. Merger-related data external to the annual plan are needed to

---

Strategic Planning Steps in a Learning Resources Consolidation

- Prepare combined staff, particularly senior members, for changes in accustomed practices
- Encourage individual and group problem-solving initiatives
- Monitor staff comfort levels
- Design in-service training sessions to address the dislocations of merging
- Experiment with new personnel configurations and pilot service programs
- Expect crises; seize opportunities
- Evaluate staff acceptance of new merger goals over a three-year time frame at minimum
- Ask the new director to design and implement a plan for self-evaluation over this same period

---

develop and affirm the library's mission and to fulfill that mission by refining and enhancing its available services. What is essential is a planning process that responds to changing circumstances and remains open to new developments rather than becoming trapped in a defense of past practices.

Strategic planning in this context incorporates the entire library personnel structure. It must answer the question, "What does this library now need to become, and what resources will be required to accomplish this goal?" Additional topics for consideration by the task force and key staff members, as well as the director, can include the information needs of the merged curriculum; new requirements for computerized information resources; expanded access to electronic text and information services; necessary user service charges; expectations for, and limits to, postmerger collecting programs; formats to be collected; new space requirements for collection storage; and the role of the combined staff of librarians as teachers, information specialists, and administrators.[1]

During merger implementation, a fundamental dilemma for the director is reconciling the forces of stability and change while managing an efficient facility (or facilities) during the transition and simultaneously shaping the new institutional structure. Research suggests that organizations resolve these opposing forces by attending first to one and then to the other.[2] The various short-term and long-term guidelines that follow are built on the premise that the first order of business is to maintain stability and to serve users' basic needs, and that in those actions a response pattern will emerge that will enable the library to

---

**Library and Learning Resources Diagnostic Checklist
for Mutual-Growth Mergers**

- How will the original missions of the two institutions be affected by the merger plan?
- How fully will the two administrations merge?
- Will all current degree programs be retained?
- Will the institutions seek accreditation at a new degree level from the regional accrediting association?
- Will the combined library prepare one or two budget recommendation statements and receive one or two appropriations? Will the two staffs be paid by one office?
- How are the physical plants to be merged? Will operations cease on one campus and function under one plant operations manager?
- How are the key library and learning resource interfaces to be merged? Will there be one or two facilities?
- To what degree will collections development now be merger driven and for how long?
- To what extent must a reassessment and potential expansion of user services be made an immediate priority?

---

define more clearly its postmerger direction (see "Strategic Planning Steps" checklist). Whatever the planning model, its results will define the nature of the merged library and learning-resource center while acknowledging that the final process depends more on a common institutional vision than on overly precise planning techniques. The new facility will develop its best strategic plan by accurately incorporating the new institution's mission, faculty strengths, student market share, administrative history, and present financial resources.

A Mutual-Growth Model for Merging College Libraries

Comprehending the shape and characteristics of the type of merger model being contemplated is essential to the eventual success of those developing the learning-resource strategy. From the perspective of the library, growth mergers divide into two structural categories, with several variations within each—full merger or consolidation, and resource affiliation or consortial agreement.

The affiliation or consortium model allows both institutions, without moving to a full merger, to address selective goals such as increasing their market share of student enrollments in specific programs or achieving selected economies of scale and operating efficiencies. In a consortium, no institution is expected unilaterally to relinquish its autonomy or to unite its overall mission with those of the other members, yet each has a stake in the others' success. Information technologies often are central ingredients in attaining consortium goals. Conversely, a full merger or consolidation formally links the institutions in a permanent enterprise and produces a new institution in the process. A central goal of the mutual-growth concept is a stronger, more flexible institution that incorporates the academic heritage of all partner colleges or universities.

The first responsibility for each library director is to secure and disseminate accurate and timely information. It is sometimes surprising how uninformed library directors are about the focus and magnitude of the merger strategy in which they are involved. The library director must have comprehensive information in order to act with the authority needed by an organization undergoing significant change. Written agreements can help explain the merger plan, but grasping the agreement alone is not sufficient for successful directors. Ongoing conversations with the members of the Merger Task Force are also recommended as an information-gathering activity, for the more deeply the merger plan and process penetrates the institution's academic programs, faculty development, and student life activities, the greater the impact on the library and learning-resource center. During even a mission-complementary merger process staff members should be counseled to expect significant dislocation over the short term. The library director needs to cultivate and manage the expectations of faculty, students, and staff members with an effective model to maintain present collections, services, and budget priorities during the uncertainty of implementation.

Affiliations and Consortia

From an organizational point of view, affiliations and consortia, in the words of Rosabeth Moss Kanter, "do not lose their legal identity; they retain their own culture and management structure, and they can pursue their own strategies, but they reduce their autonomy by strengthening their ties with other organizations, thus sharing authority over certain decisions."[3] In an affiliation or consortial agreement, the partner institutions work toward mutually developed goals for the combined learning-resource facility. The success of their agreement will usually depend on accomplishing three objectives: (1) securing economies of scale through shared purchasing services, technical processing, subject collections, and staff specializations, such as conservation, com-

puter support and subject specialists; (2) accessing computer-based systems and services, including on-line public access catalogs and remote
data bases that neither partner could afford alone, individually; and
(3) increasing the speed and reliability of document delivery with dedicated vehicle support and electronic transmission systems, such as facsimile transfers.

In fact, recent mission-complementary affiliations and consortia
have accomplished some of the most significant advances in contemporary library services. The premier example is the Online Computer
Library Center (OCLC) founded by a consortium of fifty-four Ohio
facilities in 1972 to further user access to information resources and
reduce the rising rate of information costs. Despite such an accomplishment and *Library Literature*'s multiple listings of similar cooperative
projects, dozens of issues may still emerge to challenge a new partnership. For even a mutual-growth affiliation or consortium to survive, its
partners from the outset need to adopt and adhere to clearly defined
yet flexible guidelines based on capacities for organizational trust and
tolerance.

In this context, several recommendations have been drawn from
recent successful library and learning-resource consortia and affiliations. First, library staff members, particularly at mid-level and below,
should be offered the opportunity to work together while the details
of the final agreement are still in formation. As well, there should be
times arranged for unscheduled, casual interactions and community
development activities. Second, each library affiliation or consortial
agreement should be recorded in a separate written document. Language should be library based and as nonlegal as possible as an additional way to address concerns or cultural differences. Third, during the
course of implementation, initial circumstances and situations change;
although the library may not be central to the strategic revisions, it can
only facilitate the process for staff members to become familiar with
the traditions and concerns of their institutional partner during such
periods of uncertainty. Finally, if the affiliation or consortium is dis-
banded, the dissolution may not necessarily be evidence of failure. Partners may have achieved their original objectives, and further individual
development may call for only a periodic commitment to joint activities.

To a significant extent, affiliations and consortia have the best of
both worlds: independence, flexibility, and yet the scale to achieve what
could not be done alone. To be successful over the long term, however,
the library must continually reinforce the partnership's purposes and

articulate its benefits both on its own campus and within the broader institutional agreement.

Full Mergers and Consolidations

The merger or consolidation of two or more college libraries for growth purposes needs to accommodate the collections, services, staff cultures, and organizational structures of all partners. For the merger to be successful, the merged library must immediately ensure access to its collections and to the same levels of lending and information services. Additionally, the combined staff needs to have clear and authoritative information regarding new job descriptions and the broader implications for their offices. In some cases, new programs or advocacy groups may arise in search of collections, facilities, and services, while computer technologies may make other services obsolete. Key staff members may refuse to accept the merger's mutual-growth concept and purpose.

These challenges are addressed here through the description of a merger implementation plan. At this stage, the library director must be responsible for articulating the vision and purposes of a growth merger and its nuances, but the condensed time line will probably make it impossible to communicate all of the information to staff members and engage them in a dialogue of choices. Thus, a second issue that rapidly emerges is the need to translate the new institutional vision into the mission and goals of its library. The ability of the combined staff to articulate this immediate responsibility is often an indicator of the merger's long-term potential for mutual growth.

Implementing the Merger Plan

Satisfying user needs, securing financial support, and developing a broad-based personnel plan will be the principal first tasks. Concerns are three: (1) Who is now to direct the merged library? (2) What are the merged institution's mission, goals, and priorities, and how do they affect the new learning-resource "environment"? (3) What are the immediate plans for ensuring user services, staff support, educational programs, and financial stability? (A sample work plan and a brief case study of the merger of two college libraries appear later in this chapter.)

The Leadership Decision

Members of the Merger Task Force quickly realize that an ineffective strategic plan may leave one, two, or even three library directors in place and essentially at odds until the leadership question is resolved.

Matrix management—one director supervising functional areas, such as technical services or information services, and another supervising library projects, such as automation or building renovations—may seem attractive, but it neither clarifies overall authority and the balance of power nor integrates the library staffs with each other and then the merged staff with the larger organization.

The merged facility needs the vision of one director able to provide leadership in consonance with the new institutional mission, to set the library's long-term objectives, and to coordinate the facility's resources for higher levels of productivity. With this appointment, the merged college or university should also provide the new director with financial and organizational support to address immediate needs and to develop the library's plans for the future.

The Internal Scan

Once appointed, the overall director needs to formulate and conduct an internal scan to assess the primary conditions within the merged institution affecting the library. This process should acknowledge the legacy of each institutional partner while incorporating the major factors now influencing collections, services, and library staff, including curricula, teaching practices, facilities, and funding.

Initially, the library staff needs to become familiar with the merged institution's principal teaching and research purposes through a comprehensive review of all catalogues, reports, and written agreements covering the combined instructional programs and teaching faculty. Equally important, the library director should participate in departmental conversations and colloquia with senior faculty members and academic administrators to assess more formally the emerging institutional culture and its educational goals. During merger implementation, it is not unusual for differences to exist in the definition of those goals by administrators, faculty, and students while ongoing documents remain models of clarity. The director's task is to clarify areas of consensus and difference to achieve a synthesis that the merged facility can reinforce.

The internal scan constitutes the core of the library's strategic planning process, as it identifies situations and characteristics that demand immediate adjustment or change. In many cases, its results reveal issues requiring specific action rather than broader definitional parameters, as the scan focuses on the library's primary mission—support for the institution's curriculum, research, and instructional methodologies—in its assessment of the facility's services and resources to achieve these purposes.

Questions the combined staff must consider in preparation for the internal scan include:

—Who is generating the main use of the library?

—Where does this direct principal staff attention and energies?

—What on-site collections, by subject field and type (books, serials, documents, nonprints), presently support the merged institution's curriculum?

—What collections are inadequate?

—What collections no longer address curricular programs? What should be done with them?

—Are all collections readily accessible to their users?

—Given library and program locations, should separated collections be unified or unified collections separated in appropriate instances?

Components of the Internal Scan

What Will Students Learn?

In responding to the foregoing questions and in identifying the general scope and purpose of the merged curriculum, the following factors will need to be reviewed:

—Core curricular requirements

—Course listings

—Subject fields and majors

—Certification areas (technical, specialized, or professional fields with unique accreditation or licensing requirements)

—Student learning contracts

—Graduate level programs

—Community service programs for nonmatriculated students

—Distribution of faculty by subject fields and majors

The director and combined staff then must consider

—Off-site information sources: Does the library provide access to on-line data bases or other external collections sufficient to support curricular needs? Is the access timely and convenient in addressing student needs?

—Staffing needs: Are the credentials, professional experience, diversity, and personal commitments of present staff members sufficient to provide the necessary library services to support the merged curricula?

—Organization and administration: Are the library's personnel structures, prospective organizational model, and connections with the merged faculty adequate for inclusive participation in collections development and the selection of off-site information sources?

The quality of the new facility's services depends primarily on the availability of well-selected, well-maintained collections that provide materials in adequate numbers and formats to the curriculum and instructional programs. Staff analysis of information collected through the scan will place the highest priority on the maintenance of collections, materials, and the off-site information services most used by the combined students and faculty. At the same time, even in a growth merger, staff responses must be keyed to the fiscal goals and decision-making parameters of the Merger Task Force and administrative leadership team. If growth without facilities expansion and significantly increased funding are key institutional objectives, for example, the new team must adhere to them.

How Will Students Learn?

In identifying the principal instructional methodologies of the post-merger college or university, these areas will typically be considered:

—The formal learning environment: classroom lectures, seminars, laboratory research, independent study, collaborative projects, case studies, technologically-supported instructional materials

—The learning support environment: academic support tutorials, mentored study groups

—The research and scholarship environment: faculty professional activities, faculty development programs, experimental teaching models, research commitments and grants

In formulating the library's responses to these findings, the director and combined staff will need to consider the following points:

—The library's orientation and information literacy programs: Do the library's orientation, bibliographic instruction, and information literacy programs address emerging curricular goals? Are present instructional methodologies congruent with the merged institution's prospective educational goals?

—Reference and instructional services: Are staff members informed of and experienced with the merged institution's instructional methodologies and research commitments? Do planned service objectives and performance criteria adequately address student and faculty needs in the combined structure?

—Nonprint and media services: In what specific areas is the library expected to increase its development of nonprint collections, such as audiocassettes, videotapes, and compact disks, and to provide equipment for use of these materials? To what extent should the library support the use of audiovisual equipment and materials in the classroom? To what extent will the library assist faculty in the production of their classroom materials, such as transparencies and videotapes?

—Organization and administration: What are the academic priorities most clearly reflected in the library's administrative model? In what ways will the library administration provide leadership to support the new institution's principal teaching and learning styles?

—High-tech learning technologies: Does the library currently support academic programs through the use of technologies such as computer-aided instruction and interactive video; will they be appropriate to the merged institution's prospective methodologies?

—Does the library provide computer laboratories, scholars' carrels, and other technology-based work stations appropriate to pending curricular goals and objectives?

Where Will Students Learn?

In identifying the sites and mechanisms for delivering instruction on the merged campus or campuses, the following factors should be considered:

—Campus sites: Will there be a designated main campus site? Will the new institution maintain instructional areas, such as studios and laboratories, at more than one site? Will Local Area Networks connect classrooms, offices, and residence halls to library and information resources on the merged campuses?

—Off-campus sites: Will various academic programs require students to learn on more than one site to complete their degree requirements? Will curricular offerings be duplicated at each site or will some sites emphasize particular programs and deemphasize others? How will projected delivery and transportation systems link students and materials? Will there be experimental, distance, or telecommunicated course offerings?

—Facilities: How many full-service facilities to house collections and provide access and information services will the library operate? Will the library also plan to support limited facilities such as reading rooms, departmental collections, and data-base service centers?

—Equipment and computer support: If the facilities plan calls for library operations on more than one site, what equipment, such as photocopiers, microform reader-printers, terminals, and telecommunications connections, will be needed?

—Access Services: What will the merged library's service hours and schedules be? If the library is a component of the campuswide Local Area Network, does it feature such aspects as an On-line Public Access Catalog, E-mail, BITNET, Internet, and CD-Rom data bases? Are borrowing policies and loan periods adequate for the merged general and reserve collections? How will service hours and personnel schedules need to be adjusted? Are user-access photocopying services sufficient? Will interlibrary loan services be available on an equitable basis to students and faculty at all merger sites? Will new reciprocal borrowing agreements with external libraries be necessary to support both off-campus students and instructional sites? Will new document-delivery systems, such as facsimile transfer services, need to be enhanced between campuses and instructional sites?

Based on the analysis of several recent mutual-growth mergers, several final site-related observations may be helpful. First, even during the dislocations of a merger, students will continue to access the collections and services most convenient to them, whether that site is best suited to their needs or not. Second, off-campus satellite locations offering courses supported by workbooks and manuals, such as accounting, statistics, or chemistry, may require only minimal changes in on-site library collection support and thus be relatively unaffected, from a learning-resource perspective, by the merger process. Finally, humanities courses and programs, in particular, lag behind other disciplines in telecommunication support and technologies, as their content does not readily yield to keyword indexing. Depending upon the academic histories of the merger partners, this factor may most easily be addressed by a work group from the Merger Task Force's subcommittee on learning resources.

What is the Library's Funding Support?

To assess the fiscal status and growth potential of the merged learning-resource systems, the following materials will be helpful:

—A summary of the constituent libraries' current budget appropriations for staffing, operations, and resource acquisitions

—A description of the procedures and calendar to be used in preparing the new facility's overall budget request, along with the principal priorities to incorporate in the development of a funding strategy

—The merged institution's budget projections for income and expenditures for the current and two projected years

Additional merger-related financial opportunities may emerge in the application and coordination of computer and telecommunication technologies, in the development of more efficient procedures for standardizing routine library functions (acquisitions, circulation, interlibrary loan), and in the development of a more effective personnel plan to accomplish these procedures. Viewing the growth merger as an opportunity rather than a threat is a critical component to the staff's achievement of economies of scale while preserving an harmonious working environment.

What Are the Library's Staffing Goals?

In drafting the staff development plan for the merged personnel structure, the library director needs to review the following institutionwide documents relating to these issues:

—Overall organizational chart

—Ongoing staff personnel policies

—Faculty promotion and tenure policies

—Agreements with collective bargaining units

—Specific personnel policies defining compensation, leave, benefits, and retirement provisions

—Faculty and staffing budgets, including pertinent plans for the centralization or decentralization, by campus or department, of their administration

In assessing this information, the director needs to consider both broad indicators of long-term staff planning goals as well as merger-specific factors such as the grandfathering of benefits provisions or preexistent travel restrictions for some employees.

In my recent experience, even complementary mergers can create some personnel overlap of library staff functions or responsibilities, leading to potential dissatisfactions among some employees. As mentioned earlier, to the degree possible, the recommended procedure has been an agreement that no library staff member will be retrenched for merger-related reasons. A procedure or policy such as this can become especially significant in light of a task force's goal of mutual-growth for both of the institutional partners. This policy does not prevent, nor should the library leadership team feel restrictions concerning, the reassignment of many staff members' functions and responsibilities during the merger process and afterward. Those affected should also be offered support for professional training and development. Most library directors also aggressively reconfigure the newly combined staff during a merger process through strategic planning for retirements and administrative sabbaticals, leaves, and other reassignments.

Merger-related apprehensions may still permeate staff performance, however, and affect the essential task of staff team building. If a retrenchment does appear to be necessary, the process should follow guidelines developed by the director in coordination with the Merger Task Force and senior managers of the combined institution. This process should maintain as its highest priority the preservation of quality library services to students and faculty, and it should also include counseling and out-placement support for the designated staff member. Any traumas associated with the personnel decision may thus be addressed immediately and persuasively in order to encourage remaining staff members to invest in the new organizational structure and not to associate too readily the loss of one colleague with what may or may not have been circumstances connected to the merger plan.

Finally, the director needs to inform ongoing staff members of projected compensation and benefit plans, along with other new and revised personnel policies. Throughout a typical merger process, rumors will arise regarding promises and expectations connected to pending changes in personnel policies. These need to be responded to rapidly to allay anxieties and refocus staff energy and attention on building the merged facility and its services. The library director's commitment to clarify all staff members' understanding of their compensation packages, often on an individual basis, and to provide a transitional library personnel manual, will be a critical contribution not only to the welfare of the new library but also to the success of the larger merger model.

A Sample Library Work Plan

After analyzing the results provided by the Internal Scan, the next stage of the implementation process for the director, combined staff, and members of the task force will be to formulate a specific merger work plan to accomplish the following growth objectives:

1. Mission: the alignment, in substance as well as public perception, of the merged library's programs and activities with the combined institution's mission and goals

2. Access to library services: the development of facilities, services, a staffing plan, new technologies, and policies that ensure enhanced access to necessary services

3. Resources: the development of collections and technologies that reflect anticipated user demand and increase the facility's ability to meet student and faculty needs in the postmerger institution

4. Services to users: the development of enhanced lending policies, information services, orientation programs, and instruction in library use activities

5. Staff development: the development of programs for acclimating staff members to the merged facility and personnel structure, including the development of appropriate skills and competencies to achieve the library's service and productivity goals

6. Public relations: the development of a plan to foster the academic community's understanding of the merged library's abilities to meet student and faculty needs. Experience indicates that the reliability and timeliness of these communications shape the larger community's perceptions of the success of the merger concept in the learning resources area.

7. Assessment: the development of measures to be used to assist the library in evaluating its effectiveness in strategic planning and overall decision making

8. Network and consortial arrangements: the development of agreements and memberships that enable the combined facility and its users to obtain necessary information and resources from other institutions and off-site data bases. This may typically include an inventory of all current arrangements with bibliographic networks, regional networks, off-site data base subscriptions, CD-ROM acquisition and licensing arrangements, and document delivery services and be followed by the selection of those most affordable and suited to the needs of the merged college or university, including the negotiation of a member's fee as one institution.

9. Critical issues: the identification of critical issues, their expected time frames, and the team of staff and faculty members responsible for their resolution

10. Number of service sites: The identification of sites the library will support and the range of activities to be provided on each, including the delineation of staffing costs for each operation. Acquisition and technical cataloging services are not driven by the number of sites and can be centralized on one campus. Bibliographic networks such as OCLC and computer-based technologies of book and periodical vendors also typically support this consolidation, as membership fees and access changes can be substantially reduced for single-site use.

11. Cost accounting: the development of a model that incorporates the merger of lending and information services, acquisition and cataloguing services, and the library purchasing program

12. Business procedures: the designation of a set of procedures for overall purchasing and financial accounting. These functions may be integrated independent of cooperative acquisition and collection development agreements.

13. Public services: the development of a program to assure the continuation of lending, information, reference, and instructional services through the merger process and beyond. Every opportunity should be seized to enhance these areas during implementation while simultaneously addressing perceived concerns about potential reductions in service by assigning the most experienced employees on the combined staff to high-profile positions in the new facility.

14. Ownership: the designation of a special staff work group to clarify original ownership of the principal collections, endowments, and contributed materials, and to formulate a set of recommendations ad-

dressing the long-term implications of these agreements for the new facility and its operating plan

15. Assessment: the development of a basic assessment procedure to gauge early success and failure in merging library systems. A more comprehensive management information system should be planned and implemented after the completion of the merger process. Toward this end, staff members charged with assessment responsibility may find useful the assessment publication of their regional accrediting association and *Measuring Academic Library Performance: A Practical Approach,* by Van House, Weil, and McClure, published by the American Library Association.

A Mutual-Growth Case Study: Merging the Libraries of Cedar Crest and Muhlenberg Colleges

The case study briefly outlined in this concluding section describes more specifically the range of planning activities included in the merger for mutual growth of the college libraries. The guidelines drawn from this experience, which I have directed for over fifteen years, provide evidence that this strategy can open new horizons for library services to accomplish more while conserving resources and controlling costs.

The Cedar Crest–Muhlenberg merger was implemented through the founding of Educational Ventures, Inc., a nonprofit corporation formed by the colleges in Allentown, Pennsylvania, in 1973. The partnership goals of Educational Ventures, Inc., were (1) to increase overall educational opportunities at both colleges, (2) to build and capitalize on economies of scale in library operations, and (3) to explore through cooperative arrangements more efficient ways to address specific questions of student learning styles at both institutions. The intent of the organization has been to assist each college through cost economies and program enrichments to better realize its independent academic goals. Combined business and financial decisions are controlled by a board of directors, including the presidents of both colleges, four members from each board of trustees, and a faculty member and student from each institution. The organization is funded by annual apportionments from Cedar Crest and Muhlenberg with additional foundation funding for development purposes and specific projects.

The initial step in merger implementation for Educational Ventures, Inc., consisted of the appointment of a director of libraries. Interested candidates for the position were asked to submit working papers identifying the benefits and constraints of a joint library system, a plan of action, and a listing of crucial issues and challenges. With my 1973 appointment as director, I was given the authority to administer the libraries with reporting relationships to each college's academic dean and tangential relationships to the colleges' financial officers.

I then began the process of developing a strategic plan for the merger of the Cedar Crest and Muhlenberg libraries, which included the following components:

1. Mission: to make readily available to Cedar Crest and Muhlenberg constituents library materials in a cost-effective manner, proportionate to levels of demand and use, and to enable the combined faculty and students to develop skills in finding, using, and evaluating information

2. Site development: to maintain two full-service sites with a library building at each college, each of which maintained the same level of services and the same number of public services hours (105.5) per week

3. Centralization of services: to maintain technical (acquisitions, cataloging, and processing), interlibrary loan, and computer laboratory capacities in one of the two facilities

4. Bibliographic access: to maintain one On-line Public Access Catalog (OPAC), Union List of Serial Subscriptions, and Mediagraphy (Nonprint Index) identifying the libraries' holdings for its users at either campus location and within the OCLC and PALINET networks

5. Financial support: to fund staffing, collections, and program support for each college based on formula agreements. Support for staff compensation is based on a five-year, postmerger personnel plan and operating appropriations are based on use. Funding for collection development is based on collection development program agreements, and furnishings and equipment funding addresses building-specific upgrades and renovations.

6. Ownership: each college owns the facilities, collections, furnishings, and equipment it funds. Use dictates subject collection, furnishings, and equipment in the partner's facility.

7. Document delivery: The colleges operate a van service that carries specific materials as well as faculty and students to and from each campus facility twice a day.

The Cedar Crest–Muhlenberg merger has become a framework in which the libraries serve one educational mission and seek to achieve a unified set of academic and learning resource goals annually. The libraries are identified as a single entity in reports to Integrated Postsecondary Education Data System, accrediting agencies, and Higher Education Data Sharing Consortium.

While I was appointed to develop a new administrative and staff organizational plan, the Educational Ventures, Inc., board, recognizing that the loss of staff commitment could threaten the success of the mutual-growth model, immediately implemented a staff retention policy through which both colleges encouraged individual library staff members to contribute to the combined organizational planning effort and assured each that no one would be retrenched for merger-related reasons. At the same time, all staff members were counseled that as the merged library took shape, job functions would change and many would be expected to adjust their responsibilities with training and professional development support. In retrospect, within two years every staff member had been affected by a changed job function as computer-based cataloging, bibliographic support, and interlibrary loan systems were implemented, and technical and interlibrary loan services became merged and centralized.

As a result of the retention policy, staffing costs during the first three years of the postmerger structure remained approximately that of two independent libraries. Staff reductions were coordinated through voluntary departures and retirements, and within five years a combined staff of thirty-eight had been streamlined to twenty-six. Automation of selected library services played a significant part in reducing staff costs by 32% while increasing both staff productivity and flexibility. Automation also provided the means to standardize services and implement identical user procedures at both facilities. In this model, staffing schedules were also reconfigured to enable employees at all professional levels to learn the systems on both campuses by working at least one shift in each building every week.

CHAPTER TWELVE

Mergers, Institutional Advancement, and Alumni Relationships

Victor F. Scalise, Jr.

From the perspective of an office such as institutional advancement, the guiding principles to be followed by various campus constituencies within the mutual-growth process are sometimes not fully articulated at the outset of merger planning. Rather, they are shaped and coordinated with those of other offices through the stages of premerger discussion. This chapter outlines the goals and responsibilities of such institutional advancement components of a mutual-growth college or university merger as alumni affairs, institutional fund-raising, and public relations.

As Victor Scalise, Jr., notes in *Merging for Mission,* a book outlining a planning strategy for church mergers, more human and financial resources are available for strategic planning purposes in a mission-complementary growth merger than in the traditional bankruptcy-bailout model.[1] In the recent college and university mergers I have researched, for example, combined offices have been rapidly transformed in some cases from staffs of one or two persons to teams of a dozen or more. Single fund-raisers have become members of planning groups, including a vice president for institutional advancement, a director of advancement, an alumni fund director, and a director of public relations.

In my experience, growth mergers have provided resources to each combined institution that would have been impossible for them to marshal individually. Partially for this reason, a merger adjustment period is usually necessary as persons with particular abilities and aptitudes are matched with the new and ongoing tasks, but once this has occurred, an integrated, highly motivated team can often be identified. Even more

---

Shaping an Effective Institutional Advancement Team

Goals

- Blend institutional traditions
- Develop a new vision for the institution's future
- Coordinate expanded staff into more productive organizational unit
- Cast a new institutional culture

Challenges

- Overcome midmanagement fear of job and power loss
- Stimulate staff colleagueship and information sharing
- Articulate differing institutions' work styles and cultures
- Overcome tendency toward operational inertia and status quo
- Coordinate conflicting leadership styles

Methods

- Address loss of personal and place connections for many staff members
- Provide opportunities for intrainstitutional communication
- Offer vertical consultation between executive leadership and first-level managers
- Create opportunities for professional trust building

---

importantly, the combined institution is able to address challenges of a new magnitude with increased confidence and assertiveness.

In the merger of two or more institutional advancement offices, a number of immediate goals can be accomplished: traditions of both institutions can be joined and strengthened, an enhanced vision for the combined institution's future can be developed, an expanded staff can be shaped into a more effective organizational team, and a new institutional culture can be cast. Merging the personnel of two or more institutional advancement offices also presents a set of challenges: fear among many mid-managers of losing their position, power, and prestige; an instinctive unwillingness among some staff members to share "their" knowledge, even after the merger agreement has been signed; an inability of staff to work together toward common goals; a contentious attitude characterized in some merger plans by the statement, "We never did it that way before."

Meeting the Challenges of Merging Institutional Advancement Offices

Even among senior managers, including those on the Merger Task Force, fear of change is a natural aspect of the merger process. Successfully assessing and managing this fear is essential to the success of the mutual growth approach. Rosabeth Moss Kanter recently stated in the *Harvard Business Review:* "The chance to learn new skills or apply them in new areas is an important motivator in a turbulent environment because it's oriented toward securing the future. . . . The new security is not employment security (a job which is guaranteed under any circumstances) but employability security—increased value in the internal and external labor markets."[2]

Academic managers will observe the need to encourage staff as well as faculty members to discover the opportunities for professional growth to which they may be temporarily blinded by their fear of change.

Combatting the Loss of Personal Connection

As examples, two of the deepest concerns voiced by staff members during the merger process often emerge as the prospective losses of both individual and institutional identity. Paul Tournier in his book *A Place for You* has described the strong yearning for "place" increasingly found among contemporary individuals: "I sometimes wonder whether the relationship of people with places is not more stable than that with their fellow human beings. . . . All the places we have lived in remain with us, like pegs in a vast storehouse, on which our memories are hung. . . . We all have places which mean more to us than others, because of the particular experiences with which they are connected."[3]

Even during a growth merger, when alumni from both colleges sense a pending loss of "place," the Merger Task Force as well as both institutional advancement offices need to implement an immediate course of action that persuades the majority of alumni from both institutions they have gained a new educational home that will respond sensitively to the dislocation of their prior valued relationship.

Mount Ida College, during its mergers with Chamberlayne Junior College, the Coyne School of Electricity, the New England Institute of Funeral Service Education, and a division of Newbury College, provided several creative responses to the question of alumni relationships during the four merger transitions. From revenues received through the mergers, Mount Ida constructed on its campus new classroom and professional buildings that bear the names of two of its merger partners, Chamberlayne and New England Institute. New England Institute alumni participating in the annual fund and making a leadership contribution have had their names inscribed on a plaque at the entrance of the new Funeral Service Education Professional Building. Through the creation and installation of symbols like these, a number of hesitant alumni have come to believe that their connection to the Mount Ida campus will be a lasting one. Additionally, at the first united commencement of the three colleges, an alumnus from each institution who had contributed significant service over several decades was recognized with an honorary doctoral degree. These three immediate actions, coupled with a number of other measures, gave assurance to the majority of alumni that they had not lost their identity and that there continued to be a meaningful and authentic place for them within the evolving tradition of the merged institution.

In sum, managing change, shaping appropriate attitudes, and maintaining a focused identity are essential for an effective Office of Institutional Advancement during the uncertainties of merging. In many cases, they become critical necessities to achieve the new, complementary structure, as human factors more than financial considerations form the long-term foundation of the successful growth merger model.

Improving Operations during the Merger

The transitions accompanying a college or university merger also provide an opportunity to review and revise basic office procedures in institutional advancement. Chief among these are communication among colleagues, consultation with staff members, and the establishment of professional trust.

I have observed that anxieties during the merger's implementation can be reduced when colleagues in both advancement offices communicate accurately and frequently. They will find it useful to receive or participate in the development of a revised job description and to hear on numerous occasions what will now be required of them. This will assure a standard by which their efforts can be fairly evaluated and rewarded. It is surprising to note the lack of job descriptions on some campuses during crucial periods of transition.

Both formal and informal communication systems can also prove effective. A formal approach could include a weekly staff meeting for a prescribed period of time with a rotating chair and recorder. This enables each person to bring different talents and focus to the ongoing agenda and ensures that emerging objectives are not controlled by one vested interest during periods of anxiety and dislocation.

Overall, it would be fair to say that the single most important factor in successfully merging the Offices of Institutional Advancement is effective communication with all levels of the staff at all points of the process. Early success in this area usually dictates later levels of creativity and risk taking within the newly identified personnel structure.

Presidents involved in the growth merger process sometimes do not consult adequately with the combined leadership team or the members of the Merger Task Force. If the perception is that the institution's managerial system is autocratic or isolated, resentments and resistance grow and hinder the merger process. The belief develops and persists that decisions are made at the highest level of the institution with no consultation invited or expected. The members of the Merger Task Force must remain aware of these predictable process-related anxieties and coordinate ongoing forms of dialogue and consultation to involve those who feel excluded.

Even during a complementary merger, trust in the workplace assumes unprecedented dimensions. Staff members at every level of the college or university hierarchy need more than ever to believe they can trust those in positions of responsibility and authority. Administrative leaders, board members, and members of the task force initially symbolize the human dimensions of the merger concept to those in offices such as institutional advancement, and if personnel in an area such as this believe they are being both treated fairly and invited to participate, they will contribute significant hours to refine and implement the mission of the new institution.

Shaping the Identity of the Merged Institution through Institutional Advancement

From the perspective of their external constituencies, growth mergers can sometimes provoke a form of identity crisis on one or all campuses. In this sense, the Office for Institutional Advancement, particularly its public relations function, can serve as a microcosm of the larger structure, as its staff members direct the larger merger-related forces at work throughout the institution in their examination of such factors as separate institutional language systems, differences in organizational culture, and conflicting leadership styles.

The language of merging institutions is a study in itself. During the merger, each campus subgroup typically develops code words, and others remain outsiders until they decipher them. One of the major barriers to postmerger unity and progress can be simple terminology, and those on each campus need to learn the code words, as well as the nuances and priorities they indicate, before the new institution can move for-

---

Alumni Affairs Goals During the Merger Process

- Blend organizational models and institutional goals
- Develop plan of coordinated activities
- Manage new institutional expectations
- Implement coordinated information sources (newsletters, brochures, regional meetings, commencement ceremonies) for newly combined alumni

---

ward in an integrated manner. In our experience, this process can take as long as two to two and a half years.

The organizational cultures of the merging campuses often differ as well, even if their academic missions are complementary. One may be more formal than another and require more direct supervision of staff members or a more clearly defined workday. Other campuses may have chosen to operate with flexible hours in some or all offices to enhance productivity. On the merged campus, these styles can clash, and Merger Task Force members, as well as those in the merged Office of Institutional Advancement, need to exercise patience and innovation in forming a new and harmonious work force.

As noted in the chapter on presidential leadership, in developing the merger plan, perceptive chief executive officers recognize there may be an immediate need to adjust their leadership styles. It has been my observation that for a mission-complementary merger to succeed it will be necessary to acknowledge that effective leadership styles vary and that the two chief executive officers need to agree on coordinated and coherent institutional objectives that can be publicized immediately by the Office of Institutional Advancement to three constituencies: the campus community, the combined alumni, and the local and regional publics.

In creating a new vision for each institution through merger, the Office for Institutional Advancement needs to address and resolve these matters of language, style, leadership, and culture daily.

The Alumni Affairs Office and the Mutual-Growth Merger

Blending Organizational Models

Merger Task Force members rapidly recognize that alumni organizations vary in their nature, stages of maturity, and administrative structures. Three years before its merger with Mount Ida College, Chamberlayne Junior College hired a director of alumni who organized the alumni data base and files for the first time in the college's history and introduced a major publication, the *Alumni Bulletin*. Conversely, Mount Ida College's alumni association was comprised of a small, closely knit group of female graduates (the college had introduced coeducation in 1976) whose organization provided them with a strong personal social and support system. They were principally responsible for the planning and organization of a highly successful annual Alumni Day.

At the point of its merger with Mount Ida, the New England Institute of Funeral Service Education (the name taken upon merging by the New England Institute of Applied Arts and Sciences) maintained a model of an annually elected coeducational alumni board. Membership on the board was limited to two three-year terms. The election ballot and biographical sketches of candidates were distributed to all alumni through its *alumni bulletin* with elected alumni assisting the college in developing educational seminars as well as participating in fundraising. In fact, academic managers at all of the institutions involved in the Mount Ida mergers quickly grasped the importance of developing a comprehensive communication system with all of the merged alumni. The cornerstone of this strategy became the new biannual *Alumni Bulletin*. This publication became the most efficient means the institution had under its control to tell the story of the mergers. Perhaps the only section of any bulletin read by all recipients is the class news section, and for this reason, it became imperative to publish items on as many alumni as possible from each of the three merging traditions.

As a demonstration of sometimes hidden merger sensitivities, it was noted by some alumni regarding one recent issue of the *Alumni Bulletin* that one of the merging colleges had received a disproportionate amount of discussion. An analysis was done of the column space devoted to each alumni tradition, and it was acknowledged that less than 10% of that issue had been dedicated to the college in question. In areas such as this, alumni quickly and accurately perceive the quality of the new administrative team's commitment to their legacy by coordination of press coverage and publications. If financial support is to be secured during the uncertainties of merger, this commitment will have to be demonstrated accurately and often. Alumni will be naturally resistant to significant changes they cannot control that are accentuated by their perspectives of increased geographic distance and diminished daily contact.

In addition, no two institutional partners have alumni organizations and identities at the same stages of development, as their stages of development reflect each college or university's age and unique history and culture. For example, some participants in the merger of Mercer University and Tift College in Georgia initially stated that they had only one thing in common: roots in the Baptist church. Members of the academic communities at St. Mary's College and the College of St. Catherine in Minnesota came to a similar conclusion in affirming their common origins in Roman Catholicism. Echoing these concerns, Anthony Buono and James Bowditch wrote in their recent book, *The Human Side of Mergers and Acquisitions:* "An understanding of cultural similarities and differences between merger partners should be a significant component in selecting an appropriate integration strategy."[4]

Cultural differences such as these can produce a broad range of structures for alumni associations. Some may be in an early nurturing model, while others are approaching full maturity. In another instance, an association may have identified and empowered a dedicated group of volunteers who graduated within the same decade. For a successful and comprehensive alumni organization, however, the incorporation of members of diverse graduating classes will most likely be necessary. In addition, the association may want to consider systematizing its schedule for rotating leaders, for without such a system, an organization can become closed and limiting.

Some associations provide for the regular election of alumni and the clear rotation of leadership while lacking an effective model for the promotion of and participation in alumni reunions and social events, yet another aspect that needs to be developed and managed by a successful association. For example, in response to one organization's proposal to assimilate completely the alumni of a less-developed institutional model, the smaller group or clique may become threatened by the merger and its portent of significant change, including the possible dissolution of its board. Merger managers need to remain sensitive to the psychological needs of these alumni while candidly preparing for the few defections from the association which sometimes follow.

The recent Mercer University–Tift College merger produced a classic confrontation. Groups of Tift alumni rose up against both their own college and the university with which it had merged by bringing a law suit against the board of trustees of Tift College. The group won its case in a lower local Georgia Court before the state supreme court reversed that decision. Some Tift alumni, however, were undaunted and continued their resistance. The small dissident group organized its own alumni association, which continues to collect dues and publishes its own newsletter. Although this case may appear extreme, it demonstrates levels of institutional commitment and intensity that should be studied by all those contemplating a college or university merger. Idealism and rhetoric cannot mask the need to address institutional differences patiently and constructively.

At the same time, these dynamics and conditions present opportunities for new alumni involvement and growth. Often, rejuvenation in a given area of operations identifies one or more graduates who are ready to make a new contribution to their institution in the form of time, resources, or talent. Without the occasion of merger, their involvement might not have materialized. Where collegiate athletic team competition identification, single-sex history, or other differentiating characteristics exist, however, the strategic planning process needs to anticipate and incorporate these differences in order to achieve a harmonious outcome.

From a legal perspective, the members of both Institutional Advancement Offices and the Merger Task Force must also develop an appropriate set of organizational bylaws, while remaining aware of the potential pitfalls and residual liabilities arising from postmerger alumni functions and such activities as fund-raising events and telethons over which the institution may have little actual control. This residual liability problem may be addressed in several ways, including professional liability, property and general liability insurance coverage, indemnification and hold-harmless bylaw provisions, and self-insurance arrangements aimed at protecting the actively involved alumni directors, officers, and agents of the combined institution.

Beyond this, the institution must make clear the lines of reporting and protocol between the postmerger form of the alumni association and the new college or university to ensure against unauthorized pledges of credit or other commitments binding the institution to alumni fund-raising activities. Simply stated, alumni association leaders must define sponsored events so that the institution does not inherit liability exposure for association-sponsored events beyond the college or university's control and supervision. Whatever its format, the postmerger organization should develop standard liability waivers and disclaimers that, to the extent enforceable, can serve as effective deterrents to adverse liability exposure and resultant claims and demands.

Finally, the alumni leadership needs to give renewed consideration to their stewardship, policy-making, and managerial responsibilities through the coordination of activities such as an annual certified independent financial audit, corporate filings, public charities registration, and preservation of nonprofit tax status by avoiding political activities and unrelated business income. The discharge of all these responsibilities assumes due diligence, prudence, and the avoidance of conflict of interest.

Developing a Plan of Coordinated Activities

After issues such as organizational structure, personnel development, and legal liability have been addressed, task force members and advancement officers must undertake a second challenge: melding each association's schedule of annual activities into a cohesive whole. From the beginning of the planning discussions for the merger of St. Mary's– College of St. Catherine, those involved realized they were merging two diverse, although Roman Catholic, cultures. St. Mary's was a coeducational, occupational, and career-oriented two-year-school, while the College of St. Catherine was a liberal arts, four-year college for women.

Furthermore, because of a concern that St. Mary's might disappear in a merger with the larger, more well-known College of St. Catherine, the decision was made to maintain separate alumni organizations after the merger. This model has enabled St. Mary's graduates to preserve the heritage of their institution while communicating more directly and openly through their own organization their support for the growth merger concept. In more than one mission-complementary merger, alumni who are often willing and able to work for the common goals of the newly integrated institution still may desire the ongoing opportunity to work, plan, and socialize with graduates of their own degree programs. The experience of many merged institutions is underscored by the findings of Buono and Bowditch: "Cultural change is one of the most difficult transitions for people to accept. . . . There is no single model for change nor one intervention that will encompass all concerns and issues." [5]

With regard to planning functions, special events that elicit powerful memories and meanings for particular classes can provide a continuity that meets the special needs of one or more constituencies during the merger's implementation. In a recent notable example, Tift House was erected on Mercer University's Macon campus. At the dedication ceremony, the closing words of the individual presiding were followed by a sound familiar to all Tift graduates: the Tift Bell. The great Tift tradition of ringing the Senior Bell had been preserved by placing the instrument permanently in Tift House. Reenacting this tradition in a new context proved to be a powerful public act in the critical first year of their merger agreement.

To build an immediate investment in the growth merger strategy, experience recommends continuing the unique annual events of each alumni association, such as a fashion show, lecture series, awards banquet, or athletic event. This continuation of popular events sends a clear message that the constituency has not lost its collective identity. In fact, graduates from the other merging colleges or universities may discover by attending these events a deeper appreciation of the complementary qualities of their new educational partner. In this manner, the legacies of one institution assume new shape and character as members from the partner association contribute their ideas and experiences to the larger whole.

Assessing and Managing New Institutional Expectations

The expectations of various alumni constituencies vary based upon their institutional and association histories, and although it is unrealistic to convey to the membership of either association the notion that the merger will not produce significant change, alumni leaders from both campuses may serve as extremely effective change agents during the merger process through vehicles such as class correspondence and phonathons. These individuals can disseminate accurate and supportive information regarding the growth merger concept while simultaneously collecting the opinions of fellow graduates toward their former college or university's evolving identity.

In this context, patience on the part of alumni affairs and institutional advancement personnel may eventually persuade the majority of skeptical alumni more effectively than other, more aggressive campaigns by the members of the new administration or the Merger Task Force. Most graduates are ultimately won over by the goodwill of other graduates. As Buono and Bowditch observe, "Even in friendly mergers five to seven years must pass before organizational members feel truly assimilated into a new life."[6]

Invariably, no matter how well conceived the merger may be, there will be unmet alumni expectations. At the close of the merger process, participants measure their individual and collective expectations against the current reality reflected in the new alumni organization, and, similar to an employee's anxiety about job retention, some alumni leaders are bound to voice concerns about their place in the new organizational structure. Perceptive merger managers interpret these questions as reflecting a deeper and broader uncertainty about their connection to the new institution's emerging identity. One option to consider in building a well-coordinated merger transition in this area might be the formation of a multiple-alumni organization. The chair of each organization could serve on a joint council or commission that would reflect the unified institutional identity. Each chair might also be invited and encouraged to serve as a spokesperson for the overall association. Graduates from each of the merger partners would hold membership in both an individual institutional affiliate and the combined, expanded association.

In this model, each alumni affiliate group can fashion creative ideas for enhancing its individual traditions while still participating in the complementary overall association. Some combined colleges have inaugurated programs for designating an Alumnus of the Year award from each of the merger partners. In other instances, a university may carry the name and seal of one or more of its institutional partners on its new degree diplomas while also holding individualized commencement ceremonies to bring a special focus to the value and traditions of the constituent institution.

Sometimes an act or statement that appears insignificant in the moment has caused a reverberation and bonded new institutional partners more closely. Upon merging, St. Mary's College and the College of St. Catherine had decided to maintain separate graduation ceremonies; however, a small but powerful symbol of their joined community occurred at one of the first St. Mary's commencements. The president of the College of St. Catherine, the new chief executive of the overall institution, was participating in the exercises when a blind St. Mary's graduate processed across the stage with her guide dog. When the student and dog paused at the podium, the new president shook the hand of the graduate and took a moment to acknowledge the dog with an affectionate touch of recognition. In retrospect, this very brief gesture was perceived by many present and those who heard about it as an affirmation of involvement and respect as much as many of the community-building discussions that had preceded it. During the significant dislocations of the merger process, particularly among those who are not on a Merger Task Force or in leadership positions, small gestures and acts such as this one can subtly signal the intention and concerns of the partner college or university more strikingly than position papers and other merger documents. As Peter Cohen, chief executive officer at Shearson/Lehman Brothers recently commented on these situations, "There's no one grand stroke that does it. It's a lot of little steps."[7]

A continuing challenge, therefore, for the members of the Merger Task Force is to convince the alumni associations and the combined institutional advancement staffs that the merger's potential benefits outweigh its risks. For example, in the merger of Widener College, Brandywine Junior College, and the Delaware Law School, Widener was able to add the resources of both a school of law and junior college to create the critical mass of personnel and curricular resources necessary to achieve university status. The junior college and the law school gained central administrative resources and a general education core, as examples, which allowed them to expand within the new structure beyond their freestanding identities.

In the Tift College–Mercer University merger, although the transition has been a difficult one for some members of the Tift alumni association, Tift was nevertheless able to preserve its emphasis on quality women's and teacher education within a new university setting, while Mercer gained the resources of an additional campus and accomplished faculty personnel in Tift's acknowledged areas of strengths. In the mergers of St. Mary's College and the College of St. Catherine, of Gannon University and Villa Maria College, of Iona University and Elizabeth Seton College, and of Mount Ida College and Chamberlayne Junior College, the larger institution in each instance gained a curricular identity in an academically complementary area.

In these instances, the addition of Elizabeth Seton College provided Iona University with a new focus on, and school of, associate's degree studies. Villa Maria College brought to Gannon's university environment a new emphasis on nontraditionally aged, part-time, and female students. Chamberlayne Junior College contributed a reputation as one of New England's quality schools of commercial design to Mount Ida's academic structure; in return, Mount Ida was able to give Chamberlayne students a new professional building, a residence hall, a dining facility, and, most importantly, the opportunity to earn a bachelor's degree in its two-plus-two academic structure without having to transfer, losing credits in the process, to another institution.

It is instructive in this context to review an example of a higher education merger that did not achieve its growth objectives from the perspective of the Alumni Affairs Office—the merger of Boston College and Newton College of the Sacred Heart in 1974–77. In retrospect, their planning strategy highlights the fact that not all college and university mergers of the past two decades have been based on *mutual* growth. Realistically, there will always be a percentage of higher education mergers, similar to agreements in the corporate sector, which are principally institutional acquisitions. Although this book is dedicated to examining the more recent phenomenon in higher education management of voluntarily joining two or more complementary institutions to stimulate forms of mutual growth, I have been asked increasingly during my research by those contemplating or developing a higher education merger strategy to describe an example either of a model that was not mutual growth in origin or of a plan that failed in strategy or implementation.

In U.S. higher education, there has always existed a pejorative, non-collegial quality to the concept of acquiring another college or university. *Merger* is typically the word employed in these instances, often inaccurately, for frequently more than adequate signs are revealed in the early discussions to indicate the long-term objectives of the institution initiating the process. In the arrangement between Newton College of the Sacred Heart and Boston College, merger does not, in retrospect, accurately convey the nature of the model. Rather than being enhanced educationally or in reputation, Newton College of the Sacred Heart disappeared as a partner institution during the process of being "taken over," in the words of one observer.

Although both colleges shared a Roman Catholic heritage similar to other merging institutions discussed in this chapter, the similarity extends no further. During the 1960s and 1970s, Boston College was viewed as little more than a parochial school, although enterprising in nature. Conversely, Newton College of the Sacred Heart had maintained a reputation for quality liberal arts education and selectivity, academically and socially. Since 1977, Boston College has developed into a powerful institution with national, research-university aspirations and the ability to raise academic standards consistently, whereas Newton College of the Sacred Heart is no longer a part of the New England higher education world; its campus remains, but only to serve as the site of the Boston College Law School and Fine Arts Department.

Looking back, the results of this purported merger were predictable and understandable. Even though its employees at the time were provided for with generous packages of support, Newton College of the Sacred Heart was acquired by a more powerful, entrepreneurial institution and, in the process, suffered its educational demise. Some alumni still recall with sadness the loss of their institution's identity, while many Boston College graduates now view this transition as one of the necessary components in the resource development program undergirding their institution's national reputation.

Even if some of the growth mergers discussed in this book, by consensus of those involved, have exceeded participants' expectations, it is more important for the majority of students, staff members, and alumni to believe simply that their expectations have been met through the mutual-growth approach. Unfulfilled expectations among some constituencies will be an inevitable aspect of each merger's implementation; however, from the perspective of the Alumni Affairs Office, for staff members and recent graduates who are willing to demonstrate trust, patience, and accommodation regarding a complementary educational partner, the academic and financial resource rewards can increase exponentially.

Fund-raising Challenges in the Mutual-Growth Context

I have observed in several recent merger plans that members of the Merger Task Force and each Institutional Advancement Office rapidly recognize the point of a merging as a propitious moment to expand a heretofore limited program of institutional fund-raising. Before raising of any dollars connected to the growth merger concept, however, experience suggests the importance of cultivating its human rather than financial resources.

If a plan is not immediately implemented to address office-based concerns such as job security and consensus regarding basic fund-raising themes, they will become precisely the reasons why the combined college or university loses some of its most talented fund-raisers during the merger process. Paradoxically, at the moment of a new institution's greatest fund-raising opportunities, staff members may find themselves unsettled and distracted from the goal of developing the model for a more powerful, broad-based capital campaign. The challenge for directors of advancement will be to balance a necessary focus on expanded budgets and long-range planning with that of forging a productive team spirit among anxious staff members. Buono and Bowditch discuss this set of issues in their chapter, "The Human Toll of Mergers and Acquisitions": "While organizations may give lip service to the idea that 'people are our most important asset,' research indicates that human resource considerations play a relatively small role in merger . . . decisions." As a consequence, they report, "research . . . has shown . . . the better employees, whose skills and expertise are valuable to the company, are the ones most likely to leave. These people tend to be quite marketable and enjoy the most career options. . . . The most expensive aspect of human resources turnover is replacement."[8]

Academic managers and the new institutional advancement team have a one- to three-year period in which to articulate and implement a personnel development plan that uses the momentum generated by merging. Postmerger colleges or universities that remain dependent on a tuition-driven philosophy quickly develop strategies to cultivate sources of additional revenue.

Initial Fund-raising Strategies

Once combined, the new team of fund-raisers is likely to go through several stages of adjustment before it is prepared to dedicate its full energy and attention to the primary task of raising capital for the new

> **Fund-raising Challenges in the Mutual-Growth Context**
>
> - Retain loyalty of past givers
> - Transfer loyalties of merged alumni
> - Coordinate separate alumni and other fund-raising constituencies
> - Develop postmerger support from alumni who have never contributed
> - Cultivate support from nontraditional populations, such as female and commuter graduates

college or university. It may take as long as two or more years of intensive staff development before the new team feels unified and focused on its postmerger goals and objectives. Once through this transition period, the group may begin to address the following questions:

—How can we retain the loyalty of past givers whose institution is no longer "primary"?

—How can we involve merged alumni in fund-raising when their institution had maintained no systematic program of activities?

—How can we develop support from alumni who may never have been solicited?

—How can we cultivate new contributions from the more nontraditional institutional advancement populations such as commuter and female students.

Experience has confirmed that the key to growth in alumni contributions following a merger remains a system of clear and credible communications. An efficient Institutional Advancement Office will often implement a highly publicized plan of "new" alumni invitations, visitations, telephone interviews, recognition dinners, and awards ceremonies, all of which are then documented in an enhanced alumni bulletin.

Successfully Transferring Alumni Loyalties

For all of its uncertainties and public relations challenges, a college or university merger can provide a critical mass of experienced personnel to increase the range of financial opportunities for the new institution, including the development of a comprehensive annual fund, a capital drive, corporate and planned giving programs, and federal grant applications.

These larger institutional initiatives require patience on the part of entrepreneurial advancement officers, however, as they acknowledge the fact that institutional mergers subvert business as usual for fundraising at the very point of providing the potential to attract greater levels of alumni commitment to the new institution's expanded mission.

Staff members need to let graduates move forward at their own pace regarding the merger process and to understand the larger importance of cultivating alumni loyalty to the new institution over requiring an immediate compliance with new check-submission procedures, for instance. Although this approach might seem to contradict some of the public relations guidelines discussed later in this chapter, it only serves to reinforce them through encouraging the forms of support alumni are most comfortable providing during the merger's period of greatest dislocation.

Retaining Seasoned Insiders at Board and Staff Levels

In some merger models, it is fair to expect annual giving to decline for an unspecified period due to the reasons discussed earlier. An effective response on the part of the new director of advancement can be the retention and promotion of veteran members of both staffs, where appropriate, to positions of leadership in the postmerger personnel structure.

In most cases, following the model for integrating the combined boards of trustees discussed in chapter 3, it will be strategically important to coordinate the partners' efforts for a meaningful program of fund-raising eventually to flourish. Because one merger partner may have had a history of trustees as leadership givers and another may have enlisted trustees principally to be financial contributors, the simultaneous and collegial integrations of the board and the advancement leadership teams can set examples for broader aspects of the implementation plan.

Finally, the director of the new advancement team should prepare its members for a sense of potential postmerger letdown, or even failure, during which the perception emerges that the new college or university still must overcome many of the challenges that spurred its constituents to consider merging in the first place.[9] Concerns such as a declining pool of college applicants, the rising cost of employee health care plans, shrinking federal aid revenues, and increasing requests by municipalities for payments in lieu of taxes are a few of the factors that constrain large advances in annual giving while simultaneously causing the need for them. Merger Task Force members, and more specifically, new directors of institutional advancement, cannot allow themselves to be lulled into thinking their strengthened, mission-complementary college or university has resolved all of its longstanding problems by merging, or that its need for aggressive development dollars has been reduced. In fact, the reverse is true. For a period of time, the postmerger institution is as vulnerable or more vulnerable than were its constituent partners and can be counted on to demonstrate an even more significant need for alumni loyalty, increased annual giving, and positive public relations.

The Public Relations Office in a Higher Education Merger

Colleges and universities may vary as to the placement of their office of public relations. Many incorporate this function into institutional advancement, but, regardless of location, strong, well-coordinated public relations and information services have been focally important to the long-term success of both the concept and individual plan of almost every mutual-growth merger I have researched.

To the degree that public perception affects the reality of college or university merger negotiations, the evidence is clear that fundraising campaigns are driven by a positive picture of the institution's place in the higher education marketplace. In this manner, public relations and information services play an influential role in creating a supportive merger environment. For both institutional communities, the prospect of merger typically raises anxieties over loss of job security and credit disenfranchisement; even complementary partnerships can quickly dissolve when a fragile trust is confronted by press reports of impending institutional discontinuance and loss of identity.

Starting at the board level, trustees must adhere to consistent rules of public information dissemination through faithful observance of public participation, prudent disclosure, and open dialogue. As a practical matter, merger discussions involving real estate and campus facilities acquisitions must, of necessity, be carried out in executive session with subsequent reports to the community.

For the faculty, administrators, and students involved, it will be important for members of the various Merger Task Force subcommittees on curriculum, faculty welfare, and student life to be included in key discussions of the merger's larger objectives so that an appropriate degree of vertical integration may be achieved both during the implementation process and within the new structure. One year before the New England Institute–Mount Ida merger, for example, the agreement had been reached in principle and a thorough public relations program had been developed. Through the *Alumni Bulletin*, alumni were informed of the pending merger and its benefits, and a college catalogue supplement informed potential students of advantages to the anticipated plan. Several professional funeral service journals also carried advertisements and articles explaining the pending strategy. At conferences, conventions, and alumni reunions, both presidents shared the educational rationale and justification for the growth merger concept.

In all three of Mount Ida's mergers, a well-coordinated public relations and information effort was eventually reflected in international news publications (the *London Times Higher Education Supplement*), national higher education news media (the *Chronicle of Higher Education, Community College Week*), regional journals (the New England Board of Higher Education's *Connection*), and local newspapers (the *Boston Globe* and *Boston Herald*).

More importantly, however, students, faculty and staff received ongoing task force reports and invitations to all-college meetings to clarify the merger's overall time line. This communication resulted in a sense of increased ownership of the new model, no doubt supported by the preservation of prior institutional name identity with Chamberlayne, Coyne, and the New England Institute continued as freestanding schools under the administrative and financial aegis of Mount Ida College.

In contrast, the attempted merger of the University of Detroit, Mercy College, and Marygrove College appeared to some observers to be sidetracked by an uncoordinated series of press leaks that ultimately witnessed a departure from the proposed merger plan by Marygrove, leaving only the University of Detroit and Mercy College as active participants. In the Tift College–Mercer University merger discussed earlier, various alumni publicly attacked the plan before and after its implementation, and in a later stage of the process faculty groups raised concerns in the press regarding the massive growth of Mercer University potentially at the expense of its own constituent colleges. In each of these mergers, press coverage periodically exerted a negative, even adversarial, impact on the original mutual-growth objective.

In sum, an effective public relations strategy will build upon both the reality and the perception of mission complementarity and shared institutional vision between the prospective merger partners. If students, faculty, and staff members are faithfully kept informed and experience a natural affinity with their institutional partner, the merger concept typically gathers increasing support. Based on my research, if skillfully formulated, the overall public relations program serves as an influential force within the larger growth merger process.

A mutual-growth merger produces a more powerful, flexible structure that poses significant challenges to an alumni association, public relations office, and ongoing fund-raising campaigns. The merger process should be expected to alter familiar agendas, but, if managed prudently by the chief executive officer, Merger Task Force members, and the director of institutional advancement, it can also enfranchise previously uninvolved graduates, increase levels of annual giving over prior combined totals, and provide a source of unprecedented media attention.

Experience suggests nine strategies that stabilize and enhance the combined Office of Institutional Advancement in a mutual-growth model:

1. From the earliest merger discussions, emphasis should be placed on developing new institutional advancement objectives as *common* goals to be achieved by the combined staffs of the two institutions.

2. Carefully managing the simple fear of change in all its potential manifestations, even among senior staff members, should be an early focus for the new director of institutional advancement.

3. The loss of valued, familiar relationships with a campus, a staff member, a building, even a former address can become negative forces in the merger for various alumni and should not be minimized. Rather, alumni affairs officers should respond with a program of expanded services in the postmerger structure including opportunities for new friendships and activities reinforcing the mutual-growth approach.

4. Senior staff members in the restructured Institutional Advancement Office may use the merger process proactively as a quality control instrument to review and improve the ongoing communication and consultation techniques presently being used by the combined staffs.

5. As early in the premerger discussions as possible, it is wise to acknowledge that new educational and corporate identities need to be developed and that managing the mission of the emerging educational enterprise involves refashioning its academic culture for alumni and faculty members simultaneously.

6. In most cases, constituent alumni associations are in different stages of maturation and development, and the merged staff in alumni affairs will need, while streamlining services and activities that overlap, to preserve and distinguish the distinctive histories of the constituent alumni organizations.

7. Even though the expectation may be that fund-raising levels will decline for a transitional period, doubling the number of development professionals through a complementary merger, if only for a transi-

tional period of consolidation, is a rare opportunity in the life of even a major university. With this expanded human resource base, the combined institution may seize the moment of mutual growth to implement an aggressive program of institutional development activities while simultaneously articulating the educational mission of the new institution to the community.

8. In order to achieve these goals, the new director should not hesitate to promote seasoned members of both advancement staffs as a public confirmation of the new institution's commitment and loyalty to those who made the merger concept a reality.

9. The public relations theme that has proven most effective in the merger models researched is one that remains true to its mutual-growth, mission complementary foundation through the enhancement of academic quality and educational services as expected results of the merger process.

CHAPTER THIRTEEN

An International Perspective: Recent Growth Mergers in British Higher Education

Paul Temple and Celia Whitchurch

As the form and frequency of college and university mergers have been greatly influenced by the history, organization, governance, and financial structure of the system of higher education in question, we have organized this chapter to emphasize for readers in both Britain and the United States key aspects of the British system relevant to a study of recent mutual-growth mergers within it.

The structure of higher education in Britain has been altered radically by the Further and Higher Education Act of 1992. As this chapter necessarily examines interactions that took place earlier, however, it is important to realize that before 1992, higher education in Britain—undergraduate and postgraduate studies, and some work at slightly less advanced levels—was provided by two parallel systems: universities and polytechnics. All 140 or so of these educational organizations (55 universities; 80–90 polytechnics that following the 1992 act have been redesignated as universities) were (and are) heavily dependent on government funds channeled primarily through two funding councils, one for each sector. Private institutions not reliant on government support, a central component of the U.S. model, are numerically insignificant in the British system.

The pre-1992 pattern of British higher education described here dates from the 1960s, when government policy led to a major expansion of numerous existing universities, the creation of eight completely new universities, the transformation of a number of technologically based colleges into universities, and the merging of a large number of other institutions into some forty polytechnics. This remarkable and rapid process of expansion and change is associated with the report of a 1963 royal commission chaired by Lord Robbins.[1] An important outcome of this report was the establishment of a university/polytechnic divide—which became known as the "binary line"—as a policy parameter that became a fundamental characteristic of the organization of British higher education. Under this binary policy, universities were to concentrate on "academic" students and "pure" research, while polytechnics focused on the practical and applied. Although this division became somewhat blurred over time, it created a two-tiered structure with the widely held perception that universities were "on top." This perceived superiority of universities was reinforced by the histories of the two sectors in matters of funding arrangements, internal governance, and degree-granting powers. Until the passage of the 1988 Education Reform Act (the legislation that began the process of change leading to the 1992 act), another aspect of the binary policy was particularly relevant to the prospect of mutual-growth mergers in Britain.

Universities, although largely dependent on central government money, were fully autonomous under their royal charters, while polytechnics continued under the control of the elected local government bodies in whose areas they were located. This fact became particularly irksome to polytechnic managements when, as increasingly happened, a polytechnic aspiring to a national or even international reputation was governed by a small local authority whose educational expertise was largely in the operation of primary and secondary schools. Prior to the 1988 Education Reform Act, this relationship made the local authorities key players in any merger proposals involving polytechnics, as they were deeply involved in the policies and finances of each institution. As part of a wider restructuring of educational policy on all levels, the 1988 act removed polytechnics from the control of local authorities and made them similar but not identical to universities in terms of government and funding. Local authorities retained responsibility only for colleges teaching courses below the undergraduate degree level.

Expansions initiated in all sectors of higher education during the 1960s were, in many cases, the first phases of planned long-term developments. A series of continual cutbacks in government funding from the mid-1970s onward, however, reflecting both a weaker national economy and revised political priorities, seriously disrupted almost all of these plans. (Figure 13.1 illustrates the reduced level of capital investment in real terms from the late 1970s.) The overall result was that many universities and polytechnics were frozen in an uncompleted state with unviably small departments, inadequate buildings, and problematic cost structures. (A similar picture emerges from a study of developments in other European countries.)[2] Thus, the stage was set in British

£ million

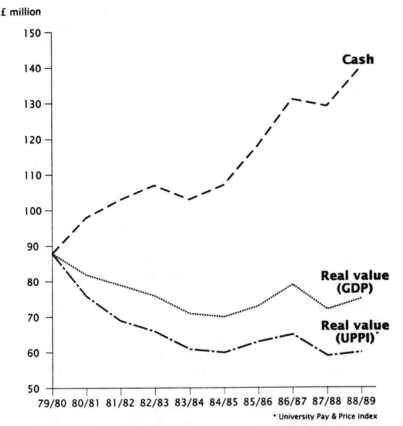

Figure 13.1. Government Capital Investment in British Universities, 1979/80–1988/89. The GDP (gross democratic product) line shows how capital investment has varied in terms of inflation in the economy generally, while the UPPI (University Pay and Price Index) line shows how it has affected universities more particularly. *Source:* Association of University Teachers, *Investment in Universities,* 1989.

higher education for growth merger proposals that could effectively rationalize this unbalanced picture.

The Pressures to Merge

In addition to these structural issues that could encourage or discourage university mergers, a number of other notable factors were impacting on British higher education in the 1970s and 1980s. Underlying the great expansion of the 1960s had been the population bulge of children born in the immediate postwar years for whom many parents had developed increasingly ambitious expectations. In contrast, later demographic projections showed a steep downturn in the number of eighteen-year-olds from the mid-1980s (figure 13.2), from which the assumption was widely but erroneously drawn that fewer places would be needed in higher education.[3] In fact, a major portion of the decline resulted from a reduction in the birth rate among groups mainly in manual occupations whose children have not traditionally participated to a significant extent in higher education. The decline in the number of eighteen-year-olds from families with professional backgrounds was relatively small, and offset by a rising participation rate. Even so, this new national demographic picture was influential in altering perceptions about the demand for higher education, and in increasing politicians' willingness to pay for its further expansion.

At roughly the same time—from the mid 1970s—successive governments began to adopt more questioning and critical attitudes toward public spending on higher education than had been apparent in what, with hindsight, appeared as the "golden age" of the 1960s. The tacit understanding that government would fund higher education but would not otherwise involve itself in its management had broken down; academic autonomy was no longer accepted as a desirable end in itself. This evolution became sharply apparent when the *Report of the Steering Committee for Efficiency Studies in Universities,* under the direction of Sir Alex Jarratt, appeared in 1985.[4] Although commissioned by the universities themselves, it was widely seen as a response to government concern about the effectiveness of their planning and managerial operations, and, although criticized by some for importing a commercial management model into academic life, it has since provided a baseline of effective managerial standards. Across the binary line, a joint government/local authority body, the National Advisory Body for Local Authority Higher Education, was organized in 1982 to oversee the funding and planning of the polytechnics, again in response to government concern about value for money and effective planning in higher education.

An increasingly managerial approach to the operation of higher education, along with heightened political concern about its costs and effectiveness, naturally focused attention on existing institutional patterns and on the emerging possibilities of achieving both strategic growth and enhancement as well as increased operational effectiveness through the mergers of universities or polytechnics. Viewed from a purely academic standpoint, mergers had also begun to look more attractive as the costs of undertaking satisfactory advanced teaching and research in science and technology escalated, and as the importance of having stronger academic teams to conduct research of an international

thousands

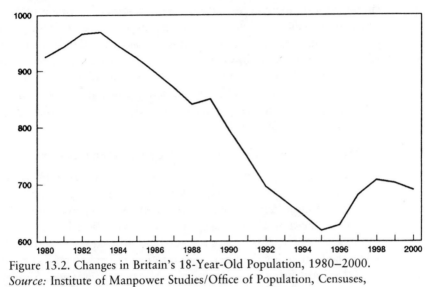

Figure 13.2. Changes in Britain's 18-Year-Old Population, 1980–2000.
Source: Institute of Manpower Studies/Office of Population, Censuses, and Surveys.

standard came to be viewed as an institutional asset from external as well as internal perspectives. In fact, this particular pressure is likely to be further intensified as a result of the new government-backed, formula-based research funding mechanisms now operating on both sides of what was the binary line.[5] Such relatively rigid approaches determine an institution's entitlement to public funds on "objective" criteria such as numbers of students and their subjects of study, together with a basic level of support for research, in which a higher level of research quality secures a higher level of financial support. In universities, detailed "research selectivity" exercises are conducted by the funding council to grade the research quality of all departments.[6] This formula-based funding model contrasts dramatically with the incremental, some would say more collegial, funding model employed on both sides of the binary line before the 1980s and clearly provides incentives for institutions to grow in size, thereby reducing overhead costs per student, and to increase research quality.

The binary line, as both concept and reality, has no doubt hindered the development of several transbinary, growth-oriented merger proposals, while in the university sector the strength of institutional identities, fostered by a tradition of autonomy, has stalled other merger plans in their discussion stages. However, the mission-complementary, mutual-growth merger strategy has stimulated increasing interest among academic staff and administrators as a planning instrument that can simultaneously increase the size of funding sources, formula or otherwise, for expanded teaching and research, as well as provide the increased managerial accountability now being required of British higher education. In what follows, we present several examples of creative academic merger models, and we indicate how mutual-growth mergers can create stronger, more effective academic institutions. We begin with a typology of the factors that have affected the shape of recent higher education merger proposals in Britain.

Mergers as a Manifestation of the Changing Environment

British institutions of higher education are, as we have shown, part of a highly structured national education system that owes its present form to tradition and postwar government policy. Perceptions of the binary line became clearly associated with institutional status as well as function. Polytechnics were regarded as "aspiring to be universities" when they expanded their activities into less practical and less technological subject areas and developed a research orientation. Similarly, colleges of professional and continuing education "aspired" to become polytechnics by undertaking more advanced level teaching. Within each sector has also emerged an unofficial yet powerful pecking order, with universities now publicly ranked on an annual basis according to research performance, attractiveness to students, and ability to earn income from industry, among other factors (see table, p. 215).[7] These elements of status consciousness have obviously affected considerations surrounding the concept of complementary mergers within the British system.

Within the university sector, the traditional concept of an institution as offering a wide and balanced range of subjects at a highly specialized level remains strong. Oxford and Cambridge remain in both popular perception and subconsciousness the ideal of what a British university should be. This has meant that universities have, by and large, tried to be all things to all people and have assumed, given the resources available, highly ambitious missions and programs. These lingering attitudes and beliefs have been critical factors in influencing searches for suitable merger partners.

The 1980s, however, saw a freeing of the educational environment to accommodate the stronger interplay of market forces. The political and financial climate of the decade posed many questions for the British higher education system as it moved from an environment of expansion through steady state, to the contraction of its resource base. At the same time, institutions were expected to respond to pressures to diver-

The Top Ten British Research Universities		
Rank	Institution	% Score
1	Cambridge	93.08
2	Oxford	91.43
3	Imperial College	91.25
4	University College London	85.83
5	Warwick	81.54
6	London School of Economics	80.00
7	Bristol	75.38
8	Manchester Institute of Science and Technology	73.85
9	York	73.85
10	Manchester	71.20

Note: These research universities were ranked following an analysis of the 1989 research selectivity exercise.

Source: Universities Funding Council.

sify their activities by introducing new modes of delivery such as part-time teaching models, credit-transfer provisions, and new areas of study. Such attempts to diversify at a time of financial contraction created tensions within many institutions. These tensions led to feelings of instability as universities experienced both the threats and opportunities market pressures were now posing, and this in turn contributed to a climate of change. Once this climate had been established, exploratory talks between institutions on both sides of the binary line became more common. Merger proposals can, therefore, be seen as one manifestation of an increasing turbulence in British higher education. That such talks should occur (and we know only of those made public), even though in many instances no definite proposals may have emerged, indicates an acknowledgment of the significant possibilities that might be brought about by strategic mutual growth. In Britain, we may view complementary institutional mergers as a particular form of the management of change, and in implementing them, academic managers must cope with classic "change" problems.[8]

Factors Conducive to University Mergers in Britain

The trigger for a higher education merger is likely to be found in a combination of external pressures and local aspirations; however, even if the merger plan is an attractive one from the missional and financial viewpoints, it will most likely only be realized if geographical locations are also proximate. Improved communications technology makes distance less of a challenge, as in the mergers of some campuses within the Australian and U.S. systems which were hundreds of miles apart; however, in Britain, partly because of the higher density of both population and of higher education institutions, colleges and universities tend to be more merger sensitive if they are in closer contact with a partner, a factor that facilitated several University of London mergers in the 1980s.

Questions of institutional viability and reputation also form major considerations, although the personalities and inclinations of the institutions' chief executive and academic officers are likely to have a stronger influence on the final outcome. Their perceptions of the advantages to be gained are crucial, although both sides do not have to see the *same* advantages. From our observations of British higher education, we have identified the following typology of external and internal factors that, to varying extents, have stimulated the mutual-growth approach to institutional mergers in recent years.

Internal factors

—Desire to concentrate academic, personnel, and financial resources

—Desire to adjust academic profile and market niche

—Desire to diversify existing degree programs in response to widening markets

—Ambitions to improve status in institutional rankings, nationally and internationally

—Desire to achieve economies of scale, such as through common library, computing, or purchasing services

External factors

—Decline in the number of traditional eighteen-year-old students (see figure 13.2)

—Reductions in government funding

—Search for new, alternative sources of funding

—Change in markets, such as the greater demands for part-time and modular courses to attract mature and nontraditionally qualified students

More detailed and pragmatic considerations having to do with the relativities between institutions become factors once negotiations are underway. These are closely allied to questions of competitive advantage and incentives, and they can have a decisive effect on the outcome of some negotiations no matter what forces have brought the institutions together. In this respect, the following key issues appear to us to be critical:

Institutional culture, mission, and objectives. This might include a strong teaching or research orientation, an interdisciplinary focus, or an "enterprise" culture that conveys the dominant identity of the institution. Collectively, these beliefs, aspirations, and expectations hold the pulse of the college or university, and sensitivities to these factors are likely to be strong. Successful negotiations depend on the opportunities offered by a potential merger partner to enhance these characteristics in the contexts of job security and career opportunities.

Academic quality and reputation. As noted earlier, British institutions are highly conscious of their quality in relation to each other, as evidenced by research selectivity exercises, competition among school leaders for places, and the standards of achievement expected of applicants. The effect of a merger, including one for mutual-growth purposes, on their ranking in the system is therefore likely to be considered extremely carefully. The mix of arts and sciences is regarded as particularly significant for an institution's standing, and it may wish to enhance its academic position by offering a balanced range, thereby creating new dynamics between subject areas, or to pursue a more highly specialized direction in technology or business, for example.

Size. Hitherto, institutional viability has depended on adequate government funding related to the factor of size. In the move from a more elite to a more diverse system, questions of size will increasingly become topics of debate. In contrast to the U.S. model, universities in Britain of fewer than 4,000 full-time equivalent students are considered small. Schools of this size may need to develop a strategic focus on doing a smaller number of things well academically in order to preserve financial and academic viability. Becoming larger may mean achieving critical mass and economies of scale, or, more critically, diffusion of effort and uncoordinated diversity.

Leadership styles and management structures. In the past, British institutions have balanced their top-down managerial tendencies with extensive academic participation and collegiality, although, as we have noted, there are indications that the balance is now adjusting in favor of a stronger managerial stance. Other emerging influences are the strength of such power bases as departments, faculties (i.e., groups of academically related departments), and the senior management team; the use of task-oriented project groups; and, at the implementation stage, the use of business planning and portfolio techniques for managing increasingly entrepreneurial institutions.[9] Opportunities for internal restructuring, the efforts of a persuasive senior management figure as influential change agent, and the institution's history of significant change are also likely to be critical factors in ultimately managing the merger.

Final success in managing a merger of two or more colleges or universities depends on an optimal blend of individual factors, and timing is often the most critical factor. What now may be achievable given a set of circumstances and personalities may not be a year earlier or later. Similarly, the degree of congruence between strategic and operational views of the future will have a decisive influence. The odds would be against the merger of a small arts-oriented "greenfield" university with a larger urban technological polytechnic, although such schemes have been proposed.[10]

As will be noted in the next section, we suggest two broad categories of growth mergers in Britain. Into the first fall mergers in which institutions enter negotiations as more or less equal partners offering equivalent benefits. As defined in our typology, these benefits may be similar or different in nature, such as an arts- and social science-based institution merging with a science-based college, or two balanced multifaculty institutions merging. Into the second category fall mergers in which a large broad-based institution assimilates a small specialist one, such as a teacher-training institution merging with a university to create a department of education, because the perceived benefit to the teacher training college is so great that it is willing to give up institutional autonomy. The recent merger of the University of Reading and Bulmershe College serves as an example of this type.

Mergers as a Strategic Planning Tool at the University of London: An Application of the Typology

The University of London is a large federal university with over 60,000 students and an operating budget of $1.5 billion. The component colleges of the university have always enjoyed a distinctive degree of autonomy. New developments at the university during the 1980–90 period demonstrate a convergence of the macro and micro aspects of our typology: a co-aligning of federal university policy and the interests of its component institutions with the intent to achieve mutual institutional growth through merger.

A number of large-scale subject reviews conducted by the university in the early 1980s confirmed the desirability of concentrating effort on a reduced number of campuses due to strategic resource considerations, such as London's traditional bias toward research and expensive science and medical subjects and the rapidly escalating costs of operating in the capital. To respond to these pressures, the university adopted the five science sites policy in 1982, halving the number of locations at which science was taught and reducing the London Medical Schools from twelve to eight in number.[11]

Compounding the general understanding and acceptance of these problems were local difficulties that led some institutions in the federation to seek closer partnerships with others, either through full merger or departmental consolidations. Bedford College was obliged to seek a new site when the lease on its buildings expired, and it finally merged with Royal Holloway College on the latter's campus. Westfield College, a smaller institution that had relinquished its science faculties, felt increasingly vulnerable and eventually merged with the larger, more science- and technology-oriented Queen Mary College near the revitalized London Docklands area. Ironically, when Westfield's science professors had been relocated five years previously, most had settled at Queen Mary.

During the early 1980s, merger discussions developed between many University of London constituents, and in a number of cases, although growth mergers eventually occurred, they were not with the original planning partner. This fact is seen in retrospect as indicative of the university's readiness as a whole to move forward with its accountability-based managerial and entrepreneurial planning model. The principal university mergers that occurred during the 1980s are listed here (and see figure 13.3 for a diagram of the restructuring that took place within the university).

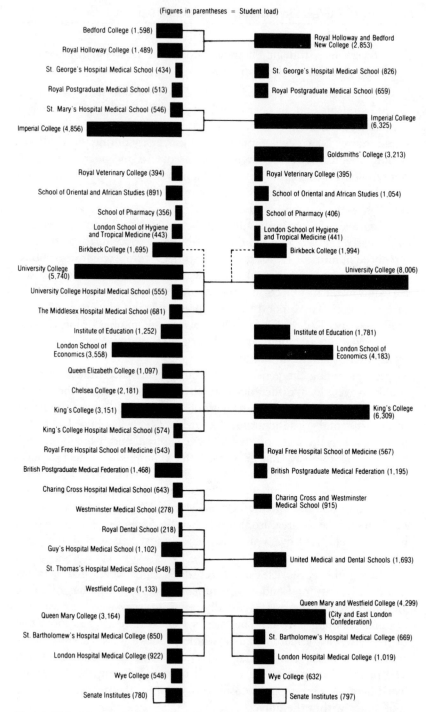

(Figures in parentheses = Student load)

Bedford College (1,598)

Royal Holloway College (1,489)

Royal Holloway and Bedford New College (2,853)

St. George's Hospital Medical School (434)

St. George's Hospital Medical School (826)

Royal Postgraduate Medical School (513)

Royal Postgraduate Medical School (659)

St. Mary's Hospital Medical School (546)

Imperial College (4,856)

Imperial College (6,325)

Goldsmiths' College (3,213)

Royal Veterinary College (394)

Royal Veterinary College (395)

School of Oriental and African Studies (891)

School of Oriental and African Studies (1,054)

School of Pharmacy (356)

School of Pharmacy (406)

London School of Hygiene and Tropical Medicine (443)

London School of Hygiene and Tropical Medicine (441)

Birkbeck College (1,695)

Birkbeck College (1,994)

University College (5,740)

University College (8,006)

University College Hospital Medical School (555)

The Middlesex Hospital Medical School (681)

Institute of Education (1,252)

Institute of Education (1,781)

London School of Economics (3,558)

London School of Economics (4,183)

Queen Elizabeth College (1,097)

Chelsea College (2,181)

King's College (3,151)

King's College (6,309)

King's College Hospital Medical School (574)

Royal Free Hospital School of Medicine (543)

Royal Free Hospital School of Medicine (567)

British Postgraduate Medical Federation (1,468)

British Postgraduate Medical Federation (1,195)

Charing Cross Hospital Medical School (643)

Westminster Medical School (278)

Charing Cross and Westminster Medical School (915)

Royal Dental School (218)

Guy's Hospital Medical School (1,102)

St. Thomas's Hospital Medical School (548)

United Medical and Dental Schools (1,693)

Westfield College (1,133)

Queen Mary and Westfield College (4,299) (City and East London Confederation)

Queen Mary College (3,164)

St. Bartholomew's Hospital Medical College (850)

St. Bartholomew's Hospital Medical College (669)

London Hospital Medical College (922)

London Hospital Medical College (1,019)

Wye College (548)

Wye College (632)

Senate Institutes (780)

Senate Institutes (797)

Figure 13.3. Mergers in the University of London, 1980–1989. Blocks are proportionate to student numbers.

—St. Thomas's Hospital Medical School, Guy's Hospital Medical School, and the Royal Dental Hospital School of Dental Surgery to form the United Medical and Dental Schools, 1983

—Chelsea College, Queen Elizabeth College, and King's College to form a new King's College, 1985

—Bedford College and Royal Holloway College to form Royal Holloway and Bedford New College, 1985

—The London Hospital Medical College, St. Bartholomew's Hospital Medical College, and Queen Mary College to form the City and East London Confederation for the purposes of preclinical medical teaching, 1988

—Queen Mary College and Westfield College to form Queen Mary and Westfield College, 1989

King's College was already a relatively large multifaculty institution and as such had been wooed by a number of smaller, more specialist institutions. Its eventual partnership with Chelsea College and Queen Elizabeth College made it the second largest college in London, with nearly 7,000 students. Chelsea College and Queen Elizabeth College were small, science-based institutions that had become increasingly unviable due to the various pressures, governmental and otherwise, on smaller institutions. Their profiles were complementary to that of King's, however: Queen Elizabeth College was rooted in practical science, such as nutrition and dietetics, and Chelsea College brought with it a strong health sciences bias. The cultures of the two smaller colleges became subsumed into the King's College culture, although a major postmerger internal reorganization was needed to enhance overall academic quality.

In contrast, the merger of Bedford College and Royal Holloway College formed a more equal partnership. The relocation of Bedford College from Regent's Park in central London to the Royal Holloway campus in Egham, twenty miles from the inner city, involved a huge capital investment that created a new set of financial and resource challenges for the combined institution. Additionally, in light of the fact that both colleges had not been strong in various science areas—an increasing governmental priority—the Universities Funding Council decided not to fund chemistry at the merged institution from 1990 onward. Thus, Royal Holloway and Bedford New College will develop a new set of academic priorities in its next ten-year master plan, and, although certain science disciplines will no longer be emphasized, various language, literature, and social science areas, among others, will most likely emerge as academic priorities to be developed by the college's expanded faculty and student constituencies. Interestingly, since this merger, discussions have developed between Royal Holloway and Bedford New College and other institutions back in the London area about the possibility of affiliations in a variety of subjects to build on the college's new identity and potential.

The larger University of London experience has illustrated a number of practical lessons for other institutions contemplating mutual-growth mergers:

1. Central administration and task force planning initiatives can help to encourage an agenda for change by providing pump-priming funding and a crucial structure for support and confidence building to address external pressures and resource considerations.

2. The combination of two or more weak departments or institutions, particularly if science-oriented, does not necessarily create a stronger, less vulnerable entity despite increased size. A deeper restructuring is likely to be necessary to increase viability.

3. Academic and physical restructuring both necessitate long-term investments, and results are unlikely to be immediate, with consequent implications for faculty, student, and alumni morale.

4. Even complementary, mutual-growth mergers require difficult curricular, resource, and staffing decisions and are unlikely to please all constituencies. Thus, a consistent managerial vision that can create opportunities from threats and articulate specific incentives will provide the basis for each merger's potential for success.

Polytechnic Mergers and Transbinary Issues

We now examine a large-scale merger among nonuniversity institutions in London: the formation of the London Institute for Art and Design from seven separate colleges under the control of the Inner London Education Authority (ILEA). The ILEA, abolished by the 1988 Education Reform Act, was unique among British local education authorities in terms of the large national proportion of higher education which its colleges and polytechnics provided. As with the University of London, it was therefore well placed to look beyond the interests of a single institution and to assess both needs and growth potential widely; and it possessed the power to put its conclusions into effect.

Following a review of all its post–high school institutions in 1984, the ILEA decided that art and design subjects could be pursued more

effectively by bringing together four art colleges and three other specialist colleges under the control of a single governing body and management team as the London Institute for Art and Design.[12] The ILEA
saw the academic and financial advantages to be gained in this model
and also realized that a multiplicity of small institutions would have
poor long-term prospects, particularly in the light of the new formula-funding arrangements then being introduced nationally. This was
a highly controversial proposal. Some of the art schools had been
founded in the last century and had developed distinguished individual
artistic traditions with high public profiles and many eminent alumni.
Most schools deeply feared their distinctiveness would be lost in the
larger grouping.

At the same time, the London Institute for Art and Design would
be by good measure the largest specialist art and design college in
Britain and would be eligible for polytechnic (and now, university)
status. Thus, the then three-tiered nature of British higher education,
with two tiers (polytechnics and the rest) on one side of the binary line
and universities on the other, has provided a significant incentive for
some farsighted management teams to support mutual-growth mergers
as a strategy to raise institutional profiles toward university levels exter-
nally while internally achieving enhanced quality within the curriculum
and faculty staffing. Still, longstanding personal attachments to existing
institutions and a natural reluctance to embrace the unknown cause
many British academic managers to fall back from implementing a
merger strategy, even though difficulties such as maintaining academic
standards, coping with higher costs, and responding to national pressures for reduced budgets are rapidly becoming more insistent. In this
instance, because the ILEA was closely involved with the funding and
management of the colleges concerned yet distanced from their institutional loyalties, and because it maintained politically agreed policy
objectives along with the authority to implement them, a merger as
significant as this one was achieved. The ILEA had developed the persuasive vision of a strong, dominant world-class art and design institution forged from seven smaller schools with complementary missions
which was politically marketable to many of the faculty and staffs of all
seven colleges. As discussions continued, the curricular and managerial
plans became refined in response to each new concern until the momentum of the concept became irresistible. The ILEA viewed it as a classic
mutual-growth merger opportunity; as the senior ILEA administrator
involved remarked, it was an idea, in its broadest sense, whose time
had come.

For the purposes of perspective, let us also examine a merger proposal in London which did not succeed, involving institutions on either side of the binary line. Discussions began in 1983–84 between City University and City of London Polytechnic with a view to creating a single, enhanced university.[13] On the face of it, the merger plan appeared to have a good chance of success. Both institutions were approximately the same size (3,000 students at the university and 4,700 advanced-level students at the polytechnic); they were geographically proximate; and both had strong links with the financial community in the City of London and had large business schools in consequence. A combined institution would have been extremely well placed to focus on the financial district's teaching and research needs and to develop a world-class business school, in addition to creating expanded departments in other fields.

These institutions, however, were never able to reach agreement on the shape of the new university. While their missions looked complementary to external supporters, to those involved they were quite different in their approaches to business education and research applications. There was also a lingering sensitivity within the university that the addition of the larger polytechnic would shift the new institution down market. At the time, there was no educational or governmental agency able to exert pressure on both sides of the binary line to reduce anxieties and to build consensus for the efficacy of merging for mutual growth.

These examples of London mergers that reached the implementation stage and those that did not again indicate the important role within the British system of an agency external to the institutions involved. Even so, as more British institutions note the successful U.S. mergers outlined in this book, and also the major growth mergers now occurring in the Australian system, issues such as the aftereffects of the binary line may become less significant, and the vision of an institution with expanded faculty and financial resources may provide support for this creative approach to institutional advancement.

In a broader geographical context, the special circumstances of Northern Ireland have given central government more scope for direct intervention in higher education than elsewhere in Britain. Following a study by a 1982 review group, it was decided that a transbinary merger should take place between the small New University of Ulster, a 1960s creation of 2,000 students, and the larger Ulster Polytechnic, with 6,500 students. The government's decision was reportedly received by the university staff with "total disbelief," and the polytechnic staff did not seem to be noticeably more receptive to the idea.[14] Nevertheless, the British government made clear that it intended to see the merger enacted promptly, and new arrangements for the governance of the combined institution were developed and approved in the following year.

Contrasts with the City University–City Polytechnic merger proposal are sharp. In Northern Ireland, external pressure was fundamental to overcoming the natural resistance to change within both institutions, as each staff and faculty felt unsettled and threatened. Unusually in that instance, the university was the institution whose identity was most at risk in the merger, as it was both small and new, even though the merged institution would retain a university profile. The new institution was dedicated as the University of Ulster in 1984 and has rapidly developed its identity as a central component of Northern Ireland's cultural and educational life; merged staff members are now said to look back on the trauma of merger as an "almost prehistoric episode."[15]

In sum, it is appropriate to note that as mutual-growth, mission-complementary mergers emerge in Britain, the guiding forces behind merger as a strategic planning instrument may emanate from separate sources. In the United States, a growing number of institutions have individually and entrepreneurially accepted merger as a strategy to achieve academic excellence and mission enhancement; in Britain, several external agencies may also assume the entrepreneurial role at present, as universities and former polytechnics, both individually and collectively, weigh the benefits of merging to improve academic quality.

The Future

Policy initiatives leading to mergers between academic institutions in Britain have been characterized by a university structure that has historically been relatively hierarchical and elitist, although there is now a thrust toward greater flexibility and accessibility in the system. The twentieth-century attitude that regards higher education as providing a public service at the government's expense has reinforced the status quo rather than embraced change in the interest of institutional development. Up to the present, successful mergers have most often occurred when, along with complementary institutional missions, an external body—in London, a corporate planning agency—has grasped academic, financial, and policy advantages in pooling resources to achieve an enhanced corporate as well as educational profile. However, the reduction of public funding for higher education and the increased market orientation of the British system over the past seven years have triggered rising concern for institutional viability while focusing greater attention on the quality and attractiveness of academic programs. The trend from a service to a business orientation in British higher education has brought with it the concepts of competitive advantage and market positioning, although there still, for example, remains a gentleman's agreement between universities not to advertise their undergraduate courses.

In the future, similar to the world of commercial enterprise, individual educational competitors will consider becoming partners if the balance of opportunity and advantages is persuasive. Building on a history characterized by resistance to change, many British academic managers are becoming more aware of their responsibilities in shaping their institutional futures. A college and university system hitherto static in nature is becoming significantly more growth-oriented and organic, encouraged by a declared government policy to move from an elite system to a mass one. As financial pressures are likely to continue, we accordingly expect to see a greater willingness to implement higher education mergers, with an assessment of benefits being made in terms of the output of the *new* institution, rather than a contemplation of lost output from the previous ones.

CHAPTER FOURTEEN

Conclusion: The Mutual-Growth Process—Myths and Realities

James Martin and James E. Samels

When we began our research and review of the literature on higher education mergers in the United States and Great Britain almost five years ago, our focus was on the goals, objectives, and results of new mutual-growth strategies. We considered factors such as "the management of decline," demographic downturns, the loss of federal student financial aid, spiraling increases in operating costs, and losses of endowment investments.

Now, as we complete this project and assess the emergence of proactive merger planning as an effective management strategy, our emphasis has increasingly shifted to the *process* of the mutual-growth model and its impact not only on the students centrally involved but also on the quality and cost of the educational opportunities they have the right to expect. Thus, in the course of our interviews with those at numerous entrepreneurial colleges and universities, we have observed the growth merger strategy serving not only as a pivotal experience in the life of two or more institutions but also as a powerful instrument to stimulate both academic quality control and educational mission enhancement.

With this in mind, we conclude our study with an outline of the principal strategic planning and management lessons drawn from our mutual-growth experience, including views on the future of higher education mergers in the United States and Great Britain. We also offer several closing thoughts on the myths and realities that have become associated with the mutual-growth concept and its potential application.

Growth Mergers and Academic Quality

As the progress of our research became a topic of discussion in the *Wall Street Journal*, the *Chronicle of Higher Education*, and the *London Times Higher Education Supplement*, we were approached by a growing number of academic managers who posed one of two familiar questions. One group asked, somewhat skeptically, "If this trend is as significant as you project it to be, how many colleges and universities will disappear by the year 2000 because of mergers?" The second group challenged us even further with the question, "What's so new about your strategy? You've simply packaged corporate takeovers for the campus. Mergers are just a clever form of asset stripping."

In this book we have addressed these questions and demonstrated how, during the coming decade, a more informed national debate might be shaped regarding the connections among strategic planning, mutual-growth mergers, and academic quality. Early in our research, it became clear that most faculty and administrators now working on U.S. campuses have never experienced a pure higher education merger. Further, pure mergers will most likely never touch many of the most successful colleges and universities in Britain, Holland, France, Germany, Sweden, and other progressive higher education systems. Whatever the number of merger plans implemented in any one year—figures from the national *Higher Education Directory* projected over a decade could reach one hundred or more completed mergers—our focus has been on the broader institutional currents in this phenomenon and the deeper policy implications they hold for future forms of collegial restructuring in all fifty states.

Our data reveal three core concepts likely to guide future merger activities: joint mission planning, multicampus resource sharing, and academic enrichment through more formal collaborations such as consolidation or merger. These three elements, along with others involving new views on student services, personnel management, financial planning, faculty governance, curricular assessment, alumni development, and public relations, have been combined at a growing number of colleges and universities to form new institutional identities and structures. Although most of these combinations fall outside the definition of pure merger, they nevertheless constitute an academic management strategy now ready for application on many campuses regardless of their current size, mission, or reputation. Driven by demands for more serious forms of accountability by students of nontraditionally-age, professional employers, parent and alumni associations, state licensing agencies, regional accrediting bodies, and the federal government, a growing number of institutions have implemented this mutual-growth strategy despite various levels of resistance from students, faculty, staff, and alumni.

In fact, while there may have only been one-hundred or more pure mergers in the past decade, the number of new *forms* of merger, such as institutional *consolidations, program transfers, consortia,* and *affiliations* for resource-sharing purposes, easily number in the thousands. Many faculty and staff members can say that mergers have not materially affected their campuses, but an even greater number might recall, for example, an ongoing teaching exchange program, a collaborative software development agreement, a cooperative purchasing arrangement for laboratory equipment, a shared library resource network, or a transfer articulation agreement with a local community college or graduate school. Thus, in answer to those who ask why we are not predicting the closure and disappearance of more colleges and universities over the coming decade, we project current examples from the new forms of merger mentioned here in approximately half the states of this country, as well as in Australia, England, Wales, Japan, and the United Arab Emirates, as examples. Mergers should be viewed in a context broader than the simple "disappearance" of a smaller college into a larger university. Ultimately, the growth merger phenomenon will best be assessed in the evolving context, nationally and internationally, of multipurpose, multicampus consortia, affiliations, federations, and resource-sharing ventures.

Recalling the distinction between mergers and asset stripping, we outline in the section that follows a sequence of institutional development stages, or phases, identified in our research as integral to a well-planned mutual-growth process and as that which distinguishes it from profit-driven, more adversarial corporate takeovers.

The Developmental Phases of a Successful Mutual-Growth Merger

In reviewing a current group of successful growth mergers, as contrasted with examples of the more traditional bankruptcy-bailout model, we have isolated the following five phases that effective institutions not only experience but actively manage to their long-term advantage, most importantly in areas of premerger planning, effective merger implementation, and postmerger community building.

Phase 1: Institutional Self-Assessment

Prior to the earliest merger-related strategic planning by either college or university, both partners complete a rigorous institutional self-

---

The Developmental Phases of a Successful Mutual-Growth Merger

- Institutional self-assessment
- Premerger strategic planning
- Premerger negotiation
- Merger implementation
- Postmerger consolidation and community-building

---

assessment process, focusing specifically on overall merger preparedness, shared mission planning, and appropriate institutional match. This assessment typically includes an institutionwide educational needs assessment, and demographic, enrollment, and competition analyses. Student affairs administrators conduct focused student group discussions and alumni preference polling as well as a broad array of business and professional career employer market surveys. The chief financial officers involved formulate extensive economic impact analyses projecting estimated revenues and expenditures to support the chosen mutual-growth merger objectives.

Only at the close of this multi-phase assessment process can members of both institutional boards, administrative leadership teams, key faculty committees, and alumni groups accumulate the necessary information to decide whether their campuses will significantly benefit from the implementation of a growth merger.

Phase 2: Premerger Strategic Planning

Strategic institutional planning, as such, does not commence until this second stage of the premerger assessment process. During this phase, the executive leadership team, key faculty, and administrative staff attempt to reach consensus on the list of institutions that might serve as mission-complementary merger partners. Initial overtures are then made to the finalist institution(s), with more well-defined mutual-growth proposals and counterproposals to follow in the process of negotiations.

Phase 3: Premerger Collaboration and Negotiation

Still within the premerger period, a Merger Task Force, joint campus in composition, is designated among key members of the board, administrative and faculty leaders, officers of student government, and members of the alumni association. In some instances, we have recommended that the task force also include local business and civic leaders.

This group should immediately be charged with outlining the mission and structure of both the postmerger institution and the process by which it will be achieved. Issues unique to either merger partner or to the specific merger plan need to be identified and addressed at this stage.

Phase 4: Merger Implementation

Only at this penultimate stage of the process does merging actually occur. In this phase, the mutual-growth blueprint is implemented by various subcommittees of the task force, particularly in the core areas of curriculum revision, department and program consolidation, integration of personnel and student cultures, licensing and accreditation self-study development, credit enfranchisement, and the design of a merger outcomes assessment instrument.

We have observed that, at this point, the most effective vehicle through which to begin the actual merging of two or more institutions is often found in the work of the Merger Task Force subcommittee focusing on educational mission review and curriculum revision. Visibly elevating curriculum content, and by extension, educational mission, to the center of the merger process affords the combined faculties and staffs an opportunity to shape a mutual vision for the new institution by exercising skill and judgment in the areas of their greatest expertise.

Phase 5: Postmerger Consolidation and Community Building

This final phase, unique to the mutual-growth model, extends over several years and often is perceived by those outside of the process as the actual merger. In fact, four phases of highly structured planning and negotiation will have been successfully completed prior to this public merger consolidation period. During this phase, the Merger Task Force completes its work, and members of the newly configured institutional leadership team turn their attention to emergent issues such as capital outlay and shared facilities utilization, endowment building, student life programming, and, most critically, the consolidation of separate campus cultures into a coherent educational community.

Orienting Merger Partners for Mutual Growth

We began the first chapter of this book with an outline of ten goals of the mutual-growth strategy as they had emerged in our initial observations of several merger models. Over the past several years, as we interviewed greater numbers of trustees, chief executive officers, students, alumni, and faculty contemplating and implementing mutual-growth mergers, we focused increasingly on the key elements of the merger process and their impact on the institutional partners. In so doing, we have identified several characteristics integral to a mutual-growth-oriented college or university, and it is through the skillful management of these planning and implementation processes that the full range of mutual growth options can best be realized during the merger phases outlined.

Campuswide commitment. Institutions implementing a mutual-growth merger have been most successfully driven by a campuswide commitment to enhance academic quality rather than to raise enrollment levels or negotiate an advantageous financial agreement. The initial force behind the most durable and creative growth mergers we have studied has been a shared institutional vision by both colleges or universities to raise the levels of academic quality they previously attained individually. Beyond short-term plans to increase the size of the first-year class or to strike a leveraged debt-sharing arrangement, the most persuasive factor for merger has been a common resolve to grow beyond conventional notions of institutional autonomy and to achieve a new level of multicampus authority and potential. In the case of the recent Kansas College of Technology–Kansas State University merger, for instance, the state Board of Regents of Higher Education determined that current educational resource levels and the potential for improved academic program quality indicated that these two institutions had more potential for complementary growth than would have been realized in an earlier proposal involving Pittsburg State University.

Merging from strength. Institutional leaders assessing the potential for mutual growth realize it can be achieved most realistically when colleges enter the merger process from positions of institutional strength and stability. Although the growth merger strategy has begun to appeal to an increasing range of academic leaders nationally, the approach will finally prove most effective for institutions who consider it from positions of relative strength and stability. For many years, mergers were implemented in higher education as an alternative to institutional closure. This bankruptcy-bailout model earned its reputation in many regions as two weakened colleges joined forces simply to create a larger weakened institution. In contrast, in the case of Tift College, for example, both the endowment and the enrollment of the college were stable, yet strategic planners foresaw that the potential diminution of both dollars and matriculants in the near future might erode decades of dedication to building Tift's academic reputation.

Thus, from a position of institutional vitality, academic leaders forged a comprehensive agreement with Mercer University which has within three years perpetuated Tift's historic levels of excellence in both women's and teacher education.

Shared vision. The final decision to merge will spring from a shared sense of institutional mission, vision, and timing more than from the recommendation of an outside accounting, law, or consulting firm. Ultimately, an effective growth merger will not be the product of an institutional planning retreat, computerized data base, or literature search, although all of these resources have played significant and positive roles for members of the Merger Task Force in several of the successful models we have studied. Finally, the decision to merge will stem from an institution's intuitive sense of its own potential as measured by key trustees, executive staff, faculty, students, and alumni during the initial stages of consideration.

In the case of Mount Ida College's merger with Chamberlayne Junior College, senior members of the faculty and administration at both institutions rapidly realized that although their colleges were relatively the same size, over three-quarters of Chamberlayne's faculty and students were concentrated in two areas, fine arts and commercial design. Fortunately, these two distinct but related fields were complementary to Mount Ida's long-range educational vision. Furthermore, Chamberlayne's chief executive officer was over eighty years of age, and the physical plant in downtown Boston was deteriorating and progressively less able to maintain a quality campus identity. A merger of these educational enterprises offered an immediate opportunity for growth and development not available to either partner through individual means.

John Sculley, chief executive of Apple Computer, recently described an analogous planning process within his corporation which draws heavily on the intuitive abilities of employees in shaping a "mature network organization":

> The old way of doing things . . . was to look at the organization and say "Here is the structure." You would talk to the leaders of the different divisions or departments and say "What do you want to know?" Then you would map the information systems onto that organizational structure. . . . We have completely reversed the traditional process. . . . We've said: "Let's look first at what we are trying to do systematically. . . . What is the information we need? . . . Then we build that same process as we expect to do it in five years, or seven years, of even ten years, if we can think that

far out. Then, regardless of what the current organization structure is, we . . . map [it] on top of the information system."[1]

Entrepreneurship. Mutual-growth mergers are entrepreneurial at root and force the new leadership team to join its responsibilities for planning and action effectively. For all of the contemporary references we hear regarding the concept of synergy, managing the personnel aspects of a higher education merger process typically requires an unprecedented combination of delicacy and perseverance on the part of the Merger Task Force and senior management team. In mergers such as those between Gannon University and Villa Maria College, and Widener College and Brandywine Junior College, for instance, those on the leadership teams at both institutions balanced the entrepreneurial initiatives of a larger college or university with the needs of the smaller partner's campus community.

As each phase of the process was completed and personnel decisions were implemented, it became apparent in these and other recent mergers that, as Peter Drucker has observed, "management is not *business* management." Rather, "management worldwide has become the new social function. . . . It needs to be applied to all third-sector institutions, such as hospitals [and] universities . . . which since World War II have grown faster than business or government." More specifically, he notes, "one important advance in the discipline and practice of management is that both now embrace entrepreneurship and innovation. A sham fight these days pits 'management' against 'entrepreneurship.' . . . Not to innovate is the single largest reason for the decline of existing organizations. Not to know how to manage is the single largest reason for the failure of new ventures."[2]

A successful mutual-growth merger plan incorporates appropriate committee involvement at every level of the organization, but it does not allow itself to become stagnated by an inability to achieve unanimity at any of these levels. Rather, mutual-growth mergers challenge both partners and their combined leadership teams to coordinate the planning and decision-making aspects of their respective institutions into a more powerful entity.

Collaborative decision making. Mutual-growth mergers integrate the combined institution's administrative, academic, and financial operations in adaptive ways capable of more effectively responding to a changing student marketplace and a more competitive employment environment. We have noted with surprise at times how little chief executive, financial, and academic officers share information on many campuses, in both public and private sectors. In our view, the success of a mission-complementary mutual-growth merger depends in large part on a collaborative decision-making model that includes not only trustees and presidents but also key staff and faculty leaders playing indispensable roles.

Coordinating pertinent financial and academic information and implementing a timely action are centrally difficult tasks on many campuses, as both faculty and administrative managers need an organizational climate that encourages leadership development.[3] In the merger between Mount Ida and the New England Institute of Funeral Service Education, a special Academic Budget Task Force was created to include the two chief academic officers, chief financial officers, and key department chairs with responsibility for implementing the transfers and mergers of core academic programs. This group was specifically charged to review the existing models for coordinating academic planning and budget oversight down to the department level and to propose a new, integrated model for the combined institution. New systems of academic and financial information sharing were also explored to significant degrees in the Kansas State–Kansas College of Technology and Widener University–Delaware Law School merger plans.

Flexibility. Mutual-growth-oriented institutions acknowledge the ongoing need to revise their original merger plan. On most of the campuses we have visited or contacted, members of the Merger Task Force and its subcommittees responded with candor regarding the challenges they faced in integrating what is often a diverse group of institutional cultures even in a mission-complementary situation. Increasing levels of experience with the merger plan and process create an awareness among participants that original strategies for the combination of departments, personnel systems, and student activities may need to be abandoned in some areas and expanded in others. The various Widener University mergers, which spanned much of the 1980s, are a case in point. The chief executive officer of the original Widener College has coordinated the simultaneous mergers of a junior college, a law school, a graduate program in clinical psychiatry, and a large college, now a small university. As these merger plans have unfolded over the course of a decade or more, the new university has experimented liberally with both the degree to which the law school and its governance structures should finally be integrated and the extent to which the university's academic structure might incorporate graduate, baccalaureate, and associate's degree programs.

Complementarity. Institutions implementing a mutual-growth merger strategy affirm the benefits of mission complementarity and shared educational planning. Throughout our research, the principle of mutual growth has been predicated on complementary educational missions, academic programming, student market bases, and long-term institutional aspirations. Colleges and universities collaborating in a growth merger acknowledge that more can be gained educationally through trading levels of institutional autonomy for the dramatically increased resources derived through the merger's overall structure.

Mergers, Management, and the Student Consumer

One higher education commentator recently offered this perspective:

> Universities need to expand their business base both as a way of making the educational experience one that actually prepares students to function at their potential, and also to make institutions more economically viable and self-supporting. . . . [Yet] while good university management today demands that schools apply basic business principles in running their institutions, many universities still don't see themselves as businesses. . . . The unfortunate truth is, however, if universities are as successful as corporations they can expect a *failure* rate of about 80–90 percent.[4]

Although Robert Zemsky, director of the Institute for Research in Higher Education at the University of Pennsylvania, has countered this impression with the comment that "higher education was less bloated and less wasteful than any form of American enterprise in the 1980s," Zemsky himself believes that the 1990s will be a decade of "unprecedented austerity" for postsecondary institutions as every organization from small, private two-year colleges to the largest public research universities revises and reduces budgets, "right-sizes," and struggles to contain costs while preserving institutional diversity.[5] Whatever level of success is achieved on each campus, it will need to overcome, as one observer has noted, a set of cumbersome operating systems, flawed decision-making procedures, and "sacrosanct" practices.[6] In sum, when the subject becomes increasing productivity, as the *Chronicle of Higher Education* reported in 1991, "colleges have not yet defined what it means to be well-managed."[7]

In reviewing the various phases of growth merger models now being implemented here and abroad, we usually begin by posing two questions to the participants: In what ways can the mutual-growth approach improve the overall academic quality and management of your institution? And how can the students be better served by the postmerger college or university? Regarding the first goal—to raise the levels of quality and management expertise on contemporary campuses—the contributors to this book dedicate considerable emphasis to the strategic advantages of the mutual-growth approach and provide specific examples of how merger plans have effectively addressed many cumbersome management and resource allocation systems.

On the issue of how growth mergers benefit the combined student populations and broader educational process, we close with several observations. Within the current movement at most colleges and universities to reduce the number of programs they provide, it has become clear that one of the first areas strategic planners implicate is student services and development. A wide range of activities and support in areas such as psychological counseling and student life programming are being gradually reduced or eliminated on many campuses. Some forecasters have described the entire middle-management tier of institutions, both large and small, as being under siege.[8] As a result, students in every geographic sector of the nation during the 1990s will experience a new and unfamiliar world of service cutbacks and reductions in the quality of their campus life. In an article that appeared during the last week of 1991 entitled "In Uncertain Times, College Students See a Bleak Future after Graduation," the *New York Times* reported that increasing concerns had emerged among many college students who "feel boxed in by anxieties and limitations."[9]

Traditionally, the method to address issues such as these has been through a thoughtful series of student development programs supported by the entire college community. Currently, on many campuses, faculty and staff members are being pressed into service in student affairs areas with part-time positions and stipends, with uncertain results when a crisis develops. As available funds dwindle to address the necessary range of student-centered issues, we would cite the benefits of combining personnel, programs, and resources through the mutual-growth approach as a powerful source of student life enhancement.

In our view, this merger model should not be constituted primarily as a management-based, financially oriented agreement. Rather, mutual growth remains a concept that carries its greatest impact in the enrichment of academic quality and student life. Thus, we believe it is appropriate to end this study with an emphasis on the center of that process—the students at colleges and universities considering a growth merger—in the belief that this concept will enhance the management and growth of their institutions while directly improving the quality of the teaching and learning processes they experience.

Principal College and University Mergers since 1975 Cited in Text

Arkansas   1991

■ Arkansas Vocational-Technical School System (24 institutions), certificates

■ Arkansas System of Technical and Community Colleges (19 institutions), associate degrees

This plan, which resulted in four institutional mergers and the creation of ten newly designated technical colleges, will ensure the availability of postsecondary degree offerings as well as enhanced transfer articulation to a significantly increased percent of the state's population in the technologically oriented decade ahead.

Delaware and Pennsylvania   1975, 1976, 1989

■ Widener College, Chester, Pa., bachelor and master degrees

■ Brandywine College, Wilmington, Del., associate degrees

■ Delaware Law School, Wilmington, Del., doctorate degree

■ Hahnemann Hospital Graduate Program in Clinical Psychology, Philadelphia, Pa., doctorate degree

Widener College merged with a career preparatory–oriented junior college, a law school located in another state, and then later with the clinical psychology doctoral degree program of a Philadelphia hospital. The new institution has been renamed Widener University with the law school named the Widener University School of Law. The university has increased during the merger years to a budget of almost $80 million and now grants doctoral degrees in four fields.

Georgia   1986

■ Mercer University, Macon, bachelor, master, and doctorate degrees

■ Tift College, Forsyth, bachelor degree

Tift, known principally for its tradition of both teacher and women's education, merged with Mercer University. The merger agreement provided for the continuation of an emphasis on the tradition of women's education within the Mercer mission. The Tift campus has been transitionally utilized by Mercer for continuing education and expanded degree program purposes.

Kansas   1991

- Kansas College of Technology in Salina, Salina, associate degrees
- Kansas State University, Manhattan, bachelor, master, and doctorate degrees

In this new structure, both campus sites have been maintained, and the smaller institution has been renamed the Kansas State College of Technology at Salina. The college of technology can draw on the more extensive course offerings of the university, and the university gains the academic and reputational strengths of one of the two technology colleges in the state system.

Massachusetts   1974

- Boston College, Newton, bachelor, master, and doctorate degrees
- Newton College of the Sacred Heart, Newton, associate and bachelor degrees

Over a three-year period between 1974 and 1977, Boston College acquired the Newton College of the Sacred Heart real estate and facilities and transformed the campus into the Boston College Law School and instructional space for its undergraduate fine arts programs. Newton College of the Sacred Heart ceased its operations. Its employees were provided with a multiyear severance arrangement, and its students at the time were allowed to earn a Newton College of the Sacred Heart degree. The college's Alumni Association has remained active.

Massachusetts   1977

- Becker Junior College, Worcester, associate degrees
- Leicester Junior College, Leicester, associate degrees

These two institutions, now named Becker College, consolidated an urban-based, career-preparatory junior college with a rural campus liberal arts–oriented junior college to provide a strengthened, more comprehensive set of academic programs.

Massachusetts   1986, 1987, 1989

- Chamberlayne Junior College, Boston, associate degree
- Coyne School of Technical Electricity, Boston, associate degree

- Mount Ida College, Newton, associate and bachelor degrees
- New England Institute of Applied Arts and Sciences, Boston, associate degree

Chamberlayne ceased its campus operation and merged with Mount Ida on the Mount Ida campus. Chamberlayne Hall, a purpose-built art and design classroom facility, was erected on the Mount Ida campus in 1988 to house the Chamberlayne art and design faculty. The ongoing Mount Ida Art and Design Division has been restructured into the Chamberlayne School of Design and Merchandising.

The Coyne School ceased its campus operation and merged with Mount Ida on the Mount Ida campus. The Coyne School was restructured at Mount Ida as one of the eight schools of the college.

The New England Institute ceased its campus operation and was re-named the New England Institute of Funeral Service Education, one of the eight schools of Mount Ida College. A purpose-built funeral service clinical teaching facility, the New England Institute Professional Building, was erected on the Mount Ida campus in 1990.

Michigan   1990

- University of Detroit, Detroit, bachelor, master, and doctorate degrees
- Mercy College, Detroit, bachelor and master degrees

In 1990, these two institutions formed the largest private Catholic comprehensive university in Michigan with enrollments of 7,850 students. The newly named University of Detroit Mercy has kept, among other graduate and professional programs, the dentistry and law schools on their respective campuses, and now utilizes the university's former main campus for traditional-aged college students, while utilizing the former college campus for returning adult student programs and continuing professional education student programs.

Michigan   1991

- Macomb Community College, Warren, associate degrees
- Wayne State University, Detroit, bachelor, master, and doctorate degrees
- Walsh College, Troy, bachelor and master degrees
- Oakland University, Rochester, bachelor, master, and doctorate degrees
- University of Detroit Mercy, Detroit, bachelor, master, and doctorate degrees
- Central Michigan University, Mount Pleasant, bachelor, master, and doctorate degrees

In 1991, these six institutions collaborated in the opening of the University Center of Macomb County. On their Clinton Township campus, Macomb Community College will now offer sixteen bachelor degree programs in partnership with Walsh College, Wayne State, Oakland, and Central Michigan universities and the University of Detroit Mercy.

Minnesota   1987

- College of St. Catherine, St. Paul, bachelor and master degrees
- St. Mary's College, Minneapolis, associate degrees

To its merger with the College of Saint Catherine, a 2,400-student liberal arts college, St. Mary's brought a history of allied health education programs. Building on the merger's resources, the combined institution has received state approval to award master degrees in nursing.

New Jersey   1991

- Camden County College, Camden, associate degrees
- Glassboro State College, Glassboro, bachelor and master degrees

In 1991, Camden County College collaborated with Glassboro State College (now named Rowan College) to open a new facility, the Camden City Center. These two colleges have established a joint academic program at the Camden City Center, which concentrates on four areas: remedial education, English as a Second Language education, traditional college curricula, and academic support services. The collaborative academic programs will enable students from Camden City and surrounding areas to earn two-year associate degrees and four-year bachelor degrees without leaving the city of Camden.

New York   1989

- Iona College, New Rochelle, bachelor and master degrees
- Elizabeth Seton, North Yonkers, associate degrees

In this structure, the smaller institution has been transformed into the Elizabeth Seton School of Associate Degree Studies within Iona College. Through this model, Elizabeth Seton's strengths in nursing and communications will be highlighted within the combined institutional structure.

Oklahoma   1993

- Oklahoma City Community College, Oklahoma City, associate degrees

- Redlands Community College, El Reno, associate degrees
- Oklahoma State University Technical Branch, Oklahoma City, associate degrees

In 1993, the State Board of Regents of Oklahoma are proposing that these three institutions consolidate their governing boards in order to eliminate program duplications and better coordinate postsecondary activities and college-level curricula throughout the state.

Oregon and Washington   1991

- Portland State University, Portland, Ore., bachelor, master, and doctorate degrees
- Portland Community College, Portland, Ore., associate degrees
- Clackamas Community College, Portland, Ore., associate degrees
- Mt. Hood Community College, Gresham, Ore., associate degrees
- Clark College, Vancouver, Wash., associate degrees

In 1990, a commission on higher education in the Portland metropolitan area began exploring possible avenues for collaboration among schools in the Portland area seeking to improve coordination among existing curricula and faculty resources in order to avoid costly expansion. In 1991, as a result of this commission, Portland State University, Clark College, and Mt. Hood, Clackamas, and Portland community colleges have received a three-year joint grant from the Department of Education in Washington, D.C., entitled "Fund for Improvement of Post Secondary Education."

This grant is enabling the faculty of these five institutions to engage in a collaborative effort, sharing methodologies, objectives, and resources in the disciplines of British literature, chemistry, and American history. Portland Community College is working toward institutionalizing this grant so that this model for collaboration can be extended to other disciplines and continue beyond the scheduled three-year time frame.

Pennsylvania   1973

- Cedar Crest College, Allentown, bachelor degree
- Muhlenberg College, Allentown, bachelor degree

The libraries of both colleges formed a partnership in 1973 while both colleges retained their degree-granting authorities and campus operations. A separate corporation, Educational Ventures, Inc., was formed, with its own board of trustees, to oversee the new structure.

Pennsylvania   1989

- Gannon University, Erie, bachelor and master degrees
- Villa Maria College, Erie, associate, bachelor, and master degrees

Villa Maria College, a 600-student Catholic women's college, merged with a 2,400-student coeducational university. The two institutions have developed a plan for the long-term placement within the Gannon mission of Villa Maria's traditions in nursing, early and elementary education, and the needs of nontraditional aged females.

Notes

Chapter One. Achieving Academic Excellence through Strategic Mergers:
A New Approach

1. Kim Cameron, Ellen Chaffee, Myung Kim, and David Whetten, "The Aftermath of Decline," *Review of Higher Education* 10, no. 3 (1987): 215–16.

2. James Martin, "More Gown, Less Town," *Times Higher Education Supplement, London,* June 29, 1990, 17.

3. *Cameron* et al., "Aftermath of Decline," 217–18.

4. Joseph P. O'Neill, "Merger as a Strategy for Growth or Increasing Market Share," in *Mergers and Acquisitions in Private Higher Education: A Report on a National Conference at Wingspread,* Decatur, Ill., June 19–21, 1987, 11–12.

5. Gail S. Chambers, "The Enterprising Alternatives," in *Mergers and Acquisitions,* 15–16.

6. Ibid., 16.

7. Interview with Dr. John McKay, deputy director for technical education, Arkansas Office of Higher Education, Feb. 8, 1993.

8. Interview with Dr. Martin Schwartz, dean of planning, research, and development, Camden County College, Camden, N.J., Feb. 1, 1993.

9. Interview with Donald Wing, associate vice president for academic affairs, Macomb University Center, Detroit, Mich., Mar. 17, 1993.

10. Mary Crystal Cage, "Michigan's 'Higher-Education Mall' Viewed as a Model for Other Communities," *Chronicle of Higher Education,* Sept. 19, 1990, 5, 26.

11. Ibid., 26.

12. Ed Wiley III, "Oklahoma Regents Approve Study of Junior College Consolidation," *Community College Week,* Apr. 16, 1990, 1, 6.

13. Interview with Patricia Stuckey, director of development and public relations, Oklahoma City Community College, Oklahoma City, Okla., Mar. 17, 1993.

14. Goldie Blumenstyk, "Public-Private Group in Portland to Help Colleges Meet Demands through Coordination instead of Expansion," *Chronicle of Higher Education,* Sept. 12, 1990, 23.

15. Interview with Barbara Murphy, dean of transfer and general education services, Portland Community College, Portland, Ore., Jan. 29, 1993.

16. "Dawkins' Way," editorial, *Times Higher Education Supplement,* Apr. 13, 1990, 40.

17. Interview with Dr. Lawrence Buck, provost and vice president for academic affairs, Widener University, Widener, Pa., Jan. 24, 1991.

18. R. Kirby Godsey, "Case Study: The Merger of Tift College and Mercer University," in *Mergers and Acquisitions,* 26–28.

19. Iona College undergraduate bulletin for baccalaureate programs, New Rochelle, N.Y., 1989–90, 88–89.

20. Gannon University catalogue, Erie, Pa., 1990–91, 3.

21. Interviews with Dr. Robert Wall, vice president for academic affairs, Gannon University, Erie, Pa., Feb. 1, 4, 1991.

22. Interviews with Barbara Milbauer, vice president of administration and institutional planning, University of Detroit Mercy, Detroit, Mich., Jan. 22, 1993; Aug. 9, 1993.

23. "Detroit Colleges to Merge to Save 'Catholic Presence,'" *Chronicle of Higher Education,* July 5, 1989.

24. Educational Ventures, Inc., *EVI Biennial Report, 1984–86* (Allentown, Pa.: EVI, 1986), 2.

25. Kent Weeks, "Creative Options: College Mergers and Institutional Reassessment, *Lex Collegii* 11, no. 2 (1987): 1–5.

26. On job security and collective bargaining, see American Association of University Professors, "Governance Standards in Institutional Mergers and Acquisitions," *AAUP Policy Documents and Reports* (Washington, D.C.: AAUP, 1990), 119–20.

27. On Mercer and Widener, interviews with Gloria Marshall, development officer, University Development Office, Mercer University, Macon, Ga., Jan. 29, 1991, and Peter Caputo, development officer, University Development Office, Widener University, Widener, Pa., Feb. 1, 1991.

28. J. Kitching, "Why Do Mergers Miscarry?" *Harvard Business Review* 46, no. 6 (1967): 92.

29. Ibid., 85, 91.

30. D. B. Jemison and S. B. Sitken, "Acquisitions: The Process Can Be the Problem," *Harvard Business Review* 64, no. 2 (1986): 107. Also see Kitching, "Why Do Mergers Miscarry?" 84; Weeks, "Creative Options," 1; and "Introduction," in *Mergers and Acquisitions,* 2–4.

31. *Jemison and Sitken,* "Acquisitions," 107.

32. *Kitching,* "Why Do Mergers Miscarry?" 94, 98.

Chapter Two. Higher Education Mergers, Consolidations, Consortia, and Affiliations: A Typology of Models and Basic Legal Structures

1. Kent Weeks, "Creative Options: College Mergers and Institutional Reassessment," *Lex Collegii* 11, no. 2 (1987): 3–4.

2. Hugh L. Thompson, "Considering a Merger?" *Planning for Higher Education* 13, no. 3 (1985): 21–26.

3. Association of Governing Boards, *Illustrative Bylaws for Independent Colleges,* article 14, Conflicts of Interest, revised, Aug. 1981, 15.

4. Edward A. Johnson and Kent Weeks. "To Close a College: Independent College Trustees and Decisions on Financial Exigency, Endowment Use, and Closure," *Journal of College and University Law* 12 (1986): 455. See also James Martin and James E. Samels, "Ethical Implications of Higher Education Mergers," paper presented at the 24th Annual Northeast Region Academic Affairs Administrators Conference, Providence, R.I., Nov. 8, 1989.

5. Ronald J. Burke, "Managing the Human Side of Mergers and Acquisitions," *Business Quarterly* 52, no. 3 (1988): 18.

6. John B. Cannon, "The Organizational and Human Implications of Mergers," paper presented at the American Educational Research Association, Montreal, Apr. 13, 1983, 5 (ERIC Document Reproduction Service, Ed. 254142).

7. J. D. Millett, *Mergers in Higher Education: An Analysis of Ten Case Studies* (Washington, D.C.: Academy for Educational Development, 1976).

8. James Martin and James E. Samels, "College Mergers Have Become Creative and Effective Means of Achieving Excellence and Articulating New Missions," *Chronicle of Higher Education*, Nov. 1, 1989, B2.

9. Donald L. Zekan, "Mergers in Public Higher Education in Massachusetts" (Ed.D. diss., University of Massachusetts, Amherst, 1990); see also James R. Mingle, et al., *Challenges of Retrenchment* (San Francisco: Jossey-Bass, 1981), 273.

10. Joseph P. O'Neill and Samuel Barnett, *Colleges and Corporate Change: Merger, Bankruptcy, and Closure. Sourcebook for Trustees and Administrators* (Princeton: Conference University Press, 1980).

11. James Martin and James E. Samels, "The Small College Entrepreneur," *Connection* (New England Board of Higher Education) 5, no. 4 (1991), 47–49.

12. Robert J. Bruce, "College Mergers: An Emerging Alternative," *Mergers and Acquisitions in Private Higher Education: A Report on a National Conference at Wingspread*, Decatur, Ill., June 19–21, 1987, 12.

13. Weeks, "Creative Options," 2.

14. Brochure for the Great Lakes Colleges Association, Ann Arbor, Mich., n.d.

15. Interview with Galen C. Godbey, director, Lehigh Valley Association of Independent Colleges, Bethlehem, Pa., September 1992, February 1993.

16. James E. Samels, "Protecting the Citadel: A Proactive Approach to Avoiding Major Campus Liability Pitfalls," *Eastern Association of College and University Business Officers Newsletter* 104, no. 1 (1991): 6–7.

17. Ibid., "Higher Education Graduates to Preventive Law," *Preventive Law Reporter*, June 1989, 23.

18. J. A. Kirby, "Legal Audits for Non-Profit Organizations," paper presented at the 3d Annual Legal Audits Seminar, Massachusetts Bar Association, Newton, Mass., Mar. 13, 1991.

19. Title 34—Education; revised July 1, 1988; chapter 6—Office of Postsecondary Education, Department of Education; part 600—Institutional Eligibility under the Higher Education Act of 1965, as amended, 34 C.F.R. 600.10.

20. New England Association of Schools and Colleges, *Commission on Institutions of Higher Education Accreditation Handbook*, 1983 ed., Guidelines on Substantive Change (1989), 109–13.

Chapter Three. The Role of Trustees and Governing Boards in College and University Mergers

1. Barbara Taylor, *Working Effectively with Trustees: Building Cooperative Campus Leadership.* ASHE-ERIC Higher Education Research Report No. 2 (Washington, D.C.: Association for the Study of Higher Education, 1987), 37.

2. Gail S. Chambers, "Negotiating Mergers between Institutions," in *Challenges of Retrenchment*, ed. James R. Mingle and Associates (San Francisco: Jossey-Bass, 1981), 93.

3. Louis T. Benezet, "Resurveying the Downward Slope," *AGB Reports*, Mar.–Apr. 1983, 40–41.

4. Hugh L. Thompson, "Considering a Merger?" *Planning for Higher Education* 13, no. 3 (1986): 21.

5. Robert Waterman, *Adhocracy: The Power to Change* (Knoxville, Tenn.: Whittle Direct Books, 1990).

6. Gail S. Chambers, "The Dilemma of College Merger," *AGB Reports,* Nov.–Dec. 1983, 17.

7. John D. Millett, *Mergers in Higher Education: An Analysis of Ten Case Studies* (Washington, D.C.: Academy for Educational Development, 1975), 43–44.

8. Thompson, "Considering a Merger?"

9. Kansas Board of Regents, *Minutes* (June 1990).

10. J. F. Wyatt, "Institutional Identity and Its Extinction," *Higher Education Review* 18, no. 2 (1986): 31.

11. For interesting discussions about the negative consequences of poorly designed communication strategies, see Benezet, "Resurveying the Downward Slope," 41, and Thompson, "Considering a Merger?" 24.

12. Scott Jaschik, "Citizens Campaigns Are Foiling State Plans to Shut Down or Merge Public Colleges," *Chronicle of Higher Education,* June 24, 1987, 20–21.

13. Thompson, "Considering a Merger?" 24.

14. V. L. Meek, "Comparative Notes on Cross-Sectoral Amalgamation of Higher Educational Institutions: British and Australian Case Studies," *Comparative Education* (1988), 348.

15. Chambers, "Dilemma of College Merger," 16.

16. Thompson, "Considering a Merger?" 24. Millett, *Mergers in Higher Education,* 97.

Chapter Four. Presidential Leadership and the Mutual-Growth Concept

1. Harry J. Gray, "The CEO: Takeover Hardball–A Tough Leader Tells How to Play the Expansion Game," *Success,* May 1987, 18.

2. George Roche, *A World without Heroes: The Modern Tragedy* (Hillsdale, Mich.: Hillsdale College Press, 1987), xii, 44, 353.

3. Barbara Kellerman, "A President Is a President Is a President," *Leadership Abstracts* 1, no. 6 (1988): n.p.

4. Pew Higher Education Research Program, "The Lattice and the Ratchet," *Policy Perspectives* 2, no. 4 (1990): 7.

5. Estela M. Bensimon, "Transactional, Transformational, and 'Trans-Vigorational' Leaders," *Leadership Abstracts* 2, no. 6 (1989): n.p.

6. George Keller, *Academic Strategy: The Management Revolution in American Higher Education* (Baltimore: Johns Hopkins University Press, 1983), 106.

7. David Ravenscroft, "The 1980s Merger Wave: An Industrial Organization Perspective," in *The Merger Boom,* ed. Lynn E. Browne and Eric S. Rosengren, proceedings of a conference held at Melvin Village, N.H., October 1987, 48–49.

8. Robert Birnbaum, *Responsibility without Authority: The Impossible Job of the College President* (Washington, D.C.: Office of Educational Research and Improvement, Department of Education, March 1988), 14.

9. Warren Bennis, *Why Leaders Can't Lead: The Unconscious Conspiracy Continues* (San Francisco: Jossey-Bass, 1989), 17.

10. Ibid., 22.

11. James L. Fisher, *Power of the Presidency* (New York: American Council on Education and Macmillan, 1984), 9.

12. Perry Pascarella and Mark A. Frohman, *The Purpose-Driven Organization: Unleashing the Power of Discretion and Commitment* (San Francisco: Jossey-Bass, 1989), 8.

13. Birnbaum, *Responsibility*, 19–20.

14. Michael D. Cohen, James G. March, and Johan P. Olsen, "A Garbage Can Model of Organizational Choice," *Administrative Science Quarterly* 17, no. 1 (1972): 11.

15. Keller, *Academic Strategy*, 123–24.

16. Ann E. Austin and Zelda F. Gamson, *Academic Workplace: New Demands, Heightened Tensions*, ASHE-ERIC Higher Education Research Report No. 10 (Washington, D.C.: Association for the Study of Higher Education, 1983), 13 and foreword; Birnbaum, *Responsibility*, 8; and Birnbaum, "The Latent Organizational Functions of the Academic Senate: Why Senates Do Not Work but Will Not Go Away," *Journal of Higher Education* 60, no. 4 (1989): 437; Keller, *Academic Strategy*, 35.

17. Joseph P. O'Neill, "Merger as a Strategy for Growth or Increasing Market Share" (rationale 10), in *Mergers and Acquisitions: A Report of a National Conference at Wingspread*, Decatur, Ill., June 19–21, 1987.

18. Fisher, *Power of the Presidency*, 86.

19. Ernest Boyer, "Faculty's Lack of Trust in Management," *London Times Higher Education Supplement*, Nov. 17, 1989, 18.

20. Robert K. Greenleaf, "The Leadership Crisis—A Message for College and University Faculty." Pamphlet reprinted from *Humanities: Journal of the Institute of Man* 14, no. 3 (1978).

21. Anthony F. Buono and James L. Bowditch, *The Human Side of Mergers and Acquisitions: Managing Collisions between People, Cultures, and Organizations* (San Francisco: Jossey-Bass, 1989), 60, 62, 63, 89.

22. Ravenscroft, "The 1980s Merger Wave," 20.

23. Chambers's categories are cited in the introduction to *Mergers and Acquisitions*, 4.

24. Gray, "The CEO," 18.

25. Buono and Bowditch, *Human Side of Mergers*, 11.

26. Price Pritchett, *The Employee Survival Guide to Mergers and Acquisitions* (Dallas: Pritchett and Associates, 1987), 4.

27. Buono and Bowditch, *Human Side of Mergers*, 20.

28. Ibid., 133.

29. Keller, *Academic Strategy*, 113.

30. Pascarella and Frohman, *Purpose-Driven Organization*, 126.

Chapter Five. An Academic Action Plan for Faculty Involvement, Curriculum Revision, and Professional Development

1. Gail S. Chambers, "Maybe There's a Reason: A Theoretical Model for Institutional Mergers," in *Mergers and Acquisitions in Private Higher Education: A Report on a National Conference at Wingspread*, Decatur, Ill., June 19–21, 1987, 20.

2. Godsey is quoted in the introduction to *Mergers and Acquisitions*, 4–5.

3. Ibid., 32.

4. Chambers, "Maybe There's a Reason," 22.

5. Ibid., 24.

6. John D. Millett, *Mergers in Higher Education: An Analysis of Ten Case Studies.* University: University of Alabama Press, 1976, 6.

7. Interview with Dr. Marylou Eldred, academic dean and vice president for academic affairs, College of St. Catherine, St. Paul, Minn., Jan. 31, 1991, and telephone interview with Dr. Robert Wall, vice president for academic affairs, Gannon University, Erie, Pa., Feb. 1, 4, 1991.

8. Interview with Dr. Robert Richardson, chair, Education Department, and Tift student adviser, Mercer University, Macon, Ga., Jan. 25, 1991.

9. Kenneth Mortimer, Marque Bagshaw, and Andrew Masland, *Flexibility in Academic Staffing: Effective Policies and Practices,* ASHE-ERIC Higher Education Research Report No. 1 (Washington, D.C.: Association for the Study of Higher Education, 1985), 76–77.

10. Ibid., 74.

11. Interview with John F. Welsh, associate director of academic affairs, Kansas Board of Regents, Topeka, Kans., Nov. 1990.

12. Interview with Dr. Lawrence Buck, provost and vice president for academic affairs, Widener University, Widener, Pa., Jan. 24, 1991.

13. Jack H. Schuster, Lynn Miller, and Associates, *Governing Tomorrow's Campus: Perspectives and Agendas* (New York: American Council on Education and Macmillan, 1989); Michael Shattock, ed., *The Structure and Governance of Higher Education* (Surrey, Eng.: Society for Research into Higher Education, Surrey University, 1983).

14. Courtney Leatherman, "Colleges' Failure to Tackle Pressing Academic Problems in 1980s Laid to Lack of Collaboration by Professors and Administrators," *Chronicle of Higher Education,* Jan. 23, 1991, A13.

15. Ann E. Austin and Zelda F. Gamson, *Academic Workplace: New Demands, Heightened Tensions,* ASHE-ERIC Higher Education Research Report No. 10 (Washington, D.C.: Association for the Study of Higher Education, 1983), 32.

16. Buck and Eldred interviews.

17. Interview with Teresa Ballan, assistant to the vice president for academic affairs, Gannon University, Erie, Pa., Feb. 1, 1991.

18. Interview with Karen Markoe, chair, Faculty Senate, State University System of New York, Fort Schuyler, N.Y., Mar. 4, 1991.

19. Ibid.

20. "Faculty Handbook Revision: Content and Process," *Higher Education Resource Center Conference Handbook* (Denver: Higher Education Resource Center, 1987), 63.

21. Austin and Gamson, *Academic Workplace,* 24–25.

22. Interview with Richardson.

23. Interview with Wall.

24. Buck interview and telephone interview with Dr. Kenneth Goudy, associate dean, College of Engineering, Kansas State University, Manhattan, Kans., Jan. 24, 1991.

25. R. Kirby Godsey, "Case Study: The Merger of Tift College and Mercer University," in *Mergers and Acquisitions,* 26, 40.

Chapter Six. Strategic Planning for Growth Mergers

1. George Keller, *Academic Strategy: The Management Revolution in American Higher Education* (Baltimore: Johns Hopkins University Press, 1983).

2. The concept of institutional culture in higher education, first discussed by Burton Clark in *The Distinctive College* (Chicago: Aldine, 1970), has most recently been addressed in William G. Tierney, ed., *Culture and Ideology in Higher Education: Advancing a Critical Agenda* (New York: Praeger, 1991).

3. James E. Elsass and Paul E. Lingenfelter, *An Identification of College and University Peer Groups* (Springfield, Ill.: Illinois Board of Education, 1980).

4. Robert G. Cope, *Strategic Policy Planning: A Guide for College and University Administrators* (Littleton, Colo.: Ireland, 1978), 8.

5. See, for example, James L. Morrison, William L. Renfro, and Wayne I. Boucher, *Futures Research and the Strategic Planning Process: Implications for Higher Education* (Washington, D.C.: American Association for Higher Education, 1984); and James L. Morrison, "Establishing an Environmental Scanning/Forecasting System to Augment College and University Planning," *Planning for Higher Education* 15, no. 1 (1987): 7–22.

6. See, for example, Norman P. Uhl's "Editor's Introduction" in *Using Research for Strategic Planning* (San Francisco: Jossey-Bass, 1983).

7. This methodology has been developed most extensively by Joseph Stafford and his colleagues in the University of Texas system.

8. Dennis P. Jones, *Data and Information for Executive Decisions in Higher Education* (Boulder, Colo.: National Center for Higher Education Management Studies, 1982), provides an introduction to the decision support field.

9. *Keller, Academic Strategy*, 61ff.

10. This section is based upon a number of interviews and discussions conducted from 1991 to 1993. In the interest of confidentiality, the institutions concerned are not identified.

Chapter Seven. The Implications of a Public Institutional Merger

1. Gail M. Chambers, *Mergers between Private Colleges: An Empirical Analysis* (Ph.D. diss., University of Rochester, 1987), 187; Joseph P. O'Neill and Samuel Barnett, *Colleges and Corporate Change: Merger, Bankruptcy, and Closure* (Princeton: Conference University Press, 1980), 28.

2. John D. Millett, *Mergers in Higher Education: An Analysis of Ten Case Studies* (University: University of Alabama Press, 1976), 53.

3. Larry L. Wade and Robert L. Curry, *A Logic of Public Policy: Aspects of Political Economy* (Belmont, Calif.: Wadsworth, 1970), 5; Christopher Jencks and David Riesman, *The Academic Revolution* (Chicago: University of Chicago Press, 1977), 286.

4. John E. v. C. Moon, *Boston State College: A Memory and A Meaning*, report of the American Federation of Teachers, AFL-CIO, item no. 64 (Washington, D.C.: American Federation of Teachers, 1983), 4.

5. On the sequence of events, see Donald L. Zekan, *Mergers in Public Higher Education in Massachusetts* (Ed.D. diss., University of Massachusetts, 1990).

6. Interview with Robert Quinn, former speaker of the Massachusetts House of Representatives and at the time of the merger chair of the University of Massachusetts Board of Trustees, Boston, Mass., Feb. 7, 1989.

7. Interview with Michael Creedon, former state representative and at the time of the merger chair of the House Committee on Ways and Means, Brockton, Mass., Jan. 31, 1989.

8. Franklin Patterson, former interim president of the University of Massachusetts

and at the time of the merger professor at the University of Massachusetts at Boston, Needham, Mass., Mar. 15, 1988.

9. John E. v. C. Moon, "The Boston State Fiasco: A Personal View," *New England Sociologist* 4, no. 1 (1982): 51, 60.

10. Millett, *Mergers in Higher Education*, 10.

11. Interview with John Duff, at the time of the mergers chancellor of the Massachusetts Board of Regents of Higher Education, Boston, Mass., June 5, 1989.

12. Edward R. Hines, *Higher Education and State Government: Renewed Partnership, Cooperation, or Competition?* ASHE-ERIC Higher Education Research Report No. 5 (Washington, D.C.: Association for the Study of Higher Education, 1988), 112–13.

13. Michael D. Cohen and James G. March, *Leadership and Ambiguity: The American College President*, 2d ed. (Boston: Harvard Business School Press, 1986), xvii.

Chapter Eight. The Business Aspects of College and University Mergers: A Plan for Merger Financing and Resource Sharing

1. Robert T. Forrester, *A Handbook on Debt Management for Colleges and Universities* (Washington, D.C.: NACUBO, 1988), 4–5.

2. National Association of College and University Business Officers, *Capital Formation Alternatives in Higher Education* (Washington, D.C.: NACUBO 1988); State Higher Education Executive Officers, *Creative Financing for Higher Education Facilities and Equipment* (Denver: SHEEO, 1985).

3. Teresa P. Gordon and Mary Fischer, "Reporting Performance: Using Financial and Nonfinancial Data," *NACUBO Business Officer Magazine* 24, no. 1 (1990): 28.

4. Robert T. Forrester, Coopers and Lybrand, Certified Public Accountants, personal correspondence, Aug. 27, 1990. The explanation of accounting and combinations in this section is derived in pertinent part from this correspondence.

Chapter Nine. Merger Licensure and Accreditation

1. Council on Postsecondary Accreditation, policy statement, "Disclosure, Confidentiality, and Institutional Integrity"; see William A. Kaplan, "Accreditation and the Public Interest," Council on Postsecondary Accreditation, COPA Occasional Paper (COPA: Washington, D.C., 1988); see also COPA, policy statement, "Accreditation and the Public Interest."

2. American Association of University Administrators, "Managing Survival in Higher Education," proceedings of the 16th Annual Assembly, Toronto, June 28, 1987; on the accrediting process, see Council on Postsecondary Accreditation Professional Development Committee, "A Case of Accreditation, *cum grano salis*," COPA Mock Trial, Apr. 12, 1989, Boston, Mass.

3. William A. Kaplan, *The Law of Higher Education*, 2d ed. (San Francisco: Jossey-Bass, 1985), 573.

4. New England Association of Schools and Colleges, *Commission on Institutions of Higher Education Accreditation Handbook*, 1983, Guidelines on Substantive Change, section A.1, 110. On inception, section C.1.a., 111–12; on ninety days premerger, section C.1.b., 112; on evaluation, section C.2., 112–13.

5. Massachusetts General Laws, chap. 69, sec. 30 *et. seq.*; and Board of Regents of Higher Education, "Degree Standards for Independent Institutions of Higher Education," 610 Code of Mass. Regulations, section 2.22.

Chapter Ten. Merging Diverse Student Cultures

1. For purposes of the discussion here, "students" refers to a traditional 18- to 22-year-old population.

2. Anthony F. Buono and James L. Bowditch, *The Human Side of Mergers and Acquisitions: Managing Collisions between People, Cultures, and Organizations* (San Francisco: Jossey-Bass, 1989).

3. Interviews with Dr. Barry Jenkins, dean of student affairs, Mercer University, Macon, Ga., Dec. 1990, and Dr. Colleen Hegranes, dean of students, College of St. Catherine, St. Paul, Minn., Jan. 1991.

4. Interview with Paul Lamontia, associate dean of students, Iona College, New Rochelle, N.Y., Feb. 1991.

5. Elisabeth Kubler-Ross, *On Death and Dying* (New York: Macmillan, 1969).

6. Interview with Rev. Charles Drexler, dean of student affairs, Gannon University, Erie, Pa., Jan. 1991.

7. Jenkins interview.

8. Ibid.

9. Hegranes interview.

10. Interview with Dr. Noel Cartwright, director of the Counseling Center, University of Massachusetts–Lowell, Lowell, Mass., Jan. 1991.

Chapter Eleven. Consolidating Library Collections and Learning-Resource Technologies

1. Robert G. Cope, *Opportunity From Strength: Strategic Planning Clarified with Case Examples.* ERIC Clearing House on Higher Education, George Washington University (Washington, D.C.: Association for the Study of Higher Education, 1987).

2. Danny Miller and Peter H. Friesen, *Organizations: A Quantum View* (Englewood, N.J.: Prentice Hall, 1984), 209.

3. Rosabeth Moss Kanter, *When Giants Learn to Dance: Mastering the Challenge of Strategy, Management, and Careers in the 1990s* (New York: Simon and Schuster, 1989), 120.

Chapter Twelve. Mergers, Institutional Advancement, and Alumni Relationships

1. Victor F. Scalise, Jr., *Merging for Mission* (Valley Forge, Pa.: Judson Press, 1972).

2. Rosabeth Moss Kanter, "The New Managerial Work," *Harvard Business Review* 67, no. 6 (1989): 85–92.

3. Paul Tournier, *A Place for You* (New York: Harper & Row, 1968), 14.

4. Anthony F. Buono and James L. Bowditch, *The Human Side of Mergers and Acquisitions: Managing Collisions between People, Cultures, and Organizations* (San Francisco: Jossey-Bass, 1989), 311–23.

5. Ibid., 253.

6. Ibid., 194.

7. Ibid., 229.

8. Ibid., 22–23, 246.

9. James M. Needham, "Paying the Postmerger Piper," in *The Mergers and Acquisitions Handbook,* ed. Milton L. Rock (New York: McGraw-Hill, 1987), 286.

Chapter Thirteen. An International Perspective: Recent Growth Mergers in British Higher Education

1. John Carswell, *Government and the Universities in Britain: Programme and Performance, 1960–1980* (Cambridge: Cambridge University Press, 1985), 52–67; *Report of the Committee on Higher Education,* Cmnd. 2154 (London: Her Majesty's Stationery Office, 1963).

2. John Davies, "New Universities: Their Origins and Strategic Development," in *International Encyclopedia of Comparative Higher Education* (forthcoming).

3. *The Development of Higher Education into the 1990s,* Cmnd. 9524 (London: Her Majesty's Stationery Office, 1985), 5.

4. *Report of the Steering Committee for Efficiency Studies in Universities* (London: Committee of Vice-Chancellors and Principals, 1985).

5. Paul Temple and Celia Whitchurch, eds., *Strategic Choice: Corporate Strategies for Change in Higher Education* (Reading, Eng.: Conference of University Administrators, 1989).

6. *Research Selectivity Exercise: The Outcome,* UFC Circular 27/89 (London: Universities Funding Council, 1989).

7. A. H. Halsey, "The Best Places," *Times Higher Education Supplement,* Feb. 2, 1990.

8. Temple and Whitchurch, *Strategic Choice.*

9. Ibid.

10. "Thames and Kent Consider Sharing Canterbury Campus," *Times Higher Education Supplement,* June 2, 1989, 1.

11. University of London, "Medical Education in London. Revised Proposals, March 1981" (London: *University of London Senate Minute 748,* Mar. 25, 1981); University of London, "Non-Medical Activities and Central Services—Academic Advice Relating to the Grant Allocation for 1982–83 and Subsequent Sessions" (London: *University of London Senate Minute 852,* Apr. 28, 1982).

12. *Review of Advanced Further Education in Inner London—Proposals* (London: Inner London Education Authority, 1984).

13. Ibid.

14. John Hunter, unpublished paper. Hunter is the secretary of the University of Ulster.

15. University of Ulster, *Report to Court, 1988–89.*

Chapter Fourteen. Conclusion: The Mutual-Growth Process— Myths and Realities

1. Paul Leinberger and Bruce Tucker, *The New Individualists: The Generation after the Organization Man* (New York: HarperCollins, 1991), 344, 345.

2. Peter F. Drucker, *The New Realities* (New York: Harper & Row, 1989), 226, 227.

3. Ann F. Lucas, "The Department Chair as Change Agent," in *How Administrators Can Improve Teaching,* ed. Peter Seldin (San Francisco: Jossey-Bass, 1990), 82.

4. Ralph Alterowitz, "Viewpoint: 'All Beginnings Are Hard,'" *Journal of Higher Education Management,* Summer/Fall 1990, 77, 78.

5. Liz McMillen, "'Cut Staffs but Not across the Board,' Strapped Colleges Are Advised," *Chronicle of Higher Education,* Feb. 13, 1991, 431.

6. Alterowitz, "Viewpoint," 78.

7. Liz McMillen, "Increasing Productivity at Colleges Is a Hot Topic for the 1990s," *Chronicle of Higher Education,* Mar. 6, 1991, 423.

8. Robert L. Jacobson, "Academic Leaders Predict Major Changes for Higher Education in Recession's Wake," *Chronicle of Higher Education,* Nov. 20, 1991, 435.

9. Anthony DePalma, "In Uncertain Times, College Students See a Bleak Future after Graduation," *New York Times,* Dec. 25, 1991, 38.

Bibliography

Alterowitz, Ralph. "Viewpoint: 'All Beginnings Are Hard,'" *Journal of Higher Education Management*, Summer/Fall 1990, 77, 78.

American Association of University Professors. "Governance Standards in Institutional Mergers and Acquisitions." *AAUP Policy Documents and Reports*. Washington, D.C.: AAUP, 1990.

American Institute of Certified Public Accountants. *Audits of Colleges and Universities*. New York: AICPA, 1975.

Anderson, Richard E., and Joel W. Meyerson, eds. *Financial Planning under Economic Uncertainty*. San Francisco: Jossey-Bass, 1990.

Association of University Teachers. *The Case for Increased Investment in Our Universities*. London: AUT, 1989.

Austin, Ann E., and Zelda F. Gamson. *Academic Workplace: New Demands, Heightened Tensions*. ASHE-ERIC Higher Education Research Report No. 10. Washington, D.C.: Association for the Study of Higher Education, 1983.

Becher, Tony. *Academic Tribes and Territories*. Milton Keynes, Eng.: SRHE and Open University Press, 1989.

Benezet, Louis T. "Resurveying the Downward Slope." *AGB Reports* 25, no. 2 (1983): 38–41.

Bennis, Warren. *Why Leaders Can't Lead: The Unconscious Conspiracy Continues*. San Francisco: Jossey-Bass, 1989.

Bensimon, Estela M. "Transactional, Transformational, and 'Trans-Vigorational' Leaders." *Leadership Abstracts* 2, no. 6 (1989).

Birnbaum, Robert. *How Colleges Work: The Cybernetics of Academic Organization and Leadership*. San Francisco: Jossey-Bass, 1988.

———. "The Impossible Job of the College President." *Leadership Abstracts* 1, no. 16 (1988).

———. "The Latent Organizational Functions of the Academic Senate; Why Senates Do Not Work but Will Not Go Away." *Journal of Higher Education* 60, no. 4 (1989): 423–43.

———. *Responsibility without Authority: The Impossible Job of the College President*. Wahsington, D.C.: Office of Educational Research and Improvement, Department of Education, March 1988.

Blumenstyk, Goldie. "Public-Private Group in Portland to Help Colleges Meet Demands through Coordination instead of Expansion," *Chronicle of Higher Education*, Sept. 12, 1990, 23.

Boyer, Ernest. "Faculty's Lack of Trust in Management." *Times Higher Education Supplement*, Nov. 17, 1989, 18.

Browne, Lynn E., and Eric S. Rosengren. "The Merger Boom: An Overview." In *The Merger Boom*, ed. Browne and Rosengren.

———, eds. *The Merger Boom.* Proceedings of a conference held at Melvin Village, N.H., Oct. 1987.

Bruce, Robert J. "Widener University's Acquisition of the Delaware Law School and Brandywine College." In *Mergers and Acquisitions in Private Higher Education,* 1987.

Brueder, Robert L. "College Mergers: An Emerging Alternative." *AACJC Journal* 60, no. 1: 37–40.

Buono, Anthony F., and James L. Bowditch. *The Human Side of Mergers and Acquisitions: Managing Collisions between People, Cultures, and Organizations.* San Francisco: Jossey-Bass, 1989.

Burke, Ronald J. "Managing the Human Side of Mergers and Acquisitions." *Business Quarterly,* 52, no. 3 (1988): 18.

Cage, Mary Crystal. "Michigan's 'Higher-Education Mall' Viewed as a Model for Other Communities." *Chronicle of Higher Education,* Sept. 19, 1990, 5, 26.

Cameron, Kim, Ellen Chaffee, Myung Kim, and David Whetten. "The Aftermath of Decline." *Review of Higher Education* 10, no. 3 (1987): 215–34.

Cannon, John B. "The Organization and Human Implications of Merger." Paper presented at the American Educational Research Association, Montreal, Apr. 13, 1983.

Carswell, John. *Government and the Universities in Britain: Programme and Performance, 1960–1980.* Cambridge: Cambridge University Press, 1985.

Chambers, Gail S. *Approaching College Merger.* Bridgeport, Conn.: University of Bridgeport, n.d.

———. "The Dilemma of College Merger." *AGB Reports* 25, no. 6: 14–18.

———. "The Enterprising Alternatives." In *Mergers and Acquisitions in Private Higher Education,* 1987.

———. "Maybe There's a Reason: A Theoretical Model for Institutional Mergers." In *Mergers and Acquisitions in Private Higher Education,* 1987.

———. "Merger between Private Colleges: An Empirical Analysis." No. 87-09491. *Dissertation Abstracts International* 48. Ann Arbor, Mich.: University Microfilms, 1987.

———. "Negotiating Mergers between Institutions." In *Challenges of Retrenchment,* ed. James R. Mingle and Associates. San Francisco: Jossey-Bass, 1981.

Clark, Burton. *The Distinctive College.* Chicago: Aldine, 1970.

Cohen, Michael D., and James G. March. *Leadership and Ambiguity: The American College President.* New York: McGraw-Hill, 1974.

Cohen, Michael D., James G. March, and Johan P. Olsen. "A Garbage Can Model of Organizational Choice." *Administrative Science Quarterly* 17, no. 1 (1972): 1–25.

Cope, Robert G. *Opportunity From Strength: Strategic Planning Clarified with Case Examples.* Prepared by ERIC Clearing House on Higher Education, George Washington University. Washington, D.C.: Association For The Study of Higher Education, 1987.

Cope, Robert G. *Strategic Policy Planning: A Guide for College and University Administrators.* Littleton, Colo.: Ireland, 1978.

Cyert, Richard. Foreword to *Academic Strategy: The Management Revolution in American Higher Education,* by George Keller. Baltimore: Johns Hopkins University Press, 1983.

"Dawkins' Way." Editorial, *Times Higher Education Supplement*, Apr. 13, 1990, 40.

DePalma, Anthony. "In Uncertain Times, College Students See a Bleak Future after Graduation." *New York Times*, Dec. 25, 1991, 38.

The Development of Higher Education into the 1990s. Cmnd. 9524. London: Her Majesty's Stationery Office, 1985.

Dickmeyer, Nathan, and K. Scott Hughes. *Financial Self-Assessment: A Workbook for Colleges*. Washington, D.C.: NACUBO, 1980.

Drucker, Peter F. *The New Realities*. New York: Harper & Row, 1989.

Educational Ventures Inc., *EVI Biennial Report, 1984–86*. Allentown, Pa.: EVI, 1986.

Fisher, James L. *Power of the Presidency*. New York: American Council on Education and Macmillan, 1984.

Fisher, James L., Martha W. Tack, and Karen J. Wheeler. *The Effective College President*. New York: American Council on Education and Macmillan, 1988.

Forrester, Robert T. *A Handbook on Debt Management for Colleges and Universities*. Washington, D.C.: NACUBO, 1988.

Freyer, Thomas W., Jr. "An Overarching Purpose for Institutional Governance." *Leadership Abstracts* 1, no. 11 (1988).

Godsey, R. Kirby, "Case Study: The Merger of Tift College and Mercer University." In *Mergers and Acquisitions in Private Higher Education*, 1987.

Gordon, Teresa P., and Mary Fischer. "Reporting Performance: Using Financial and Nonfinancial Data." *NACUBO Business Officer Magazine* 24, no. 1 (1990): 28.

Gouldner, A. W. "Cosmopolitans and Locals." *Administrative Science Quarterly* 2 (1957): 281–306, 444–80.

Gray, Harry J. "The CEO: Takeover Hardball—A Tough Leader Tells How to Play the Expansion Game." *Success*, May 1987, 18.

Greenleaf, Robert K. "The Leadership Crisis—A Message for College and University Faculty." Pamphlet reprinted from *Humanities: Journal of the Institute of Man* 14, no. 3 (1978).

Handy, Charles. *Understanding Organizations*. Harmondsworth, Eng.: Penguin, 1976.

Henderson, Robert P. "Discussion." In *The Merger Boom*, ed. Browne and Rosengren.

Higher Education: Meeting the Challenge. Cmnd. 114. London: Her Majesty's Stationery Office, 1987.

Hines, Edward R. *Higher Education and State Government: Renewed Partnership, Cooperation, or Competition?* ASHE-ERIC Higher Education Report No. 5. Washington, D.C.: Association for the Study of Higher Education, 1988.

Hyatt, James A. *Presentation and Analysis of Financial Management Information*. Washington, D.C.: NACUBO, 1989.

Hyatt, James A., and Aurora A. Santiago. *Financial Management of Colleges and Universities*. Washington, D.C.: NACUBO, 1986.

Jacobson, Robert L. "Academic Leaders Predict Major Changes for Higher Education in Recession's Wake." *Chronicle of Higher Education*, Nov. 20, 1991, 435.

Jaschik, Scott. "Citizens Campaigns Are Foiling State Plans to Shut Down or

Merger Public Colleges." *Chronicle of Higher Education,* June 24, 1987, 1, 20–21.

Jemison, D. B., and S. B. Sitken. "Acquisitions: The Process Can Be the Problem." *Harvard Business Review* 64, no. 2 (1986): 107–16.

Jencks, Christopher, and David Riesman. *The Academic Revolution.* Chicago: University of Chicago Press, 1977.

Johnson, Edward A., and Kent Weeks. "To Close a College: Independent College Trustees and Decisions on Financial Exigency, Endowment Use, and Closure." *Journal of College and University Law* 12 (1986): 455.

Jones, Dennis P. *Data and Information for Executive Decisions in Higher Education.* Boulder, Colo.: National Center for Higher Education Management Systems, 1982.

Kanter, Rosabeth Moss. "The New Managerial Work," *Harvard Business Review* 67, no. 6 (1989): 85–92.

———. *When Giants Learn to Dance: Mastering the Challenge of Strategy, Management, and Careers in the 1990s.* New York: Simon and Schuster, 1989.

Kaplan, William A. *The Law of Higher Education.* 2d ed. San Francisco: Jossey-Bass, 1985.

Keller, George. *Academic Strategy: The Management Revolution in American Higher Education.* Baltimore: Johns Hopkins University Press, 1983.

Kellerman, Barbara. "A President Is a President Is a President." *Leadership Abstracts* 1, no. 20 (1988).

Kirby, J. A. "Legal Audits for Non-Profit Organizations." Paper presented at the Third Annual Legal Audits Seminar, Massachusetts Bar Association, Newton, Mass., Mar. 13, 1991.

Kitching, J. "Why Do Mergers Miscarry?" *Harvard Business Review* 46, no. 6 (1967): 84–101.

Leinberger, Paul, and Bruce Tucker. *The New Individualists: The Generation after the Organization Man.* New York: HarperCollins, 1991.

Lucas, Ann F. "The Department Chair as Change Agent." In *How Administrators Can Improve Teaching,* ed. Peter Seldin. San Francisco: Jossey-Bass, 1990.

Lyons, Nancy L. "Arkansas Vo-Tech Schools May Merge with CCs." *Community College Week,* May 28, 1990, 3.

McMillen, Liz. " 'Cut Staffs but Not across the Board,' Strapped Colleges Are Advised." *Chronicle of Higher Education,* Feb. 13, 1991, 431.

———. "Increasing Productivity at Colleges Is a Hot Topic for the 1990s." *Chronicle of Higher Education,* Mar. 6, 1991, 423.

Martin, James. "More Gown, Less Town." *Times Higher Education Supplement,* June 29, 1990, 17.

Martin, James, and James E. Samels. "Ethical Implications of Higher Education Mergers." Paper presented at the Twenty-fourth Annual Northeast Region Academic Affairs Administrators Conference, Providence, R.I., Nov. 8, 1989.

———. "The Small College Entrepreneur." *Connection* (New England Board of Higher Education) 5, no. 4 (1991).

Meek, V. L. "Comparative Notes on Cross-Sectoral Amalgamation of Higher Educational Institutions: British and Australian Case Studies." *Comparative Education* 24, no. 3 (1988): 335–49.

Mercer, Joye. "Tennessee Board Approves Community College/Vo-Tech Mergers." *Community College Week*, Dec. 24, 1990, 2.

Mergers and Acquisitions in Private Higher Education: A Report on a National Conference at Wingspread. Sponsored by Milliken University; cosponsored by AGB, ACE, CIC, and CASE. Decatur, Ill., June 19–21, 1987.

Miller, Danny, and Peter H. Friesen, *Organizations: A Quantum View.* Englewood City, NJ: Prentice Hall, 1984.

Millett, John D. *Mergers in Higher Education: An Analysis of Ten Case Studies.* Washington, D.C.: Academy for Educational Development, 1976, and University: University of Alabama Press, 1976.

Mingle, James R., et al. *Challenges of Retrenchment.* San Francisco: Jossey-Bass, 1981.

Moon, John E. v. C. "The Boston State Fiasco: A Personal View." *New England Sociologist* 4, no. 1: 51, 60.

Morrison, James L. "Establishing an Environmental Scanning/Forecasting System to Augment College and University Planning." *Planning for Higher Education* 15, no. 1 (1987): 7–22.

Morrison, James L., William L. Renfro, and Wayne I. Boucher. *Futures Research and the Strategic Planning Processes: Implications for Higher Education.* Washington, D.C.: American Association for Higher Education, 1984.

Mortimer, Kenneth, Marque Bagshaw, and Andrew Masland. *Flexibility in Academic Staffing: Effective Policies and Practices.* ASHE-ERIC Higher Education Research Report No. 1. Washington, D.C.: Association for the Study of Higher Education, 1985.

National Association of College and University Business Officers. *Capital Formation Alternatives in Higher Education.* Washington, D.C.: NACUBO, 1988.

———. *Financial Accounting and Reporting Manual for Higher Education.* Washington, D.C.: NACUBO, 1990.

Needham, James M. "Paying the Postmerger Piper." In *The Mergers and Acquisitions Handbook*, ed. Milton L. Rock. New York: McGraw-Hill, 1987.

O'Neill, Joseph P. "Merger as a Strategy for Growth or Increasing Market Share." In *Mergers and Acquisitions in Private Higher Education*, 1987.

O'Neill, Joseph P., and Samuel Barnett. *Colleges and Corporate Change: Merger, Bankruptcy, and Closure. Sourcebook for Trustees and Administrators.* Princeton: Conference University Press, 1980.

Pascarella, Perry, and Mark A. Frohman. *The Purpose-Driven Organization: Unleashing the Power of Discretion and Commitment.* San Francisco: Jossey-Bass, 1989.

Pearson, Richard, Geoffrey Pike, Alan Gordon, and Clare Weyman. *How Many Graduates in the 21st Century?* IMS Report No. 177. Brighton, Eng.: Institute of Manpower Studies, 1989.

Pew Higher Education Research Program. "The Lattice and the Ratchet." *Policy Perspectives* 2, no. 4 (1990), n.p.

Pritchett, Price. *The Employee Survival Guide to Mergers and Acquisitions.* Dallas: Pritchett and Associates, 1987.

Ravenscroft, David. "The 1980s Merger Wave: An Industrial Organization Perspective." In *The Merger Boom*, ed. Browne and Rosengren.

Report of the Committee on Higher Education. Cmnd. 2154. London: Her Majesty's Stationery Office, 1963.

Research Selectivity Exercise: The Outcome. Circular 27/89. London: Universities Funding Council, 1989.

Roche, George. *A World without Heroes: The Modern Tragedy.* Hillsdale, Mich.: Hillsdale College Press, 1987.

Schuster, Jack, Lynn Miller, and Associates. *Governing Tomorrow's Campus: Perspectives and Agendas.* New York: American Council on Education and Macmillan, 1989.

Seymour, Daniel T. "Developing Academic Programs: The Climate for Innovation." ASHE-ERIC Higher Education Report No. 3. Washington, D.C.: Association for the Study of Higher Education, 1988.

Shattock, Michael, ed. *The Structure and Governance of Higher Education.* Surrey, Eng.: Society for Research into Higher Education, Surrey University, 1983.

State Higher Education Executive Officers. *Creative Financing for Higher Education Facilities and Equipment.* Denver: SHEEO, 1985.

Taylor, Barbara. *Working Effectively with Trustees: Building Cooperative Campus Leadership.* ASHE-ERIC Higher Education Research Report No. 2. Washington, D.C.: Association for the Study of Higher Education, 1987.

Temple, Paul, and Celia Whitchurch, eds. *Strategic Choice: Corporate Strategies for Change in Higher Education.* Reading, Eng.: Conference of University Administrators, 1989.

Thompson, Hugh L. "Considering a Merger?" *Planning for Higher Education* 13, no. 3 (1986): 21–26.

Tierney, William G., ed. *Culture and Ideology in Higher Education: Advancing a Critical Agenda.* New York: Praeger, 1991.

Tournier, Paul. *A Place for You.* New York: Harper & Row, 1968.

Uhl, Norman P. "Editor's Introduction." In *Using Research for Strategic Planning.* San Francisco: Jossey-Bass, 1983.

Wade, Larry, and Robert L. Curry. *A Logic of Public Policy: Aspects of Political Economy.* Belmont, Calif.: Wadsworth, 1970.

Waterman, Robert. *Adhocracy: The Power to Change.* Knoxville, Tenn.: Whittle Direct Books, 1990.

Weeks, Kent. "Creative Options: College Mergers and Institutional Reassessment." *Lex Collegii* 11, no. 2 (1987): 1–5.

Wiley III, Ed. "Alabama Merger Paragon of Articulation, Officials Say." *Community College Week,* Oct. 29, 1990, 3.

Williams, Don, William Gore, Charles Broches, and Cynthia Lostoski. "One Faculty's Perception of Its Governance Role." *Journal of Higher Education* 58, no. 6 (1987): 629–57.

Wyatt, J. F. "Institutional Identity and Its Extinction." *Higher Education Review* 18, no. 2 (1986): 21–32.

Zekan, Donald L. "Mergers in Public Higher Education in Massachusetts." Ph.D. diss., University of Massachusetts, Amherst, 1990.

Contributors

JAMES MARTIN is vice president for academic affairs at Mount Ida College in Newton Centre, Massachusetts. He has held fellowships from the National Endowment for the Humanities, the National Endowment for the Arts, and the Massachusetts Foundation for the Humanities and Public Policy and has published articles on the evolving role of the contemporary chief academic officer, entrepreneurial academic management, and new models of effective governance, as well as mutual growth mergers. In 1988, Martin was invited to become one of the founding members of the first chief academic officers' think tank in New England, sponsored by the New England Resource Center for Higher Education at the University of Massachusetts. During the 1989–90 academic year, he was in residence at the University of London on a Fulbright Fellowship to study institutional mergers within the university while also conducting research on this subject at institutions in England, Ireland, and Wales. In 1989, he founded, with James E. Samels, the Samels Group, a Massachusetts higher education consulting firm.

JAMES E. SAMELS is recognized as an authority in the fields of higher education law, preventive legal planning, and collegiate mergers and consolidations. Samels Associates, the law firm that he founded, concentrates specifically in higher education law. He has served as a faculty member in the College of Management Science at the University of Lowell, and previously taught at Bentley College and the University of Massachusetts. He has authored and edited articles, comments, and remarks in numerous higher education publications. Samels has served as acting state controller, special assistant attorney general, and general counsel to the Massachusetts Board of Regents. He received a graduate degree in public administration from the University of Rhode Island, his law degree from Suffolk University, and a doctorate in education from the University of Massachusetts. The Samels Group higher education consulting firm, founded in 1989 with James Martin, specializes in academic master planning, licensing and accreditation, and mergers and consolidations.

263

BRYAN E. CARLSON is president of Mount Ida College. He received a B.A. degree cum laude from Northeastern University, and Ed.M. and Ed.D. degrees from Boston University. Under his leadership, Mount Ida was the fastest growing two-plus-two college in the New England states in the 1980s. The college tripled its enrollment and significantly expanded its institutional mission, developing an articulated associate's and bachelor's degree academic system while substantially expanding its personnel and physical resources. In 1987, Carlson assumed a dual presidency when he also became the chief executive officer of Chamberlayne Junior College before its merger with Mount Ida. During the 1984–92 period, Carlson directed his institution through five merger activities, becoming one of the most experienced chief executive officers nationally in the mutual-growth strategy.

ANDRÉ MAYER, vice president–communications and research at Associated Industries of Massachusetts, was formerly director of planning for the Massachusetts Board of Regents of Higher Education and Higher Education Coordinating Council. He has helped plan and coordinate several college and university mergers in a variety of roles. Educated at Harvard and Berkeley, Mayer has written on a wide range of topics in books and in periodicals including *Daedalus,* the *Atlantic, Sloan Management Review,* and *Planning for Higher Education.*

SHEILA MURPHY is vice president for student affairs and dean of students at Bradford College in Bradford, Massachusetts. She has served as dean of students at Mount Holyoke College in South Hadley, Massachusetts, as vice president for student affairs at Russell Sage College, Troy, New York, and as dean of students at Mount Ida College during its initial merger planning. She has presented papers at professional conferences on subjects such as women and leadership, student development, merging student cultures, and multicultural education on predominately white campuses. She served as president of the Massachusetts College Personnel Association and on the executive committees of the Massachusetts Association for Women in Education and the College Student Personnel Association of New York. She is currently the network coordinator of the NASPA–Region 1's Women in Student Affairs Network. Throughout her fifteen years in student affairs, she has managed the student development component of two-year, four-year, single-sex, co-ed, and multicampus operations.

PATRICIA ANN SACKS received her A.B. degree in history and government from Cedar Crest College and her M.L.S. from Drexel

University. She has also served for the past ten years as an organizational development consultant and regional accrediting team member with a specialty in library cooperation and partnerships. Sacks is completing *Preparing for Accreditation: A Handbook for Academic Librarians,* which will be published by the American Library Association in spring 1993. She developed the Building Program Statement for Muhlenberg's Trexler Library, participated in the selecting and contracting of the architect and the construction manager, and served as project manager during the construction and occupancy stages. She has participated in the planning and development of the Cedar Crest and Muhlenberg College partnership (Educational Ventures, Inc.) and, with five library directors, founded the Lehigh Valley Association of Independent Colleges Libraries, a six-college consortium.

VICTOR F. SCALISE, JR., is vice president for institutional advancement at Mount Ida College. He served as president of New England Institute of Applied Arts and Sciences from 1977 to 1989, and in 1989 he directed the merger of his institution with Mount Ida. Earlier he was senior minister and chief architect of the United Parish in Brookline, Massachusetts, formed from the merger of three major religious denominations: American Baptist, United Methodist, and the United Church of Christ. Scalise's book *Merging for Mission* remains the textbook for U.S. church mergers. Scalise received his B.D., S.T.M., and D. Min. degrees from Andover-Newton Theological School and is also a graduate of the Harvard University Graduate School of Business.

PAUL TEMPLE as head of the University of London's Planning and Development Division was responsible for strategic planning for the federal University of London, which represents approximately one-fifth of the British university system. He recently coedited, with Celia Whitchurch, a handbook on higher education strategic planning for the British Conference of University Administrators, *Strategic Choice: Corporate Strategies for Change in Higher Education* (1989), and they have also published a study of entrepreneurial universities entitled *Universities in the Marketplace* (1992). He has undertaken comparative studies of the University of London and multicampus universities in the United States. Before joining the University of London, he worked on polytechnic and college planning for the Inner London Education Authority, following experience in corporate planning in London regional government.

JOHN F. WELSH is the associate director of academic affairs for the Kansas Board of Regents, a position he has held since May 1987. Before joining the board staff he taught sociology at Pittsburg State University for nine years. His responsibilities with the board of regents focus on the development of new academic policy, including strategies for institutional merger. In this regard, he has developed background research materials for board of regents' initiatives in statewide governance reform, admissions standards, and new degree proposals, as well as recent college and university mergers within the state system. In 1990 he provided professional staff work for the Governor's Commission on Reform of Educational Governance, an effort that resulted in the development of ten recommendations for the reform of the education article of the Kansas constitution. He received the Ph.D. degree from Oklahoma State University in 1978.

CELIA WHITCHURCH has worked in British universities for fifteen years, including five years as senior planning officer at the University of London, and currently as secretary of the Faculty of Medicine and Dentistry at the University of Birmingham, planning the development of medical education and hospital provision in the city. During 1987 she was assigned to the national Committee of Vice-Chancellors and Principals to work on performance evaluation and human resource investment. She has extensive experience of the political dimensions of institutional collaboration and competition. As an executive member of the Association of University Administrators, she has a longstanding involvement with the professional development of university managers and, more recently, has worked on the establishment of a national forum on corporate strategic planning in higher education. She is the author of a number of publications on staff development and strategic planning.

DONALD L. ZEKAN is vice president of business and financial affairs at St. Bonaventure University. He was previously the chief fiscal and administrative officer of Massasoit Community College and its executive vice president for four years. He also served as acting president of the college during the 1982–83 academic year. Zekan received his Ed.D. and M.P.A. degrees from the University of Massachusetts, Amherst, an M.S.A. degree from Bentley College, and a B.A. degree from the University of Pittsburgh. In the mid-1980s, he coordinated the merger of Massasoit Community College and Blue Hills Technical Institute. The subject of his doctoral dissertation was mergers in public higher education.

Index

Academic action plan, 75–99; guidelines, 99
Academic advising, student affairs program, 157
Academic governance, faculty, 86–89
Academic offerings, mutual-growth strategy, 14–16; complementary degree programs, 15; curriculum review, 15; faculty resource enhancement, 15–16; redundancy elimination, 15
Academic quality, mutual-growth strategy, 228–29
Accounting, business combination, 138–39
Accounting reference tool, 132–34
Accounting standards, 134–35
Accreditation, 40–41, 142–53; educational consumer protection, 149–51; legal issues, 143; postmerger investigation, 145–47; preparation, 143–45; report, 147–48; student financial assistance, 145; visitation, 147–48
Administrative staff: mutual-growth strategy, 17, 18; personnel review, 17–18
Administrator, Merger Task Force, 47
Affiliation: financial options, 140–41; learning-resource technologies, 173–75; library, 173–75
Alcohol policies, student affairs program, 158
Alumni: fund-raising, 202–5; Merger Task Force, 47; mutual-growth strategy, 19
Alumni affairs office, 193–202; blending organizational models, 193–97; coordinated activities plan, 197–98; goals during merger process, 193; mutual-growth strategy, 19; new institutional expectations, 198–202
Asset, 135–36
Asset transfer: defined, 27; described, 28–29; phased, 140; reasons for, 27–28

Association: defined, 29; described, 29–30; reasons for, 29
Athletics, student affairs program, 157–58

Bankruptcy-bailout, merger, 4–5
Benefits, personnel policy, 92–93
Board of Trustees. *See* Trustees
British higher education: academic quality, 217; expansion in 1960s, 209–11; goals, 217; government policy, 209–15; institutional mission, 217; leadership, 218; management structure, 218; pattern, 209; size, 217–18; strategic planning, 219–22
British higher education, merger in: factors conducive to, 215–17; polytechnic mergers, 222–25; pressures, 211–14; transbinary issues, 222–25
Business combination, accounting, 138–39

Capital outlay financing, 39
Career placement, student affairs program, 158
Chief executive officer. *See* President
Codes of conduct, student affairs program, 158
Collaboration, 228
Collective bargaining, 37
Collective bargaining, faculty, 94–96; bargaining issues vs. governance issues, 95–96; candor, 95; confrontation, 95; union loyalty recognition, 96; union vs. nonunion personnel policies, 95
College (*see also* Public college): failure rate, 3; mergers by state, 239–44
Communication, 166–67; institutional advancement office, 191–92
Compensation, personnel policy, 91–92
Complementarity: institutional missions, 12–14; mutual-growth strategy, 236

Consolidation, 228; defined, 26; described, 27; financing option, 140; learning-resource technologies, 175; library, 175; reasons for, 27
Consortium, ix; defined, 29; described, 29–30; learning-resource technologies, 173–75; library, 173–75; reasons for, 29
Contractual liability, 38–39
Curriculum review, 15; faculty, 78–82

Debt, 135–36
Decision making: faculty, 84; mutual-growth strategy, 234–35
Diversified planning, mutual-growth strategy, 20–21

Educational affiliation: defined, 30; reasons for, 30
Educational complementarity, 33–34
Educational consumer protection: accreditation, 149–51; complaint, 39; licensure, 149–51
Enrollment, mutual-growth strategy, 16–17
Entrepreneurship, mutual-growth strategy, 234

Faculty: academic governance, 86–89; curriculum review, 78–82; decision making, 84; duties and responsibilities, 93; planning, 82–86; professional development, 97–99; public college, 122–23; staffing issues, 82–86
Faculty, collective bargaining, 94–96; bargaining issues vs. governance issues, 95–96; candor, 95; confrontation, 95; union loyalty recognition, 96; union vs. nonunion personnel policies, 95
Faculty, personnel policy, 89–97; collective bargaining, 94–95; reappointment, 93; retrenchment policy, 93
Faculty handbook, 96–97
Faculty rank, personnel policy, 89
Faculty representative, Merger Task Force, 46
Federation: defined, 29; described, 29–30; reasons for, 29
Fiduciary responsibilities, 23–24
Financial base, mutual-growth strategy, 16

Financial ratios and trends, 135–36
Financial reference tool, 132–34
Fraternity, student affairs program, 159
Fund-raising: alumni, 202–5; institutional advancement office, 202–5

Good-faith cooperation, 35
Governance, faculty, 86–89
Governing board. See Trustees

Human resources, 36–37

Institutional advancement office, 188–93; challenges, 189, 190–93; communication, 191–92; fund-raising, 202–5; goals, 189; loss of personal connection, 190–91; methods, 189; operations during merger, 191; shaping identity of merged institution, 192–93
Institutional autonomy, vii
Institutional expectations, 198–202
Institutional mission: complementary, 13; Merger Task Force, 46; mutual-growth strategy, 12–14
Institutional synergy, mutual-growth strategy, 20
Institutional will, mutual-growth strategy, 14
Integration clause, 35

Joint Big Decisions Committee, strategic planning, 110
Joint mission planning, 228
Joint venture: defined, 30; financial options, 140–41; reasons for, 30

Leadership: British higher education, 218; growth of others, 74; learning-resource technologies, 175–76; library, 175–76; Merger Task Force, 60; mutual-growth strategy, 21; president, 63–64; public college, 129–30
Learning assistance, student affairs program, 157
Learning-resource technologies, 168–87; affiliation, 173–75; consolidation, 175; consortium, 173–75; leadership, 175–76; merger plan implementation, 175–83; mutual-growth case study, 185–87; mutual-growth strategy, 172–75; pressures for change, 168–69; pure

merger, 175; strategic planning, 169–72

Legal audit, 37

Legal issues: accreditation, 143; licensure, 143

Legal services, 31–41

Library, 168–87; affiliation, 173–75; consolidation, 175; consortium, 173–75; funding support, 181; leadership, 175–76; merger plan implementation, 175–83; mutual-growth case study, 185–87; mutual-growth strategy, 172–75; pressures for change, 168–69; pure merger, 175; sample work plan, 183–85; staffing goals, 181–82; strategic planning, 169–72

Licensure, 40–41, 142–53; appellate procedures, 148–49; educational consumer protection, 149–51; legal issues, 143; postmerger investigation, 145–47; preparation, 143–45; standards, 148–49; student financial assistance, 145

Liquidity, 135–36

Management structure, in British higher education, 218

Merger, ix; agreement negotiation, 50–52; bankruptcy-bailout, 4–5; business plan elements, 133; context, vii-viii; contract consummation, 38; defined, 5; feasibility, 45; financial models, 139–41; forms, 229; impetus, 3; implementation summary action plan, 76; international perspective, 209–25; national context, 69–70; negotiations closure, 37–38; stereotype, 4–5; typology, 24–31

Merger, in British higher education, 209–25; polytechnic mergers, 222–25; transbinary issues, 222–25

Merger, pure, 24–26; defined, 24–25; described, 25–26; financial options, 139–40; learning-resource technologies, 175; library, 175; reasons for, 24–25

Merger Task Force, 46–49; administrator, 47; alumni, 47; chair, 48; constituencies, 46–49; creation, 46; faculty representative, 46; institutional mission, 46; leadership, 60; strategic planning, 110; student, 47–48

Mount Ida model of academic achievement, 67–69

Multicampus resource sharing, 228

Mutual-growth strategy, ix–x; academic quality, 228–29; achieving excellence, 12–20; administrative staff, 17, 18; advancement, 70–72; alumni base, 19; alumni office, 19; campuswide commitment, 232; complementarity, 236; components, 12–20; decision making, 234–35; developmental phases, 229–31; diversified planning, 20–21; emergence, 6–9; enrollment, 16–17; entrepreneurship, 234; financial base, 16; flexibility, 235; implementation, 20–21; implementation by trustees, 54–58; institutional mission, 12–14; institutional self-assessment, 229–30; institutional synergy, 20; institutional will, 14; leadership, 21; learning-resource technologies, 172–75; legal structure, 31–41; library, 172–75; merger implementation, 231; merging from strength, 232–33; mutual institutional growth, 14; orienting merger partners, 231–36; postmerger consolidation and community building, 231; in practice, 5–9, 10–12, 239–44; premerger collaboration and negotiation, 230–31; premerger strategic planning, 230; and president, 64–65; principles, 12–20; shared vision, 233–34; student, 236–37; student market share, 16–17

Mutual-growth strategy, academic offerings, 14–16; complementary degree programs, 15; curriculum review, 15; faculty resource enhancement, 15–16; redundancy elimination, 15

Name change, 34

New facilities development, 39

Organizational dysfunction; dual hierarchy, 67; and president, 66–67

Parents, 166

Personnel policy: benefits, 92–93; compensation, 91–92; tenure, 89–91

Personnel policy, faculty, 89–97; collective bargaining, 94–95; rank, 89; reappointment, 93; retrenchment policy, 93

Personnel review, administrative staff, 17–18
Political economy, public college, 119–26
Pooling-of-interest accounting, 138–39
Postmerger growth, administrative barriers, 72–73
Power struggle, 60
Premerger financial condition analysis, 135
Premerger legal audit, 37
Premerger planning, 75–78
President, 59–74; leadership context, 61–63; leadership designation, 60; leadership style, 63–64; management exercise perspective, 65–66; merger uniqueness, 59–60; mutual-growth strategy, 64–65; national merger context, 69–70; opportunities, 61; organizational dysfunction, 66–67; power struggle, 60
Privacy law, 40
Professional development, faculty, 97–99
Program transfer, financial options, 141
Public college, 117–31; faculty, 122–23; institution-based merger initiatives, 126–29; leadership, 129–30; merger analyses, 117; merger literature, 118–19; political economy, 119–26; public sector merger initiatives, 119–26; state government, 129–30
Public relations office, 205–8

Reciprocal indemnification, 35–36
Residential life, student affairs program, 159
Residual liability, 35–36
Return on investment, 136–38

Sorority, student affairs program, 159
Staff review, process, 84–85
State government, public college, 129–30
Strategic decision, 108
Strategic legal planning, 33
Strategic planning, 103–16; analysis vs. action, 106–8; basic decision, 108–9; in British higher education, 219–22; for community, 105–6; defined, 103; elements, 108–12; evolution, 103–4;

external environment, 106–7; implementation, 112–15; information, 109–10; internal capabilities, 107; Joint Big Decisions Committee, 110; learning-resource technologies, 169–72; lessons from experience, 112–15; library, 169–72; merger planner guidance, 115–16; Merger Task Force, 110; process, 105–6, 107, 110–12; staffing, 109–10; stakeholder goals and values, 107; strategic decision, 108; structure, 110–12; SWOTS analysis, 107
Student: Merger Task Force, 47–48; merging cultures, 155–67; mutual-growth strategy, 236–37
Student activities, 159–60
Student affairs programs: academic advising, 157; alcohol policies, 158; athletics, 157–58; career placement, 158; codes of conduct, 158; fraternity, 159; learning assistance, 157; operational checklist, 157; recent growth-merger implementation, 160–66; residential life, 159; reviewing existing policies, 156–60; sorority, 159; student activities, 159–60; student financial aid, 158; student governance, 159–60
Student financial aid, 40; accreditation, 145; licensure, 145; student affairs program, 158
Student governance, student affairs program, 159–60
Student market share, mutual-growth strategy, 16–17
Student records, 40

Tenure, personnel policy, 89–91
Transfer of assets: defined, 27; described, 28–29; phased, 140; reasons for, 27–28
Trustees, 42–58, 118; merger agreement approval, 53–54; merger agreement negotiation, 50–52; merger feasibility, 45; mutual-growth strategy, implementation, 54–58; process, 43; role elements, 43

University. See College

Library of Congress Cataloging-in-Publication Data

Martin, James, 1948 Jan. 14–
   Merging colleges for mutual growth : a new strategy for academic managers /
James Martin, James E. Samuels, and associates.
      p.   cm.
   Includes bibliographical references (p.   ) and index.
   ISBN 0-8018-4666-8 (alk. paper)
   1. Universities and colleges—United States—Mergers. 2. Universities and col-
leges—United States—Administration. I. Samuels, James E. II. Title.
LB2341.M2896   1994
378.1—dc20
                                                             93-8380